Nurturing the Prophetic Imagination

Nurturing the Prophetic Imagination

Co-Editors:
Jamie Gates
Mark H. Mann

WIPF & STOCK · Eugene, Oregon

Nurturing the Prophetic Imagination

Point Loma Press Series

Copyright©2012 Wipf and Stock Publishers. All rights reserved. Except for brief quotations in critical publications or reviews, no part of this book may be reproduced in any manner without prior written permission from the publisher. Write: Permissions, Wipf and Stock Publishers, 199 W. 8th Ave., Suite 3, Eugene, OR 97401.

Point Loma Press
3900 Lomaland Dr.
San Diego, CA 92106

Wipf and Stock Publishers
199 W. 8th Ave., Suite 3
Eugene, OR 97401

www.wipfandstock.com

ISBN 13: 978-1-62032-743-2

Contents

Acknowledgments • xi
Introduction • xv

Part I: Primer on the Prophets • 1

1. Prophecy, Canon and Imagination: Walter Brueggemann's *The Prophetic Imagination* and the Contributions of Biblical Interpretation to the Prophetic Project
   Brad E. Kelle • 5

2. The Prophets and the Social and Ecological Consequences of the Monarchy
   Maria Pascuzzi • 17

3. Prophetic Imagination in the Gospel of Matthew
   Michael Lodahl • 37

4. "As if We Lived in a Liberated World": The Prophetic Vision of Dorothee Soelle
   Rebecca Laird • 43

Part II: Open our Eyes, Open our Ears • 51

5. It's Hard Out Here for a PIMP (a Prophet who Imagines Moral Possibilities)
   Michael Eric Dyson • 57

6. The Assassin of Prophetic Imagination: Imperialistic Rhetoric in Ancient Rome and Contemporary America
   Jacquelyn Winston • 69

7. Appropriating the Prophetic Visions of Du Bois and Thurman: Considerations for the Academy
   Karen D. Crozier • 79

8. Unmasking the Gods of the Marketplace: God's Economy as a Counter to the Religious Functions of Prevailing Economic Models
   Lee Van Ham • 91

9. Seeing Beyond the Economy of Appearances: Fair Trade as Phantasm of Justice
   Orlando R. Serrano, Jr. • 103

Part III: Refuse To Be Consoled • 113

10. A Voice is Heard at Ramah: Lament as the Form and Shape of the Prophetic Imagination
    Emmanuel Katongole • 117

11. When Beauty Speaks, Truth Answers
    Kathleen Norris • 133

12. Rumours of Glory: The Prophetic Music of Bruce Cockburn
    Karl Martin • 141

13. Walking Humbly
    Jin S. Kim • 163

Part IV: A Eucharistic People • 171

14. The Eucharistic Imagination of Hope and Martyrdom: The Kingdom of God
    Brent D. Peterson • 179

15. In Solidarity With the World: The Holiness of the Missionary Community
    Nathan R. Kerr • 189

16. Prophets Turning Profits: The Transforming Impact of Women's Savings Groups in Sub-Saharan Africa
    Stephan J. Bauman and Wendy Wellman Sinnema • 203

17. Interview with Bill McKibben: An Environmental Prophet Crying in the Wilderness
    Dean Nelson • 221

18. Nurturing a Prophetic Imagination: Missiology as Ecclesiology
    Jamie Gates, Larry Bollinger, Robert Gailey • 229

Contributors List • 245

Foreword for Point Loma Press Series

Point Loma Press was founded in 1992 to provide a publishing outlet for faculty and to serve the distinct theological mission of Point Loma Nazarene University (San Diego, CA). Over time the press has grown to publish authors from a wider range of institutional backgrounds, but its core mission remains the same: to encourage and extend a distinctly Wesleyan theological perspective on various topics and issues for the church today. Most Point Loma Press books are theological in scope, though many are quite practical in their focus, and some address non-theological topics but from a Wesleyan theological perspective. All Point Loma Press books are written with a broad audience in mind, intended to contribute effectively to contemporary scholarship while also being accessible to pastors, laypersons, and students alike. Our hope is that our new collaboration with Wipf & Stock Publishers will continue to allow us to expand our audience for the important topics and perspective of our work.

Point Loma Press welcomes any submissions that meet these criteria. Inquiries should be directed to PointLomaPress@pointloma.edu or 619-849-2359. When submitting, please provide rationale for how your work supports the mission of the Point Loma Nazarene University Wesleyan Center to articulate distinctly Wesleyan themes and trajectories.

Acknowledgments

This volume has been a special labor of love. Its conception began five years ago when Jamie began envisioning a year-long series of events to foster a campus-wide conversation at Point Loma Nazarene University related to his work as director for the Center for Justice and Reconciliation. Conception transformed into inception when, in 2008, Mark arrived at PLNU to become the director for the Wesleyan Center for 21st Century Studies and the vision became a shared one which resulted in the Nurturing the Prophetic Imagination Conference in March of 2010. It was out of this conference that this book arose as our shared attempt to take the dynamic conversation brought together on the PLNU campus to a much wider audience.

Our gratitude must first be expressed to the authors who have contributed to this book. They range from seasoned scholars to young, fresh voices that are being heard for the first time. We are grateful to our contributors for their ongoing persistence and patience during the long process of a collaborative volume. Most of all we are grateful for the moral courage each of our authors has shown in speaking counter-culturally into the difficult issues of our time and for the grace-filled proposals that flow from their writings.

We want to particularly recognize the contribution of our good friend, priest and professor Emmanuel Katongole. More than anyone else, the writings of Fr. Katongole provided the theological inspiration for the conference and this book. While the title and structure of the book owes much to Walter Brueggemann's classic book *The Prophetic Imagination* (1978), the spirit and the content is modeled on the works of Fr. Katongole. We are grateful for his faithfulness and his deep wisdom, and it is for this reason that we have dedicated this volume to him.

We also want to thank those who have not had any direct involvement in the book, but without whom the conference, and therefore the book, would not have come together. Essential to this collaboration was our remarkable colleague Dean Nelson. Dean runs the annual Writer's Symposium-by-the-Sea which was woven together seamlessly with the conference. This allowed us to bring to PLNU three of our main speakers—Michael Eric Dyson, Kathleen Norris and Bill McKibben—all of whom contributed to this book. This collaboration also allowed us to draw upon the wonderful administrative strengths of Edie Chapman and Jennifer Rogers, who together spent countless hours on all of the planning details that generally escape academics like us. It was fantastic to be able to focus on the big picture, and to be able to trust that all of the "details" would be taken care of.

From the beginning, fellow PLNU colleagues played a significant role in providing vision and planning support. Special thanks to PLNU Vice President of Spiritual Development Mary Paul and Chaplain Mark Carter for weaving this theme into campus spiritual life for the 2009-2010 academic calendar. Heartfelt thanks to our fellow academic center directors, including Linda Beail, who directs the Center for Women's Studies, Rob Gailey, who directs the Center for International Development, Randy Ataide, Executive Director for the Fermanian Business and Economic Institute and Norm Shoemaker, Director for the Center for Pastoral Leadership. They each helped to organize special events and sessions relating the theme to their expertise and special areas of interest. Their participation ensured a breadth of interdisciplinary reflection and participation that challenged us all to think in new categories. Readers will reap the fruit of this interdisciplinary collaboration in this book.

We would be remiss if we did not also express our gratitude to PLNU President Bob Brower, PLNU Provost Kerry Fulcher and then-president of Nazarene Theological Seminary Ron Benefiel for their support for our work. Their support stayed strong in the midst of criticism brought upon them by persons outside of the university. Our critical eye and confessional call to the church evoked criticism from within the church, and never once did these leaders express concern or frustration for the many hours they spent fielding questions from concerned constituents. To the contrary, they were some of our biggest supporters in articulating the central themes of the conference to a wider community, and we owe them all a great debt. A special thank you also to Ron Benefiel for serving as Master of Ceremonies for the conference.

Finally, we are deeply appreciative to all those who gave of their time and energy to write and slog with us through a two-year editorial process. Special thanks to Wesleyan Center/Point Loma Press staff, Sharon Bowles and Lydia Heberling, for their assistance in bringing the project to its completion.

Psalm 85

You once favored, LORD, your land, restored the good fortune of Jacob.
You forgave the guilt of your people, pardoned all their sins. Selah
You withdrew all your wrath, turned back your burning anger.
Restore us once more, God our savior; abandon your wrath against us.
Will you be angry with us forever, drag out your anger for all generations?
Please give us life again, that your people may rejoice in you.
Show us, LORD, your love; grant us your salvation.
I will listen for the word of God; surely the LORD will proclaim peace
To his people, to the faithful, to those who trust in him.
Near indeed is salvation for the loyal; prosperity will fill our land.
Kindness and truth shall meet; justice and peace shall kiss.
Truth shall spring out of the earth; justice shall look down from the heavens.
The LORD will surely grant abundance; our land will yield its increase.
Prosperity will march before the Lord, and good fortune will follow behind.

—New American Bible, 1991; italics, 1970

Introduction

Jamie Gates

What does it mean to step consciously into the stream of the prophetic traditions of ancient scriptures and Christian history? Some would say only history can judge a particular contribution to be prophetic. We disagree. With this book, *Nurturing the Prophetic Imagination*, the authors make the case that it is the responsibility of the church and its educators to draw on the deepest wisdom of the past to raise up new schools of prophetic thought and action for the present.[1] The prophetic purposes of this book are to (1) *call believers in Christ to think deeply about the ways in which the church has accommodated itself to or been marred by the influences of the dominant culture—economically, politically, morally, socially and relationally*, (2) *encourage more faithful practice of the Christian disciplines of confession and lament*, and (3) *proclaim more fully the love and hope of God in Christ who created the world, saved us from ourselves and is reconciling all things*. The authors in this work were asked to reflect on where the prophetic work of God was happening in the contemporary world, to reflect on the prophetic nature of their own work, to compare their work to the work of the Old Testament prophets who delivered tough messages to their people in order to call them back to the purposes of God and to announce the incarnation of God in Christ.

Prophetic

In his influential work *The Prophetic Imagination* (1978; 2005), the eminent Old Testament scholar and Christian poet/writer/activist Walter Brueggemann reminds us that:

> The task of prophetic ministry is to nurture, nourish, and evoke a consciousness and perception alternative to the consciousness and perception of the dominant culture around us. ... The alternative consciousness to be nurtured, on the one hand, serves to *criticize*

---

1. This book arises out of the work of scholars and practitioners who participated in the "Nurturing the Prophetic Imagination" conference at Point Loma Nazarene University in the spring of 2010. The conference was co-hosted by the university's Wesleyan Center for 21st Century Studies, the Writer's Symposium-by-the-Sea, the Margaret Stevenson Women's Studies Center, Center for International Development and the Center for Justice and Reconciliation. The conference title was based upon the work of Walter Brueggemann and his landmark book, *The Prophetic Imagination*, first published in 1978. In this book, and its more recent *2001* edition, Brueggemann attempts to call believers in Christ to regain a biblical understanding of the role of the prophets as they operated as God's messengers in Old Testament times, but also to make us more aware of the prophetic role of the church in today's world.

in dismantling the dominant consciousness [i.e., rejection and delegitimatizing of the present ordering of things]. On the other hand, that alternative consciousness to be nurtured serves to *energize* persons and communities by its promise of another time and situation toward which the community of faith may move [i.e., to live in fervent anticipation of the newness that God has promised and will surely give].[2]

Criticizing and energizing—two essential tasks of the prophets of history, two tasks in narrative and historical order, two interdependent tasks, where one falls apart without the other. The tasks of criticizing and energizing are measured by the deep wisdom of the Christian scriptures, tradition, reason and experience[3] in the context of the people of God gathered for worship, lit. *ekklesia*, the Church. These prophetic tasks are dependent on a "deep memory,"[4] remembering rightly who we are (creatures, created in the image of God) and what we are to do (to love God with all one's heart, mind, soul and strength, and to love one's neighbor as oneself). Radical prophetic action drives us, returns us, connects us to the deepest roots of love, justice and reconciliation that have been flowing since the beginning of time—the story of God and God's people. And prophetic action should drive us to the "exuberant hope"[5] of God found incarnate in Christ and poured out on God's people through the Holy Spirit.

If *deep memory* is the first act, and *exuberant hope* the culminating act of the prophetic drama, then there is a third act central to the prophetic vocation more implicit in Bruegemann's work: *confession and lament*. Remember that the Gospel of Matthew begins in lament, quoting Jeremiah 31:

> A cry is heard in Ramah
> Wailing, bitter weeping
> Rachel, weeping for her children
> She refuses to be consoled,
> For her children, who are not. (Jer 31:15)

---

2. Walter Brueggemann, *The Prophetic Imagination* (2d ed.; Minneapolis: Fortress, 2001; first ed. 1978). 3.

3. The hermeneutic assumed here is that Christian life is interpreted through the lens of scripture with the help of the history of interpreters (tradition), the power of human reason and the breadth of human experience. See Don Thorsen, *The Wesleyan Quadrilateral: Scripture, Tradition, Reason and Experience as a Model of Evangelical Theology* (Grand Rapids: Francis Asbury Press for Zondervan, 1990; Lexington, KY: Emeth Press, 2005).

4. Walter Brueggemann, *Deep Memory, Exuberant Hope: Contested Truth in a Post-Christian World* (Minneapolis: Fortress Press, 2000).

5. Ibid.

Jesus was born into a world that so feared his presence that babies were slaughtered to prevent him from existing. Writing on the centrality of lament for Christians in post-genocide Rwanda, citing this passage from Jeremiah, Father Emmanuel Katongole reminds us that:

> Beginning with the memory of [the] 1994 [genocide] not only allows lament of the many innocent Rwandans killed, it also allows Christians to lament the violence that Christianity has unwittingly performed in Africa. For what the ironic contradictions of Rwanda 1994 helped to reveal is the fact that genocide was not an event that happened outside the peaceful ways and message of Christianity. The genocide happened at the very heart of a Christian story in Rwanda. Thus lament allows Christians to begin to own the story of Christianity in Rwanda as not only the story of Easter, but also the story of an endless Passion, of a never ending Good Friday.[6]

Christians are aware that those who mourn are blessed, as Jesus preached in the Sermon on the Mount,[7] but the prophetic vocation involves habitual reminders that, in the face of suffering and injustice that breaks the heart of God, the people of God *refuse to be consoled*.[8]

We may summarize the historic pattern of the prophets as follows:

Deep memory (criticizing) > refusing to be consoled (confession and lament) > exuberant hope (energizing)

But we should be careful with this kind of over-simplification. We should never assume that this is a simple formula that enacts the prophetic drama in and of itself; prophets are raised up in the deep stories of the faith. Nor can this pattern be abstracted and pulled out of its larger narrative and historical context; it is a pattern that assumes the ongoing discipleship of a holy people, a people called out as witness to what God is doing in the world, a people with a particular history. Nor can we assume that this prophetic vocation includes all of that to which the people of God are called. While the prophetic calling may be to lament, God's people also act pastorally as witnesses to God's comfort

---

6. Emmanuel Katongole, "Violence and Christian Social Reconstruction in Africa: On the resurrection of the body (politic)," *The Other Journal*, 6 (January 2005): 2.

7. Matthew 5:4.

8. Of course, we do not take lightly that God has little interest in leaving God's people in a constant state of lament. Remember that *refusing to be consoled* is in the context of a larger story that is always moving toward *exuberant hope*. The prophetic work of confession and lament guards against the common temptation toward what Bonhoeffer called *cheap grace*, i.e., "the preaching of forgiveness without repentance," Dietrich Bonhoeffer, *The Cost of Discipleship* (New York: MacMillan, 1966).

and care. With these qualifications in mind, we have found this historic pattern useful for guiding the broad outlines of our book.

Imagination

Most of us tend to think of children and artists when we think of "good imaginations." We think of children because they have "innocent minds" that are untainted by decades of socialization, the pain of life's realities and the complexities of the thought world that adults inhabit. We think of artists as imaginative because of their penchant for creating sounds or forms or words or images that lie outside of or tangential to the normal sounds and forms and words and images of the general population. Both children and artists tend to think outside the box. They tend to surprise us and often make us aware of a different reality right in our midst. Like children and artists, prophets develop ways of helping us see the world not perceived by the general population, often challenging the dominant ways of seeing and being in the world, in ways that are more faithful to the ways God wants us to be in the world.

"Imagination" as we are using it here refers in part to perception, cognition and other fundamentally psychological aspects of understanding. This is what we often mean by "having eyes to see." But it means more than this. We are using "imagination" in a similar sense to how Benedict Anderson did in his well-known book about the rise of modern nations, *Imagined Communities*.[9] Anderson comments on the social (collective) imagination it took to bring the modern nation into existence and to maintain its viability:

> Nationality, or, as one might prefer to put it in view of that word's multiple significations, nation-ness, as well as nationalism, are cultural artifacts of a particular kind. To understand them properly we need to consider carefully how they have come into historical being, in what ways their meanings have changed over time, and why, today, they command such profound emotional legitimacy.[10]

Anderson understands that complex realities like modern nation-states are products of our own invention, change over time, are shaped by creative ideas and in turn shape the ways we not only think about things but also the emotional investments we make in them. What we make of the world arises out of how we make sense of the world. And how we make sense of the world is in turn conditioned by what we have made of the world. At some point in history humans discovered that they could make fire, and that over time opened

---

9. Benedict Anderson, *Imagined Communities: Reflections on the Origin and Spread of Nationalism* (New York: Verso, 1983).
10. Ibid., 48.

the imagination to a world of barbequed meat, slash-n-burn clearing of land for horticultural farming, the smelting of steel for railway lines and all that fire and the human imagination have made possible.

So "imagination" in the way we are using it here is much more than the fanciful dreaming stereotypically attributed to children and artists. It is more than words and symbols and ideas, although deeply dependent on such. Imagination is the means by which we construct our social and physical environment. It is the deep patterning of the ways we see the world and act in it. It is the palette we use to paint the horizons of what is possible or impossible. It is the story that others have constructed for us, that conditions the way we relate to others and the world around us, and that we now find ourselves using to creatively engage the world.

Thus, the prophetic imagination is about telling a particular story. It is about announcing the revelation that God has made another way of seeing and being in the world possible, and about beginning to point to just where that other world has already happened, and is happening, in our midst. Of course, when we start talking about "another way," those of us invested in the current ways of thinking and being become uncomfortable. As Brueggemann puts it: "[P]rophetic texts could be seen as poetic scenarios of alternative social reality that might lead to direct confrontation with 'presumed, taken-for-granted worlds' (the old liberal assumption). The canonical text, as norm for an intergenerational community, might also serve to nurture and fund obedience that is not necessarily confrontational but that simply acts out of a different perceived, differently received, differently practiced world (imagination/obedience)."[11]

The prophetic imagination is not a safe imagination and often avoids confrontation. The prophetic imagination works in the way that poetry works to disorient us, shake up our categories, release us from the chains of conventional socialization and open us up to new insights, new possibilities, a reality that has always been there but has been invisible because we did not have the eyes to see or ears to hear it.

Nurturing

When we were searching for the fitting artwork to represent the conference which led to this book we wanted to draw on the artwork representing the history of our faith. We first tapped into the history of classic art representing the prophets of old. Who could be a more fitting figure than the icon of all prophets, Moses? And who could be a more well-known artist than the Dutch Golden Age artist Rembrandt Van Rijn? So early on we settled on Rembrandt's

---

11. Brueggemann, *Prophetic Imagination*, Preface to the Revised Edition, x–xi.

Moses Smashing the Tablets of the Law, dated approximately 1659. Rembrandt was well educated in the classics and drew deeply from the texts of ancient scripture and Christian tradition for his paintings and sketches. Painting as a Dutch artist in the 1600s, Rembrandt was strongly influenced by both the Renaissance painters and the spirit of the Protestant Reformation. He knew his Bible well, and spent a good deal of his artistic energy painting action scenes from the Bible that were close to the biblical record (not common among the more common Catholic biblical art of the day). He used ordinary people, often Jewish contemporaries, as his models, a counter-cultural act by this artist. Although there is some evidence that Rembrandt was in close fellowship with the evangelical wing of the Mennonites, Rembrandt is on record as a life-long member of the Dutch Reformed Church. When he died in 1669, there was only one book in his possession, his Dutch Bible.[12]

In this painting Rembrandt depicts the moment when Moses came down from receiving the commandments of God on Mount Sinai. Moses is depicted as he is about to smash the holy tablets against the rocks, a symbol of the broken covenant between God and an unfaithful people. Rembrandt highlights the pained look of the prophet Moses. He captures the disappointment and anger of God reflected in Moses' face and demeanor. The painting itself is imposing; standing at five and one-half feet tall, four and one-half feet wide, Moses is larger than life. Standing close to the painting gives the viewer the ominous feeling of being towered over by an angry figure. While there may be timeless aspects to this image, the anger and disappointment in Moses' face evokes the fear and guilt common in the Protestant theology of the Reformation era.

While this portrait of a prophet is provocative, and while it certainly represents a dominant theme in the history of Christian interpretations of the prophetic imagination, its imagery and theology is locked into a time and theological vision that may itself be captured more by the spirit of that age than is right and good for our contemporary times. This was brought to our attention by a number of our female colleagues at PLNU who saw the imposing, angry male figure as just one more reification of an aggressive militant God, giving permission for an aggressive militant male-led people. Certainly the Christian tradition has a long history of worshipping a God whose anger is nothing to take lightly. But we came to see this image of the prophet as unidimensional, as reflecting strongly the transcendence and omnipotence of God while taking too lightly the incarnational and nurturing nature of God's revelation in Christ. And, while this image grounds the prophetic imagination in one of the most pivotal moments in Jewish and Christian traditions, strengthening our deep

---

12. For more history on the influence of Christianity on Rembrandt's life and paintings, see W. A. Visser't Hooft, *Rembrandt and the Gospel*, trans. K. Gregor Smith (Philadelphia: Westminster Press, 1957).

memory and ability to criticize, what's missing from this image is the exuberant hope. We felt in the end that this image tempted contemporary readers to miss the breadth of transformation for which the prophetic imagination calls.

Rebecca Flietstra, professor of biology at PLNU, reminded us of the works of John August Swanson. Born in 1938 to a Mexican mother and a Swedish father, his style is influenced by Islamic and Christian medieval miniatures, Russian iconography, the color of Latin American folk art and the tradition of Mexican muralists.[13] His art hangs in three museums of the Smithsonian Institution: The National Museum of American History, The National Museum of American Art and The National Air and Space Museum. He is also included in the print collections of the Art Institute of Chicago, Harvard University's Fogg Museum, the Tate Gallery and Victoria and Albert Museum in London and the Bibliothèque Nationale in Paris. His painting THE PROCESSION is one of relatively few works by contemporary artists to be selected for the Vatican Museums' Collection of Modern Religious Art. The largest collection of his works on display are currently at Emory University's Candler School of Theology.

Figure 2: *Psalm 85* by John August Swanson

In the end we chose John August Swanson's *Psalm 85* (see Figure 2) to represent our conference, this book and a fuller representation of what we mean by "nurturing the prophetic imagination." The painting contains the following words from Psalm 85:10.

> "Kindness and truth shall meet; justice and peace shall kiss.
> Truth shall spring out of the earth; justice shall look down from the heavens."

---

13. http://www.johnaugustswanson.com/default.cfm/PID=1.5

While the truth of this painting is drawn from the ancient text of the Psalms, thereby requiring a deep memory for its interpretation, the words point us to an exuberantly hopeful time when "justice and peace shall kiss," when justice, kindness and truth shall reign. These ancient words speak the central hope of what God will bring to pass. As a prophetic word for our day, no setting could be more appropriate than the Mexican countryside. Women, children, men, families dependent on domesticated animals, sowing, harvesting—an agrarian life threatened by the dominant economic and political arrangements of the day. Swanson has the prophetic words of God arise from the soil, from the ground, riding on sunbeams and nourishing the activities of some of the most marginalized people on earth.

The prophetic imagination found in Christ the suffering servant is the same imagination found in Psalm 85. Swanson's *Psalm 85* brings the Psalms and Christ into our contemporary situation. Reflected in God's love for widows, orphans and strangers, incarnated in the compassionate[14] life and teachings of Jesus, the prophetic imagination challenges in particular what Brueggemann calls an Economics of Affluence, a Politics of Oppression and a Religion of Immanence. An Economics of Affluence is where wealth for some is built on the backs of others, where the wealthy are so well-off that they can avoid the pain of the working either by refusing to acknowledge it or by consuming their way around it. We don't have to look much beyond the growing gap between the rich and the poor around the world to see such an economy at work. A Politics of Oppression is when power for some comes at the expense of the weakest, where the cries of the marginal are not heard or are dismissed as crazy or treasonous, where the weak are blamed for conditions brought on them by the powerful. These are the times we live in as small scale farmers all over the world are getting squeezed off their land by massive agri-business corporations that gobble up more and more land and profits with the backing of global trade policies in order to feed increasingly luxurious appetites for a global elite. A Religion of Immanence is when God looks an awful lot like us, where divine authority is defined by and has been appropriated for the use of a privileged few, where spirituality

---

14. This is compassion as Henri Nouwen makes use of the term in *Compassion: A Reflection on the Christian Life*. Here Nouwen breaks down the term: *com* = with, and *passion* = suffering. The compassion of Christ is God incarnate choosing to suffer with all of humanity rather than use violence to overthrow evil. This compassion is profoundly counter-cultural, prophetic. "Let us not underestimate how hard it is to be compassionate. Compassion is hard because it requires the inner disposition to go with others to place where they are weak, vulnerable, lonely, and broken. But this is not our spontaneous response to suffering. What we desire most is to do away with suffering by fleeing from it or finding a quick cure for it." From McNeill, Donald P., Douglas A. Morrison and Henri J. M. Nouwen, *Compassion: A Reflection on the Christian Life* (Garden City, NJ: Image Press, 1983), 3.

translates to a private, safe, domesticated God easily accessible, used for our own ends. Nations often claim that they are "one nation, under God," while their policies and practices bear little resemblance to a covenant relationship with God. At the more local level, God is often treated like our friend, like a "buddy" who is easily understandable and relatable. Such a god is palatable, a god that draws a crowd, grows congregations, an easily marketable god. But the prophets remind us that this is not the God of all Nations when nations and corporations can deploy these kinds of gods for their own ends. Swanson's *Psalm 85* reminds us that the hope of God's work in the world becomes far more apparent to us when we spend time with those on the margins.

We also chose Swanson's *Psalm 85* because of how difficult it would be to reduce its impact to the rational and didactic sense we make of the work. It speaks prophetically in its beauty, in its poetry. It contains bright and colorful images, full of life and joy. It visually lifts the spirits as it lifts the eyes in waves from the earth to the sun. In its imagery and in drawing on the Psalms it speaks in the mode of the poet rather than the preacher. The prophetic imagination is clever and crafty this way, finding alternative images, stories, language to broach the unspeakable beauty, truth and goodness of God. We find ourselves increasingly in desperate need of poets and artists, the ones who consistently nurture the imagination, to also take up the prophetic task of reminding us of our deep past and spiritual roots, teaching us the language of lament and lifting us up with a vision of hope that cannot be mistaken for anything other than the revelation of God.

Part I: Primer on the Prophets

Jamie Gates

In the opening essay of our introductory section, Dr. Brad Kelle invites us to reflect on the contribution of renowned Old Testament scholar Walter Brueggemann to our understanding of what it means to be prophetically engaged in the world. While this book is not specifically built around his scholarship, nor should Dr. Brueggemann take any of the blame for the direction we have taken this work, his 1978 work *The Prophetic Imagination* stands as a roadsign pointing the church in a direction the authors of this book follow, a movement toward a much deeper and richer engagement with the prophetic traditions of the past for the sake of the active, liturgical life of the church.

As Dr. Kelle reminds us:

> By bringing together elements of social-scientific exegesis, rhetoric, and liberationist perspectives, Brueggemann's *The Prophetic Imagination* constructed a way of reading that engages in social criticism of both the political, cultural, and economic dynamics in the texts and those at work in the contemporary circumstances and dominant discourses into which the texts may speak, especially the church's liturgical life and practices in the industrial West.

The present volume assumes we are to draw on the best of social-scientific research for understanding both the ancient and contemporary worlds. It assumes the power of rhetoric to generate not only new ideas, but new behaviors and new social realities. And consistently the essays assume and most often articulate the same prophetic moral concern for justice and care for those on the margins, i.e., the widow, orphan and stranger.

Dr. Maria Pascuzzi helps to ground our understanding of the prophetic imagination in the lives and activities of the Old Testament prophets. She bridges the hermeneutical gap between the ancient worlds of the Old Testament prophets and the pressing social issues of our time. She points out that "the history of the kingdoms of Israel and Judah is, with few exceptions, a litany of ineffective monarchs who abused their power and were responsible for the conditions that generated serious social inequity." Goods and resources were monopolized for the prosperity of some at the expense of others. Often forgotten in the prophetic concern for the marginalized, Pascuzzi reminds us that "the social and economic injustices went hand in hand with the disregard for the land and the environment."

The arc of the ancient prophetic imagination is seen to carry into the New Testament most directly in the life, teachings and actions of Jesus of Nazareth. Theologian Michael Lodahl helps to distinguish the prophetic imagination from the apocalyptic imagination, which "tends to operate on the strong assumption that the world can only get worse."

But as Lodahl explores the prophetic imagination in the Gospel of Matthew, he leads us to a vision of the prophetic imagination grounded in the words of God through the prophet Hosea, "I desire mercy and not sacrifice." The prophetic imagination "reveals a divine yearning ... a longing of God for the world to be different, to be a place where compassion flows toward human suffering and need, where the hungry have plenty to eat and health care truly is provided for all."

Theologian and pastor Rebecca Laird examines the life of a 20th century figure whom she believes embodies the prophetic imagination as well as any other contemporaries. Dorothee Soelle, Protestant German liberation theologian of the late 20th century, lived "bewildered by a larger question: How could her family, society and the world at large act as if the existing structures that lead to educational success and religious propriety nourish a full adult life for her if they also bred the silences that allowed six million people to die at the hands of educated, civilized people who were formed by those selfsame structures?" Her faith was formed on the anvil of her own suffering, the suffering of her family and the suffering of countless others during World War II. All of her writing, indeed her theology and living, were done remembering the ashes of Auschwitz.

Laird describes Soelle's contribution to the prophetic imagination as one that "[Soelle] did not wait for a new heaven in some immaterial future; she wanted it to be 'on earth as it is in heaven.' She understood the way to bring heaven to this earth was by 'embedding this vision' in her daily life and in her social interactions."

Tilling the Soil with Care

Kelle, Pascuzzi, Laird and the authors in this volume recognize that the prophetic work of God's people is fraught with possible missteps and dangerous paths down which other reportedly prophetic voices have led. Avoiding these dangerous paths is as important as finding the more fruitful ones.

A common misconception is to confuse the prophets with soothsayers, seers or futurists. Prophets are sometimes thought to look into a crystal ball to give some secret information about the future that only they possess. But the prophets of Christian and Jewish tradition were more commonly reading the signs of the times as interpreted through lessons from the past (scripture and tradition) that everyone in the community should already have known. Isaiah and Jeremiah speak to the reality of a people under siege, taken into exile under the Babylonians, interpreting their troubles as a function of their unfaithfulness to their historic covenant with God. While nurturing the prophetic imagination does lead to reflection on what the future might look like if the unfaithful continue down the destructive path, it is not principally about predicting the future. We'll learn more about these contrasts from Dr. Lodahl in Chapter 3 of this volume.

Those who consciously stand in the prophetic traditions must be on guard for the temptation of self-righteousness. The temptation to self-righteous moralizing always hangs over those who claim to be counter-cultural. How can we be sure that in saying "Thus Sayeth the Lord!" we are not just baptizing our own concerns and proclivities with the waters of divine authority? This temptation is particularly strong when those speaking are from the dominant culture, already vested with power that others do not share. This temptation is particularly strong when we are embedded in a dominant culture that prizes the power of the heroic individual.

Guarding against the temptation to self-righteous moralizing requires that we speak confessionally in community with those we are challenging, and from among those whose suffering is breaking the heart of God. Before pointing the finger at the surrounding culture and calling it evil, have we confessed the corruption from within? Have we examined the role that we play in others' suffering? Have we examined the faithfulness of those that call themselves the people of God, or followers of Christ? In fact, most of the prophets' energies are spent on correcting and cajoling the people of God—those that claim faith—not those that don't.

Contemporary prophets amplify the voices of the proverbial widow, orphan and stranger in our midst, but doing so from the seats of power and not the periphery can itself be a sign of self-righteousness, even hypocrisy. While the prophets speak on behalf of the poor and marginalized, rarely can they speak for those who are suffering if they are not also amidst and among those who are suffering. Christ models this in the incarnation as he lived, suffered and died in solidarity with all of humanity.

The prophetic traditions often model speaking truth to power ("prophet versus King"). At times Christians from the dominant culture may need to take advantage of their citizenship to speak in the halls of power (rarely do people on the margins have this privilege). But when such is required, we are to guard even more carefully against the temptation to self-righteous muckraking. We do not go into the halls of power hoping to take hold of the reigns of power, or with our ultimate hope in their solutions, for that would be idolatry. But prophets recognize that God may use the powers-that-be for God's purposes, often even despite their lack of faith.

At times Christians may need to be less like Amos directly confronting Amaziah (Amos 7:10–17) and more like Jesus subtly and non-violently confronting the Pharisees and Pilate with humor and sarcasm, prophetic interpretations of scripture and faithful obedience that may likely include suffering. But prophets are rarely nice ... not the kind of people you want to take home to the family. Prophets speak difficult truth into difficult situations.

In the end, it is God who raises up prophets when the time is right. While God raises up prophets, we can create a social environment that will be much more hospitable to the emergence of prophetic communities. Jesus raised up disciples; the prophets of biblical history were trained in prophetic schools. We can do our part to remove the weeds and nurture the soil from which the prophetic imagination springs. This book is just such an attempt.

1

Prophecy, Canon and Imagination: Walter Brueggemann's *The Prophetic Imagination* and the Contributions of Biblical Interpretation to the Prophetic Project

Brad E. Kelle

The conference at which many of the essays in this volume were originally delivered—and, indeed, the larger ethos and project in which they participate—stand in a legacy formed, in part, by Walter Brueggemann's brief work of biblical scholarship first published in 1978 entitled, *The Prophetic Imagination*.[1] As a work of biblical hermeneutics, Brueggemann's volume was noticeably brief and focused on a particular corpus of Old Testament (OT) material and a specific mode of interpretation. Its contribution, however, has proven to be paradigmatic, especially for defining the nature of "prophetic" engagement between church and culture. The book appeared at a time in the late 1970s when the kinds of conversations about a theology of culture, politics and economics now so well-known to the contemporary church and academy were underway in varying degrees.[2] No doubt those developing conversations within theology and ecclesiology partially evoked Brueggemann's volume—both consciously and otherwise. Within the field of biblical scholarship in the late 1970s, however, the perspectives and issues associated with theological reflection on society, politics and economics had yet to be substantially integrated into the interpretive practices of biblical scholars. And therein may be the most significant legacy of Brueggemann's initial and later work as a biblical interpreter. In a distinctive way, Brueggemann, beginning in earnest with his 1978 treatment, made the biblical texts, especially the OT prophets, available in new and profound ways to those struggling to articulate a theology of critical Christian engagement with culture, politics and economics. He "gave back" the prophetic texts in particular to theologians, ministers, sociologists and others who perhaps sensed that such ancient texts had little, if anything, constructive to offer to their critical and hermeneutical project. Moreover, he did so by helping to solidify an understanding of prophets and prophecy that moves beyond common (mis)conceptions of prophets and brings the prophetic texts into the church's liturgical life and practice in ways that can nourish and evoke new types of engagement with the dominant culture.

---

1. Walter Brueggemann, *The Prophetic Imagination* (2nd ed.; Minneapolis: Fortress, 2001; first ed. 1978). All quotations are taken from the 2d ed.

2. See, for example, the earlier work of Richard H. Niebuhr, *Christ and Culture* (New York: Harper, 1951).

The purpose of this essay is to illustrate briefly the elements of the legacy that Brueggemann, particularly in *The Prophetic Imagination*, has created concerning biblical scholarship, the notion of the "prophetic" and the potential of biblical interpretation to contribute to the conversation represented by the present volume. While much more could be said about this scholar's lasting impact upon issues touching social justice, liberationist hermeneutics, ecclesial theology and ministerial practice,[3] Brueggemann's initial and continued work offers a method of engagement with the OT prophetic texts in particular that centers on rhetoric and imagination. This approach moves beyond both popular (mis)conceptions of prophets and prophecy and merely historicist or deconstructivist options to make the biblical texts available in new ways to fund the church's struggle with a theology of culture, politics and economics.

Rhetoric and Imagination

The Prophetic Imagination stands as one representative of the large body of work that has established Brueggemann as arguably the most significant American OT scholar in the second half of the twentieth and early part of the twenty-first centuries. Impressively, his more than 50 books and numerous other articles demonstrate a tenacious cohesiveness. Each in its own way, Brueggemann's works give voice to a type of engagement with the biblical texts that combines literary and sociological modes of reading, featuring a theological interpretation involved with sociological and ideological concerns of both the texts and their past and present reading communities. The mode of interpretation is dialogical and dialectical. He reads diverse biblical texts in dialogue with one another, holding various theologies and ideologies expressed in different texts in tension and connecting them with the social and ideological forces in the ancient contexts that shaped them.[4] At the same time, he moves the biblical texts toward engagement with contemporary social and theological situations in ways that establish a dialogue between the theological impulses

---

3. Among Brueggemann's litany of books, see the following examples: Walter Brueggemann, *Living Toward a Vision: Biblical Reflections on Shalom* (Philadelphia: United Church Press, 1976; 2nd ed. 1982); idem, *Hopeful Imagination: Prophetic Voices in Exile* (Philadelphia: Fortress, 1986); idem, *Abiding Astonishment: Psalms, Modernity, and the Making of History* (Literary Currents in Biblical Interpretation; Louisville: Westminster/John Knox, 1991); idem, *An Introduction to the Old Testament: The Canon and Christian Imagination* (Louisville: Westminster/John Knox, 2003); idem, *A Mandate To Be Different: An Invitation to the Contemporary Church* (Louisville: Westminster/John Knox, 2007); idem, *The Word Militant: Preaching a Decentering Word* (Minneapolis: Fortress, 2007). Most recently, see Walter Brueggemann, *Disruptive Grace: Reflections on God, Scripture, and the Church* (edited and introduced by Carolyn J. Sharp; Minneapolis: Augsburg, 2011).

4. See especially, Walter Brueggemann, *Theology of the Old Testament: Testimony, Dispute, Advocacy* (Minneapolis: Fortress, 1997) and idem, *An Introduction to the Old Testament*.

in the texts and the social and economic realities that characterize modern Western society in particular.

As Brueggemann himself describes in the preface to the second edition of *The Prophetic Imagination*, several trends that were emerging within biblical scholarship in the late 1970s shaped his initial work in these directions and the interpretive approach that resulted from it. One such trend was the emergence of social-scientific approaches to biblical texts.[5] These approaches began by taking more serious account of the fact that the biblical texts emerged from real people in real socio-economic contexts and that these factors produced ideologies that both evoked and are evoked by the texts themselves. Such sociological sensitivities moved away from the dominance of historical criticism in biblical interpretation by calling interpreters to attend to the ideological concerns that shaped the texts, as well as the kinds of socio-cultural understandings and practices that the texts elicit. Similarly, Brueggemann's 1978 work stood near the beginning of a trend that over the following years would emphasize the importance of rhetoric and "rhetorical criticism" in the interpretation of biblical texts.[6] This mode of reading attended with care to the particularities of the language of the texts. Yet it also sought to take account of the "generative, constitutive power" possessed by that language—the ability of these texts to evoke new understandings of reality and persuade readers into those new conceptions. A third trend, which was only beginning to find a place in biblical scholarship at the time of Brueggemann's initial writing, was the hermeneutics of liberationist theologies.[7] Perhaps more so than any other hermeneutical movement, liberationist perspectives foregrounded the living and vital intersections between the biblical texts and the societal, economic

---

5. Brueggemann, *Prophetic Imagination*, ix. As examples of this approach, the years immediately following the publication of the first edition of *The Prophetic Imagination* saw the appearance of Norman K. Gottwald, *The Tribes of Yahweh: A Sociology of the Religion of Liberated Israel, 1250–1050 B.C.* (Maryknoll, N.Y.: Orbis, 1979) and Robert R. Wilson, *Prophecy and Society in Ancient Israel* (Philadelphia: Fortress, 1980).

6. Brueggemann, *Prophetic Imagination*, x. For example, the same year in which *The Prophetic Imagination* was published saw the publication of Phyllis Trible, *God and the Rhetoric of Sexuality* (OBT; Philadelphia: Fortress, 1978). For more recent discussion of rhetoric and the prophetic texts in particular, see Phyllis Trible, *Rhetorical Criticism: Context, Method, and the Book of Jonah* (Guides to Biblical Scholarship; Minneapolis: Fortress, 1994) and Brad E. Kelle, *Hosea 2: Metaphor and Rhetoric in Historical Perspective* (SBL Academia Biblica 20; Atlanta: Society of Biblical Literature, 2005).

7. For a classic example, see Gustavo Gutiérrez, *A Theology of Liberation: History, Politics, and Salvation* (trans. and ed. C. Inda and J. Eagleson; Maryknoll, N.Y.: Orbis, 1973). From within biblical studies, see more recently Anthony R. Ceresko, *Introduction to the Old Testament: A Liberation Perspective* (rev. ed.; Maryknoll, N.Y.: Orbis, 2001); Miguel A. De La Torre, *Reading the Bible from the Margins* (Maryknoll, N.Y.: Orbis, 2002); Gerald O. West, ed., *Reading Other-Wise: Socially Engaged Biblical Scholars Reading with Their Local Communities* (Society of Biblical Literature Semeia Studies 62; Atlanta: Society of Biblical Literature, 2007).

and political structures that so often dictated the experience of the world's poor. As Brueggemann describes, years of reflection and practice emerging from communities in Latin America and elsewhere generated biblical hermeneutics that were shaped in response to the "enmeshment of the United States church in the raging force of globalization and the easy accommodation of church faith and practice to consumer commoditism."[8]

By bringing together elements of social-scientific exegesis, rhetoric and liberationist perspectives, Brueggemann's *The Prophetic Imagination* constructed a way of reading that engages in social criticism of both the political, cultural and economic dynamics in the texts and those at work in the contemporary circumstances and dominant discourses into which the texts may speak, especially the church's liturgical life and practices in the industrial West. What emerged from this intersection was a mode of interpreting the prophetic texts that centers on rhetoric and, in particular, imagination. Funded by the important insights on imagination by Paul Riceour and others, Brueggemann arrived at the conviction that Old Testament prophetic texts invite imaginative interpretation that moves the texts beyond themselves. Moreover, the texts themselves are "acts of imagination that offer and purpose 'alternative worlds' that exist because of and in the act of the utterance."[9] The texts do not merely describe or speak to a "common sense world," but employ rhetoric, artistry and testimony to "posit, characterize, and vouch for a world beyond the 'common sense.'"[10] Here is a method that reads the Old Testament prophets not simply as spokespersons delivering messages to their day, but as imaginative agents that picture an alternative construal of reality and provoke new practices of justice in line with that imagined reality. The prophets' imagination then calls the church to imagine how to move from these texts to new circumstances in which the church's life and practices unfold. For Brueggemann, read in this way, the prophetic texts can "nurture and fund obedience that ... acts out of a differently perceived, differently received, differently practiced world (imagination/obedience)."[11]

For those interested in the larger conversation concerning the church's theology of culture, politics and economics, especially those who participate in that conversation from points of reference other than professional biblical scholarship, perhaps the most significant aspect of Brueggemann's interpretive moves that found early expression in *The Prophetic Imagination* is how they continue to allow one to move beyond certain tendencies in the treatment of the biblical (particularly prophetic) texts to enable those texts to contribute to the

---

8. Brueggemann, *Prophetic Imagination*, xi.
9. Ibid., x.
10. Brueggemann, *An Introduction to the Old Testament*, 9.
11. Brueggemann, *Prophetic Imagination*, xi.

conversation about church and culture in ongoing and fresh ways. At the most basic level, Brueggemann's reading moves beyond common (mis)conceptions of prophets as end-time futurists and apocalyptic prognosticators to establish an understanding of the "prophetic" as that which works within dominant cultures and discourses to evoke and nourish new conceptions of reality and new ways of ordering society. Additionally, Brueggemann's interpretive impulses move beyond the historical-critical paradigm that had so long reigned in biblical interpretation and often had the effect of relegating the biblical texts to antiquarian artifacts with little significance for contemporary societies.[12] Rather than restricting engagement with the prophetic texts to descriptive analyses of Israel's history and religion, Brueggemann's mode of interpretation enlivens these texts as shaping voices for the church that establish a "dynamic equivalent" between Israel's life and that of faith communities today.[13]

Finally, Brueggemann's hermeneutic, while originally formulated at a time when liberationist theologies were only beginning to find a place in biblical studies, provides a means by which one can keep the biblical texts as an important resource for the church even in the face of sharp and appropriate liberationist and post-colonialist critiques of the problematic elements of the Bible that have emerged over the last few decades.[14] Since the 1980s, important liberationist insights about the problematic social, economic and political ideologies that both elicited and are elicited by some Old Testament texts suggested for some that the role of biblical interpretation in the church's struggle with a theology of culture and politics is primarily deconstructive—a project to expose those biblical ideologies and criticize the beliefs and practices that they generate in modern settings. Without denying the social matrices that produced the texts, Brueggemann provides a way to highlight the diversity of the biblical testimonies and find within them the resources for the church's confrontation (both direct and subtle) with presumed worlds and their dominant discourses.[15] The church's engagement with the biblical texts can be constructive, as they evoke for the church new ways to challenge taken-for-granted operations and envision alternative scenarios. For Brueggemann, the Old Testament prophets provide the paradigm for the rhetoric and imagination that provides the church with needed ongoing resources, and he explicates just that conviction in the classic work of *The Prophetic Imagination*.

Brueggemann's *The Prophetic Imagination*

Appreciation of the paradigmatic nature of the Old Testament prophets for the church's engagement with culture begins in Brueggemann's *The Prophetic*

---

12. See Ibid., ix.
13. Brueggemann, *Hopeful Imagination*, ix, 6.
14. See Brueggemann, *The Prophetic Imagination*, x.
15. Ibid., x–xi.

Imagination with a clear and decisive move away from common misconceptions of prophecy as futuristic prediction of end-times and other scenarios. At the most essential level, Brueggemann's 1978 classic is an attempt to broaden the church's understanding of the "prophetic" task, both past and present. Necessarily, his first move in the book is to the Old Testament prophets in which he forwards the conviction that the "prophetic" task emerges from the recognition that prophetic texts envision and help to create alternative worlds and social realities that confront dominant worlds:

> [B]iblical texts ... are acts of imagination that offer and purpose "alternative worlds" that exist because of and in the act of utterance ... in particular prophetic texts, could be seen as poetic scenarios of alternative social reality that might lead to direct confrontation with "presumed, taken-for-granted worlds."[16]

The alert reader will recognize here the notions mentioned above about texts, rhetoric and the power to shape worlds from the works of Paul Ricoeur and others, but Brueggemann ultimately emphasizes that the "prophetic imagination" revolves around just that—"imagination"—not as a flight of fancy, but as a "legitimate way of knowing" and acting in the world.[17]

From this starting point, Brueggemann looks to the life of ancient Israel and its representations in the OT and locates the prophetic task at the point where two *consciousnesses* or societies collide: the royal consciousness or "normative" society of the empire and the alternative consciousness, or Mosaic community. The royal consciousness appears first in the oppressive experiences of Pharaoh's Egypt and later reappears, after a brief interruption by Moses, in the practices of Israel's monarchy in the days of Solomon and beyond.[18] Several characteristics mark this consciousness, including affluence that leads to a type of consumption, oppressive social policies that produce affluence for some and lack for others, and a static conception of society and religion that permits no newness but only a given status quo that binds the divine to the dominant social practices. As Brueggemann summarizes:

> The royal consciousness with its program of achievable satiation has redefined our notions of humanness ... It has created a subjective consciousness concerned only with self-satisfaction. It has denied the legitimacy of tradition that requires us to remember, of authority that expects us to answer, and of community that calls us to care. It has so

---

16. Ibid.
17. Ibid., x.
18. See Ibid., 21–38.

enthroned the present that a promised future, delayed but certain, is unthinkable.[19]

By contrast, Brueggemann asserts that the alternative consciousness or Mosaic community begins with an imagination that conceives a real freedom for the divine, who is not bound within the social processes but is able to break in for newness.[20] As a result, this consciousness/community features a politics of justice and compassion that produces a new way of imagining God and the world. Brueggemann explains:

> The mythic claims of the empire are ended by the disclosure of the *alternative religion of the freedom of God* ... At the same time, Moses dismantles the politics of oppression and exploitation by countering it with a *politics of justice and compassion* ... The program of Moses is not the freeing of a little band of slaves ... Rather, his work is nothing less than an assault on the consciousness of the empire, aimed at nothing less than the dismantling of the empire both in its social practices and in its mythic pretensions.[21]

The heart of Brueggemann's conception of the "prophetic" task is the assertion that the "prophetic imagination" is the means by which to move from the royal to the Mosaic consciousness. And this prophetic imagination involves two primary tasks: to criticize and to energize. In Brueggemann's conception, the act of criticism embodied by the OT prophets goes beyond denunciation and more properly means to *expose* the unjust and fraudulent character of the dominant, taken-for-granted social constructions.[22] In the act of criticism, the prophets offer symbols to a community that break through the numbness, denial and despair produced by the royal consciousness and bring to public expression the elements of "deathliness" at work in a society and the suppressed fears that accompany them.[23] Prophetic criticism is an act of speaking, often metaphorically and symbolically, about the imaginations and myths that undergird the operations of the empire, showing these imaginations and myths to be fraudulent and untrustworthy. For Brueggemann, the prophet Jeremiah gives the clearest embodiment of criticism's function to embrace pathos and pain—especially through the personal and public expression of grief[24]—and

---

19. Ibid., 37.
20. See Ibid., 1–19.
21. Ibid., 6–7, 9 (italics original).
22. See Ibid., 39–57.
23. Ibid., 45.
24. On the importance of grief for the act of criticism, Brueggemann states, "I believe that the proper idiom for the prophet in cutting through the royal numbness and denial is the *language of*

thereby refuses to deny the suffering and death caused by the present system. The criticism of Jeremiah and others "provides a way in which the cover-up and the stonewalling can be ended ... To *bring to public expression those very fears and terrors* that have been denied so long and suppressed so deeply that we do not know they are there."[25]

If criticism is ultimately an act of grief and exposure, the second and correlated prophetic task of energizing is the stirring of a new sense of wonder, amazement and possibility that leads a people not only to envision but to enact a new mode of existence.[26] Most fully embodied in the preaching now collected in so-called "Second Isaiah" (Isa 40–55), Brueggemann identifies the act of energizing as the prophet's offering of new symbols to a community (often powerful, historical symbols such as the exodus from Egypt) that contradict the feelings of despair and bring to public expression the hopes that have been suppressed. Prophetic energizing is a way of speaking—often metaphorically and symbolically, yet still concretely—about the real possibility of newness that can redefine life. As Brueggemann explains, "The royal consciousness leads people to despair about the power to move toward new life. It is the task of prophetic imagination and ministry to bring people to engage the promise of newness that is at work in our history with God."[27]

Out of the exploration of these elements of the Old Testament prophets and in keeping with Brueggemann's own commitment to the life and ministry of the church, the final sections of *The Prophetic Imagination* turn to the ways that the prophetic task can shape the contemporary Christian community. Brueggemann devotes extended attention to how his understanding of the prophetic imagination provides a lens to view the person of Jesus of Nazareth.[28] In short, he contends that Jesus embodies the prophetic imagination through the acts of crucifixion and resurrection. Jesus's crucifixion serves as the decisive criticism of the royal consciousness through which God enters into and exposes the deathliness of the dominant culture: "[W]e might see in the crucifixion of Jesus the ultimate act of prophetic criticism in which Jesus announces the end of a world of death ... and takes the death into his own person."[29] Conversely, the resurrection of Jesus stands as the ultimate act of energizing that creates the possibility of a new future: "The resurrection can only be received and affirmed and celebrated as the new action of God, whose province it is to create new futures for people and also to let them be amazed in the midst of despair."[30]

---

grief ... [C]rying in pathos is the ultimate form of criticism, for it announces the sure end of the whole royal arrangement" (Ibid., p. 46; italics original).

25. Ibid., p. 45 (italics original).
26. See Ibid., 59–79.
27. Ibid., 59–60.
28. See Ibid., 81–113.
29. Ibid., 94–95.
30. Ibid., 112.

In the final analysis, the kinds of interpretive moves that Brueggemann makes in reading the prophets toward a "prophetic imagination" and then extending those moves toward the life and faith of the church are precisely what gives his 1978 work—and his many publications that have followed in its wake—lasting significance for both biblical scholarship and the church in the conversation concerning a theology of culture, politics and economics.

Biblical Interpretation, the Church and a Theology of Culture, Politics and Economics

As suggested at the outset of this essay, Brueggemann's 1978 work has the ability not only to move beyond common (mis)conceptions of prophets and prophecy but also to give biblical scholarship, and the interpretation of Old Testament texts in particular, to the church in fresh ways that can contribute to the church's ongoing struggle to define its life in the world. Given that *The Prophetic Imagination* first appeared in the field of Old Testament scholarship more than three decades ago, there are certainly elements of the work that contemporary biblical scholars may feel compelled to nuance, critique or challenge. Indeed, Brueggemann addressed many of these areas of critique in the preface to the 2001 revised edition, and several of them involve changes in biblical scholarship's conception of the social standing and function of prophets in ancient societies.[31] Even so, Brueggemann's formulations hold a special significance for biblical scholarship in particular, as they push the field and its interpretive practices to engage explicitly the contemporary conversations around theology, culture, politics and economics. Rather than allowing biblical scholarship to adopt a telos of merely academic inquiry, antiquarian interest, or intellectual parochialism, Brueggemann's mode of reading reveals a biblical interpretation in the service of the underprivileged and marginalized—those suffering from the militaristic, consumeristic and individualistic practices of a pharaoh-like consumption society. Rather than retreating to past paradigms of historicist interpretation, Brueggemann offers a biblical interpretation that challenges, critiques and protests the "established institutions and social conventions" that lead to injustice and despair.[32] Here is a mode of biblical scholarship that can make fresh contributions to the task of critical engagement

---

31. See Ibid., ix–xxi. For instance, a long-standing criticism of Brueggemann's formulation is that he overdraws the dichotomy between the prophetic and royal traditions in ancient Israel and the OT. Moreover, he seems to operate with an abstract picture of the OT prophets that does not always line up well with the specificity of the individual texts themselves. In particular, he seems to view the "prophetic" as equal only to the stance of the so-called "peripheral" prophets, who stand outside of and opposed to the central social structures—or else he makes the unstated theological judgment that the peripheral prophets are the most important prophets for shaping the church's identity and ministry today.

32. Ibid., xv.

with the social and economic situation in the contemporary United States, in particular.

Beyond the significance that Brueggemann holds for biblical scholarship, *The Prophetic Imagination* and the modes of interpretation it represents hold perhaps an even greater significance for the church.[33] The textual engagement outlined above offers the biblical texts to the liturgical life and practices of the church in fresh ways. Moreover, these are ways in which the texts themselves take on a "prophetic" function for the church—calling the church to a "prophetic" ministry in which it operates as an alternative community with peculiar discourses of criticizing and energizing that move toward an alternative reality in the midst of the dominant culture. Toward this end, Brueggemann devotes the final section of *The Prophetic Imagination* to a move from the imagination of the prophets and Jesus to the practices of the church today.[34] His special concern here is the ministry of the church in the "First World" setting of the West, which he diagnoses as a situation characterized by the kinds of things that marked the royal consciousness: satiation of commodities and consumerism, ideologies of militarism and conformity, and so on. Against that backdrop, the prophetic imagination, he concludes, challenges the church to find ways to elicit an alternative community and practice a type of ministry that "penetrates the numbness in order to face the body of death in which we are caught," yet also evokes visions of "new futures" beyond the present circumstances.[35] Perhaps justifiably, Brueggemann's original publication did not provide many examples of the concrete practices of persons, communities and institutions that embody this task, yet a new postscript in the revised edition of *The Prophetic Imagination* offers some suggestive examples, some of which have emerged directly in response to ideas put forth in his first edition.[36] Whether those practices be the prominence given to lament in worship at the Watts Street Baptist Church in Durham, North Carolina, or the health care center for the poor and uninsured sponsored by a coalition of Memphis, Tennessee congregations, these examples underscore that ministry evoked by the prophetic imagination does not traffic in common, ready-made answers or a mere social activism that often amounts to charity. Rather, although taking various forms, both direct and subtle, "prophetic" ministry is about imagination—evoking alternative conceptions,

---

33. No doubt this concern for the church emerges out of Brueggemann's career-long involvement in theological and seminary-level education. He had a distinguished career as professor of OT (1961–1968) and dean (1968–1982) at Eden Theological Seminary before serving as professor of OT at Columbia Theological Seminary from 1986 until his retirement in the early 2000s.

34. See Ibid., 115–25.

35. Ibid., 117.

36. See Ibid., 121–25.

perceptions and consciousnesses out of which new kinds of concrete actions may flow.

As a primer on the prophets and "prophetic" ministry, Brueggemann's *The Prophetic Imagination* and the body of work that has flowed from it move beyond common (mis)conceptions about prophets and prophecy, push biblical scholarship toward deep and intentional cultural engagement and offer the biblical texts and their challenge to the liturgical life and practices of the contemporary church in fresh ways. In so doing, the "prophetic" turns out to be an imaginative reading of reality that criticizes dominant discourses and energizes new perceptions and new political, economic and social practices. With this reading of the Old Testament scripture in hand, the church may move beyond the temptation to relegate these ancient and foreign texts to the recesses of antiquity or to engage their, at times, problematic social ideologies in only a decontructivist mode. Instead, the contemporary church may find fresh ways to incorporate these texts into its liturgical life and practices as the church struggles to engage the dominant discourses of society.

2

The Prophets and the Social and Ecological Consequences of the Monarchy
Maria Pascuzzi

Introduction

Within the Old Testament there are passages scattered through the prophetic books in which a personified earth is described as mourning.[1] In five passages, the earth's suffering is directly linked to the transgressions of the people of Israel (cf. Hosea 4:1-3; Jer 12:4; 23:9-11; Isa 24:1-5; 33:1-9). The degree to which the earth is, or will be, parched, polluted, infertile and bereft of plant and animal life is generally taken as a poetic barometer of Israel's own failure to fulfill its covenant vocation to do justice. This failure is commonly attributed to Israel's imperial ambitions and to the exploitative imperial consciousness which the prophets denounced as they witnessed the monarchy come into being at the expense of the poor and underclasses.[2] The eventual downfall of Israel and Judah is viewed as the direct result of disobedience to God, actualized in the disregard for social justice. Scant attention is paid to the degree to which Israel's ambitions were actualized at the expense of the environment which the people of Israel were also charged to protect.[3] Yet, as noted in a number of recent studies, there was usually a significant ecological component to the rise and fall of ancient societies in the Mediterranean.[4] Though defeat at the hands of a superior invading force

---

1. Cf. Amos 1:2; Hos 4:1-3; Jer 4:23-28; 12:1-4, 7-13, 23:9-12; Isa 24:1-20, 33:7-9 and Joel 1:5-20. A detailed study of the use of this image in the nine passages cited is provided by Katherine M. Hayes, *"The Earth Mourns." Prophetic Metaphor and Oral Aesthetic*, by Katherine M. Hayes. Academia Biblica 8. (Atlanta: The Society of Biblical Literature, 2002).

2. Cf. e.g. Normal Gottwald, *The Tribes of Yahweh: A Sociology of the Religion of Liberated Israel, 1250–1050 B.C.E.* (Maryknoll, N.Y. : Orbis Books, 1979); id., "From Tribal Existence to Empire: The Social Historical Context for the Rise of the Hebrew Prophets," in *God and Capitalism. A Prophetic Critique of Market Economy* (eds. J. Mark Thomas and Vernon Visick; Madison, WI: A-R Editions, Inc., 1990) 11–29; Walter Brueggemann, "Trajectories in Old Testament Literature and the Sociology of Ancient Israel," *JBL* 98 (1979): 161–85.

3. The inattentiveness is probably related to the anthropocentric bias of past scholarship which has begun to be addressed only recently, cf. e.g. Norman C. Habel and Peter Trundiger, eds., *Exploring Ecological Hermeneutics* (Society of Biblical Literature Symposium Series, 46; Atlanta: Society of Biblical Literature, 2008).

4. Cf. e.g. Timothy C. Weiskel, "The Ecological Lessons of the Past: An Anthropology of Environmental Decline," *Ecologist* 19 (3/1989) 98–103; Jared Diamond, "Ecological Collapses of Past Societies," *PAPhS* 138 (3/1994) 363–70; J. Donald Hughes, *Pan's Travail. Environmental Problems of the Ancient Greeks and Romans* (Baltimore: The Johns Hopkins University Press, 1994).

was often the ostensible cause of a nation's downfall, as Jared Diamond has observed, in ancient societies, a state's ecological debilitation may have actually precipitated its conquest by an intact neighboring society.[5] Such observations invite a consideration of the ecological implications of Israel's evolution from an earth community, in which the integrity of the whole of creation seems to have been an important factor in how the early Israelites interacted with their environment, to a nation-state.[6]

In what follows, I will first consider what the limited archaeological, geographical, agricultural, ecological, social and scriptural evidence reveals about the Israelites' rapport with the land and their "ecological concern" during their pre-monarchical, or settlement, period of existence, ca.12th–11th c. BCE. (Iron Age I). Using the same set of sources, I will then consider what the evidence reveals about the ecological impact that accompanied the rise of the monarchy. Clearly, landscape transformation and ecological degradation did not begin in the land of Israel with the monarchy.[7] However, some evidence suggests that ecological degradation was exacerbated as Israel evolved into a state.

Pre-Monarchical Israel

Though little is known about their precise origin, most scholars agree that the people who later coalesced and became identified as ethnic Israel first settled in hundreds of small un-walled villages throughout the highlands of Canaan

---

5. Diamond, "Ecological Collapses," 363–4.

6. The credibility of the biblical account of the Davidic-Solomonic empire has been undermined by recent studies which have concluded that the account is a complete literary fiction, cf. e.g., Thomas L. Thompson, *The Mythic Past: Biblical Archaeology and the Myth of Israel* (New York: Basic Books, 1999); Israel Finkelstein, "The Rise of Jerusalem and Judah: The Missing Link," in *Jerusalem in the Bible and Archaeology. The First Temple Period* (eds. Andrew G. Vaughn and Ann E. Killebrew; Leiden: E. J. Brill, 2003) 81–101. Others are less inclined to dismiss the account as lacking a complete basis in history, cf. e.g., William Devers, *What Did the Biblical Writers Know and When Did They Know it?* (Grand Rapids, MI: Eerdmans, 2001); Nadav Na'aman, "Cow Town or Royal Capital? Evidence for Iron Age Jerusalem," *BAR* 23 (4/1997), 43–7, 67; Jane M. Cahill, "Jerusalem at the Time of the United Monarchy: The Archaeological Evidence," in *Jerusalem in the Bible and Archaeology*, 13–80; J. J. M. Roberts, "Solomon's Jerusalem and the Zion Tradition," in *Jerusalem in the Bible and Archaeology*, 163-70; Abraham Malamat continues to insist that the Davidic-Solomonic kingdom " ... was a super-national system of political and economic domination by a center over a periphery, ... a true empire," (*History of Biblical Israel: Major Problems and Minor Issues* [Leiden: Brill, 2001] 197 and esp. 192–99), but most scholars hold the more moderate view that Israel was a state of modest territorial and economic dimensions.

7. For an historical survey of human impact on Israel's landscape beginning with the early Pleistocene period through the contemporary period, cf. Zev Naveh and Joel Dan, "The Human Degradation of Mediterranean Landscapes in Israel," in *Mediterranean Type Ecosystems: Origin and Structure* (eds. Francesco di Castri and Harry A. Mooney; Heidelberg-Berlin: Springer Verlag, 1973), 373–90.

beginning around 1200 BCE.[8] The highlands were formed by a low mountain range running down the length of Canaan's center, like a spine. The whole highland expanse was a fragile ecological zone, comprised of multiple microenvironments, some more conducive to agriculture than others.[9]

In this period, the settlers struggled for subsistence on land where water and flat arable plots were limited.[10] Sustainable use of such land for long periods of time required ecological awareness, attention to the vicissitudes of weather, especially lack or overabundance of water, knowledge of the soil and as few ecological errors as possible.[11] The settlers' concern for soil and water conservation was evident in the practice of terrace farming.[12] They adopted this technique which had already been in use in Canaan at least since the Early Bronze Age.[13] Terracing was especially useful in areas where lack of water or rugged topography meant unfavorable conditions for subsistence farming.[14] The construction of terraces, a labor intensive undertaking, created more level arable surfaces and facilitated the absorption of rain water which would otherwise run

---

8. According to Avraham Faust, Israelite ethnic identity came about in successive acts of self conscious differentiation from the Canaanites and then the Philistines, cf. "How Did Israel Become a People? The Genesis of Israelite Identity," *BAR* 35 (6/2009), 62–9, 92–3; cf. further, Shlomo Bunimovitz and Zvi Lederman, "A Border Case: Beth-Shemesh and the Rise of Ancient Israel," in *Israel in Transition. From Late Bronze II to Iron I a.c.1250–850 B.C.E.* (ed. Lester L. Grabbe; London: T & T Clark, 2008), 21–31. On the number, location, types and social organization of the settlements, cf. Joseph A. Callaway, "A New Perspective on the Hill Country Settlement of Canaan in Iron Age I," in *Palestine in the Bronze and Iron Ages. Papers in Honour of Olga Tufnell* (ed. Jonathan N. Tubb; London: University of London Institute of Archaeology, 1985), 31–49; Elizabeth Bloch-Smith and Beth Alpert Nakhai, "A Landscape Comes to Life: The Iron Age I," *NEA* 62 (2/1999), 62–92; and further, Oded Borowski, *Daily Life in Biblical Times*, (Archaeology and Biblical Studies, 5; Atlanta: Society of Biblical Literature, 2003), 14–16.

9. On the geomorphology of the highlands, cf. David C. Hopkins, *The Highlands of Canaan. Agricultural Life in the Early Iron Age* (Decatur, GA: Almond Press, 1985), 55–75.

10. On the ecology of the Palestinian hill country, cf. Frank S. Frick, "Ecology, Agriculture and Patterns of Settlement," in *The World of Ancient Israel. Sociological, Anthropological and Political Perspectives* (ed. Ronald E. Clements; Cambridge: Cambridge University Press, 1989), 67–93.

11. Among various environmental challenges, Hopkins signals "highly variable rainfall" as the greatest challenge to subsistence farmers, cf. *Agricultural Life*, 107–08. Cf. further Daniel Hillel, *The Natural History of the Bible. An Environmental Exploration of the Hebrew Scriptures* (New York: Colombia University Press, 2006), esp. 140–63.

12. On the utility of terraces, cf. Hopkins, *Agricultural Life*, 171–87; B. S.J. Isserlin, *The Israelites* (New York, N. Y.: Thames & Hudson, 1998), 151; Frick, "Ecology," 83–7.

13. Cf. Shimon Gibson, "Agricultural Terraces and Settlement Expansion in the Highlands of Early Iron Age Palestine: Is There Any Correlation Between the Two?" in *Studies in the Archaeology of the Iron Age in Israel and Jordan* (eds. Amihai Mazar and Ginny Mathias; JSOTSS, 131; Sheffield: Sheffield Academic Press, 2001), 113–46.

14. For example, at Ai, the settlers created a subsistence base for themselves by terracing over and planting the rugged eastern slope of their settlement area, cf. J. A. Callaway, "New Perspective on the Hill Country Settlement," 33, 40.

off slopes and cause soil erosion.[15] Conserving water with terraces also helped to prevent the depletion of rivers and streams.

The highlanders were also attentive to soil conservation and fertility maintenance. Among other things, this required caution when it came to forest clearing as well as continuous care of the soil, even in areas where it offered a fairly decent environment for farming.[16] The settlers preserved the plant nutrients of their soil through a system of agricultural fallowing as well as natural fertilization. The break in farming was needed to interrupt the natural recurrence of plant pests and pathogens and to restore nutrients by leaving herds to graze the land and drop natural fertilizer. Though this method of fallowing and fertilizing was not conducive to abundant crop yields, it afforded the settlers what they needed to subsist.

In the Bible, the agricultural practice of fallowing is presented as a divine mandate to rest the land every seven years (cf. Exod 23:10-11; cf. Lev 25:2-7). This mandate carried social implications since fallowing allowed the hungry poor and wild beasts to have their share of the land's gifts (Exod 23:11). However, fallowing, which was good agricultural practice, probably occurred more frequently than every seventh year. Frick opines that a year of fallowing probably followed each year of cultivation, while Hopkins considers it more likely that farmers divided their land, alternately fallowing one-half and planting the other.[17] Whether the settlers had actually intuited the connection between caring for the land through fallowing and caring for the hungry, which was later made explicit in texts, is not certain.[18] Nevertheless, to the degree that the practice of fallowing can be taken as a reflection of attitudes about human-land relations, it suggests that the settlers viewed the land as a resource which, if

---

15. On the rigors, labor and organization entailed in terrace construction, cf. Gershon Edelstein and Mordechai Kislev, "Mevasseret Yerushalayim: The Ancient Settlement and Its Agricultural Terraces," *BA* 44 (1/1981), 53-56, esp. 55-6. On the demographic constraints that impacted village life during the settlement period, including the capacity for widespread terracing, cf. David C. Hopkins, "The Subsistence Struggles of Early Israel," *BA* (1987), 179-91, esp. 181-3.

16. For a variety of reasons, as Hopkins points out, there was less dense forest and much less forest-clearing by the settlers than is usually assumed in view of Josh 17:18, cf. *Agricultural Life*, 132-3 and Ibid, "Subsistence," 180-1. On soil care, cf. e.g. Hopkins, *Agricultural Life*, 191-210; Frick, "Ecology," 77-82.

17. Frick, "Ecology," 83; Hopkins, *Agricultural Life*, 200-202. Hopkins does not completely dismiss the possibility that a full year of fallowing could have been observed every seventh year, noting that the settlers could have concentrated on animal husbandry. However, as Roland de Vaux notes it is hard to know how faithfully Israel observed the sabbatical rest for the land since evidence is rare and late (cf. Nehemiah 10:31 & 1 Maccabees 6:49-53) and comes from periods of national and religious fervor, cf. *Ancient Israel: Social Institutions*, Vol. 1 (New York: McGraw Hill, 1965), 175.

18. The same can be said of the practice of incomplete gleaning which ensured that some of the harvest would remain for the poor, the widow, the orphan and the resident alien (cf. Deut. 24:19-22; Lev 19:9-10; 23:22).

cared for properly and respected in terms of its own limits and capacity, would afford them a stable level of subsistence.

In addition to terracing and fallowing, the settlers also mixed and rotated crops, mostly cereals such as wheat and barley, and root vegetables. Crop rotation was an old and economical means of pest and plant pathogen control which helped prevent the loss of an entire harvest. In the event that one species was completely blighted, at least the other would survive. Crop rotation also prevented over-depletion of the soil's moisture and nutrients. Since the sources of subsistence from farming depended on so many environmental variables, the settlers managed this risk by practicing animal-husbandry, mainly sheep-herding, which provided them with wool, milk, meat, leather and manure. Though the settlers had fruit sufficient for their needs, unless their livelihood absolutely depended on it, most could not afford the luxury of extensive cultivation of olive trees and vines.[19] Such cultivation required years of wait-time between planting and harvesting as well as ample irrigation for abundant yields.[20] Moreover, the settlers lacked the residential stability needed for such a long term investment, as well as the work-force, organization and facilities needed to process olive and grape and then store the oil and wine for eventual exchange for goods and services. According to Baruch Rosen, archaeological evidence from highland settlement sites reveals only crude structures for storing grain and no evidence of proto-industrial installations for the conversion of olives and grapes into secondary products.[21] Those structures would come later in the monarchical period when population increase afforded increased production capacity. Additionally, the political stability provided by the monarchy facilitated both residential stability and population spread to ecological frontier zones where new agricultural strategies would be developed to permit farming.

To summarize briefly, the early settlers appear to have been disciplined in their agricultural practices and measured in what they exacted from the land. It would be exaggerated to claim, based on these limited insights, that the settlers were always exemplary when it came to protecting the environment. However,

---

19. Due to rugged topography, scarcity of water and soil conditions, settlers in the hill country of Manasseh apparently based their limited economy on the cultivation of olives and vineyards as indicated by the archaeological evidence, cf. Adam Zertal, "The Cultivation and Economy of Olives in Mannasseh," in *Olive Oil in Antiquity. Israel and Neighboring Countries from the Neolithic to the Early Arab Period* (eds. David Eitam and Michael Heltzer; History of Ancient Near East Studies, VII; Padova: Sargon srl, 1996), 307–14.

20. Wait-time between planting and harvesting the olive is at least five years while cereals can be harvested within a year of planting, cf. Baruch Rosen, "Aspects of Oil Production in Pre-Modern Israel," in *Olive Oil in Antiquity*, 23–8, here 26. Cf. further Lawrence Stager, "The First Fruits of Civilization," in *Palestine in the Bronze and Iron Ages*, 172–88.

21. Cf. Baruch Rosen, "Subsistence Economy in Iron Age I," in *From Nomadism to Monarchy: Archaeological and Historical Aspects of Early Israel* (eds. Israel Finkelstein and Nadav Na'aman; Jerusalem: Israel Exploration Society, 1994), 339–51.

in their disciplined practices and temperate use of the land it is at least possible to see their concern for ecological balance as well as acknowledgment of their dependence on the earth and its resources.

While it is generally agreed that the biblical texts purporting to describe the entry into and settlement of the land were composed after this period in Israel's history, what is recounted is not completely at odds with the environmental ethos and concern for balance that characterized the settlers' rapport with the land as these are reflected in their agricultural practices. Though Deut 20:19–20, with its injunction against destroying fruit trees, is usually cited to illustrate heightened environmental concern,[22] the texts dealing with the distribution of land, for example, capture a concern for both social and ecological balance. According to Judges 13–19 (cf. Num 26:52–56), at the time of Israel's settlement each tribe received a portion of the land according to its size and need. The portion was then sub-divided among individual households. This biblical evidence of equitable land distribution along with the archaeological evidence of the dispersed pattern of settlements points to a situation in which competition for arable land for subsistence farming was unnecessary. According to Hopkins, "the absence of pressures on land resources stemming from competition for land suggests that no objective focusing on increasing productivity of limited land resources demanded high priority in the conduct of agriculture in the early Iron Age Highlands."[23] In brief, with their subsistence needs met at this stage in their history, the settlers had no need to over-farm the land to increase crop output.

Each family considered its allotted portion a sacred family trust. Like all peasant farmers, the settlers were deeply attached to their land upon which they depended for life. Selling one's land portion for profit or commercial interests, or being forced to give up ownership, was still unknown at this stage in Israel's early history.[24] What mattered was that one had enough and that this level of sustainability was achieved without violating the integrity of the rest of creation. This way of life is captured in the description of each family "living under its [his] vine and under its [his] fig-tree" (cf. Micah 4:4; Zech 3:10). Further, at this time in Israel's history, ca early 10th c. BCE, the settlers more or less shared the same standard of living. Excavations of 10th c. BCE

---

22. Gerhard von Rad commented that the inclusion of this text on the protection of trees in a context dealing with rules for war is "probably unique in the history of the growth of a humane outlook [on nature] in ancient times," cf. *Deuteronomy: A Commentary*, Vol. 5 (Old Testament Library; Philadelphia: Westminster, 1966), 133. For Patrick D. Miller, this law is an example of an early "environmental protection regulation," cf. *Deuteronomy Interpretation: A Bible Commentary for Teaching and Preaching* (Louisville: John Knox Press, 1990), 171.

23. Cf. Hopkins, *Agricultural Life*, 167–8.

24. Specific legislation was designed to inhibit forfeiture or tampering with one's ancestral land, (Heb. *nachalah*), cf. Num 27:9–11; Lev 25:8–34; Deut. 19:4; 27:17). Nabaoth's refusal to part with his land (1 Kg 21:1–16) suggests that, into the period of the divided kingdom, some continued to regard the land as an inalienable sacred trust.

towns have unearthed the remains of homes showing uniformity of size and disposition which reflected a modest standard of living.[25] By contrast, when dwellings built in the 8th c. BCE were later excavated on this same site (Tell el-Farah, near Nablus), archaeologists discovered larger houses, segregated from the smaller, more poorly constructed houses which suggests a move away from an egalitarian to a more stratified society. As scholars recognize, between the 10th and the 8th centuries, social and economic developments took place that coincided with the transition to monarchical rule.[26]

In sum, in their practice and in texts which purport to describe the way of life prior to the emergence of the monarchy, the settlers appear to have been responsible stewards of creation, caring for all of its resources which had been entrusted to their care by Yahweh. Moreover, in the pre-monarchical period, the settlers experienced a period of social stability characterized by inter-village cooperation and fixed socio-economic relations within and between villages.[27] This system allowed the peasant farmers to keep produce necessary for survival, exchange limited surplus for other necessities, and work together for the common good.[28] This basic level of existence was achieved without over-exploitation of the earth and its resources; but this would change as agricultural practice became impacted by the economic interests of the monarchy.[29]

From Earth Community to Monarchy

Walter Brueggemann has observed that with the rise of the monarchy, the story of the land and its resources, which belonged to the many, became the story of power and usurpation that was rooted in a "crass sense of entitlement" on the part of the few.[30] Though the monarchy would bring about political unification and oversee the rise of an independent nation state, these developments would come at a price. In an admonishment to the people of Israel against subordinating themselves to monarchical authority (cf. 1 Sam 8:1–17), Samuel warned of the socio-economic consequences that kingship would entail. The

---

25. Cf. Roland de Vaux, *Ancient Israel*, Vol. 1, 72. On the typical four-room Iron I house and what its construction entailed, cf. Douglas R. Clark, "Bricks, Sweat and Tears: The Human Investment in Constructing a 'Four-room' House," *NEA* 66 (1 / 2 2003), 34–43.

26. Cf. de Vaux, *Ancient Israel*, Vol. 1, 73.

27. Cf. Frick, "Ecology," 86–7. On the socio-political structure of the village, cf. further, Borowski, *Daily Life*, 21–24.

28. During the pre-monarchic period, what limited surplus existed was used in small-scale bartering, cf. Isserlin, *Israelites*, 151 and further Borowski, *Daily Life*, 55–6.

29. As pointed out by Miriam C. Chernoff and Samuel M. Paley, state-mandated taxes in the form of produce and high demand for particular crops can influence both the level of production and the choice of what will be planted and harvested, cf. "Dynamics of Cereal Production at Tell el Ifshar, Israel during the Middle Bronze Age," *JFA* 25 (4/ 1998): 397–416.

30. Walter Brueggemann, "To Whom Does the Land Belong?: 2 Sam 3:12," *Journal for Preachers* (2007): 28–35, here 29.

people would be conscripted for military and civil service (v. 11b–13). Their private agricultural property would be confiscated by the king to use for his own purposes, or transfer to his retainers (v.14). The king would also demand a share of their best produce and flocks (vv.14–17).[31] They would effectively be enslaving themselves (v.17b) to a system from which they would not be liberated, even by God, no matter how much they cried out (v.18). Yet despite the warning and significant opposition, the monarchy emerged.[32] Though the abuse of power and the socio-economic inequities mentioned in 1 Sam 8 and denounced by the classical prophets would be fully realized under subsequent kings, it is Solomon especially who is featured as ushering in the abusive trends and inequities that would become characteristic of monarchical rule.[33]

The biblical account in 1 Kings 3–11 is the only written source of information for Solomon's reign. After consolidating his power by murdering or detaining anyone suspected of disloyalty (cf. 1 Kgs 2:26–46) and expanding Israel's sovereignty over various kingdoms (1 Kgs 4:20–21), Solomon set out to build a capitol city with a royal complex equal to the splendor of his kingdom. Opulence and grandeur are associated with every aspect of his reign. His court's table is described as a superabundance of choice food, supplied through taxation (1 Kgs 4:22–29). His bronze stockpile was beyond weighing (1Kgs 7:47); his knowledge was encyclopedic (1 Kgs 4:29–34); his wealth continuously increased through international trade (1 Kgs 10:14–15); his architecture was monumental (1 Kgs 5–7); his kingdom's fame was international (1 Kgs 10:1–8).

Judging by the scriptural account, Solomon's reign was taken up with large state construction projects. Besides the temple and royal compound, he constructed fortifications for some cities (1 Kgs 9:15), rebuilt others (1Kgs 9:17) and built a few cities to warehouse his chariots and cavalry (1 Kgs 9:19). Solomon's extensive architectural program was likely motivated by concern to legitimate monarchic rule, consolidate his own power, and further the national unification and expansion begun under David.[34] To carry out this construction

---

31. In 1 Sam 8:11–18, the repetition (6x) of *yikkakh* (he will seize) underscores the avarice of the king who will take the best (*haṭṭōbim*) for himself (v.14).

32. The claim that 1 Sam 8 belongs to a late exilic, fictional, anti-monarchic source has been losing ground in the face of recent arguments that situate the anti-monarchic current in a much earlier historical context. See the discussion in Keith W. Whitelam, "Israelite Kingship," in *The World of Ancient Israel. Sociological, Anthropological and Political Perspectives,* ed. Ronald E. Clements (Cambridge: Cambridge University Press, 1989), 119–39, esp. 122–24.

33. It is important, however, to recognize that socio-economic stratification and inequity, though exacerbated during the monarchical period, was latent in pre-monarchical Israel. Cf. Robert B. Coote and Keith W. Whitelam, "The Emergence of Israel: Social Transformation and State Formation Following the Decline in Late Bronze Age Trade," *Semeia* 37 (1986): 107–47.

34. Cf. Carol Meyers, "The Israelite Empire: In Defense of King Solomon," *Mich. Q. Rev.* 22 (1983), 412–3 and Ibid, "David as Temple-Builder," in *Ancient Israelite Religion. Essays in Honor of Frank Moore Cross,* ed. Patrick. D. Miller, Paul D. Hanson and S. Dean McBride (Philadelphia: Fortress Press, 1987), 357–76.

program, Solomon instituted a corvée (1 Kgs 5:13–18). Attempts to exonerate Solomon from the charge of conscripting his own people (1 Kgs 9:22 and further 2 Chr 2:17; 8:7–9) along with the fact that forced-labor was a factor in the revolt and secession of the northern tribes (cf. 1 Kgs 12:1–20) suggest that the report of a corvée may be historically credible. The question of whether all the construction projects listed in the text attributed to Solomon were ever actually built during his reign is part of a complicated and controverted discussion that is beyond the scope of this paper.[35] For the purpose of this study, what needs to be noted is that Solomon is presented as someone who lusted after the best natural resources—most notably the cedar, prized for its height, durability and fragrance. The cedar forests of the Lebanon highlands had supplied various ancient empires with this choice lumber from which long boards needed for the support beams and roofing of temples and other monumental structures were made.[36] Once the trees were cut, the lumber was typically transported by sea and land to its final destination (cf. 1 Kgs 5:9 and 2 Chr 2:16). [37]

Solomon is described as contracting with the Phoenician king, Hiram, for cedar, cypress and other unidentified species of trees from Lebanon.[38] In addition to its use in the temple, cedar was reportedly used in the buildings which comprised the royal complex. One, constructed exclusively of cedar, is simply referred to as "The House of the Forest of Lebanon" (1 Kgs 7:1). Solomon is also reported to have constructed a royal fleet (cf. 1 Kgs 9:26; 10:22; further, Ezek 27:5) and chariots (1 Kgs 10:26). Cedar was known to be the preferred material for ship- and probably chariot-building as well.[39] Solomon

---

35. Cf. Gary. N. Knoppers, "The Vanishing Solomon: The Disappearance of the United Monarchy from Recent Histories of Ancient Israel," *JBL* 116 (1/1997): 19–44. J. Maxwell Miller, "Separating the Solomon of History from the Solomon of Legend," in *The Age of Solomon. Studies at the Turn of the Millennium*, ed. L. K. Handy (Leiden: Brill, 1997), 1–24.

Apropos the description of Solomon and his building activities, the fact that the account follows a conventional narrative is, in Barstad's view, insufficient to deny the existence of Solomon or that he built a temple in Jerusalem. Cf. *History and the Hebrew Bible*, esp. 18–24.

36. Since short-trunked, native trees were unsuitable for building monumental structures, Israel had to rely on imported cedar, cf., Nili Liphschitz, *Timber in Ancient Israel. Dendroarchaeology and Dendrochronology*, 26 (Institute of Archeology Monograph Series: Tel Aviv University, 2007), 16. According to Ezra 3:7, Phoenician cedar was also imported for the construction of the second temple.

37. An extant Assyrian frieze, ca. 8th c. BCE, entitled the "Frieze of the Transportation of Timber" depicts the transportation process. The frieze can be viewed on-line at:

http://www.louvre.fr/llv/oeuvres/detail_notice.jsp?CONTENT%3C%3Ecnt_id=10134198673225258&CURRENT_LLV_NOTICE%3C%3Ecnt_id=10134198673225258&FOLDER%3C%3Efolder_id=9852723696500800&bmLocale=en# (Accessed May 3, 2010)

38. According to 2 Sam 5:11–12, Hiram had also supplied cedar for the construction of David's royal house.

39. Egyptians were already importing cedar of Lebanon for ship-building in the 3rd millennium BCE, cf., Steven Vinson, "Ships in the Ancient Mediterranean," *BA* 53, (1/1990):

also imported large quantities of *almug* (var. *algum*, 2 Chr 2:8), an unidentified species of tree used for the crafting of musical instruments and decoration (cf. 1 Kgs 10:11–12).

In his study of the forest ecology of the Levantine highlands, M. W. Mikesell chronicles the devastation wrought by humans, since at least the 3rd millennium BCE, who sought, fought for and demanded as tribute the prized cedar of the Lebanon highlands, which today are "as barren as the mountains of the Sahara"[40] and " ... offer dramatic evidence of the use and misuse of a resource that was once described as the glory of Lebanon."[41] Among historical exploiters of cedar who contributed to the deforestation, Mikesell includes Solomon.[42] It is beyond dispute that a real historical pattern of ecological exploitation has resulted in the baring of the once densely forested lands of the Levant. According to archaeo-botanists N. Liphschitz and G. Biger, the dendrohistorical evidence also leaves no doubt that the over-exploitation of cedars for use in construction in Israel was a major contributor to the disappearance of the cedar forests in Lebanon.[43] Whether this history of over-exploiting cedars actually began with Solomon, who was purported to have made cedar of Lebanon as ubiquitous as the sycamores of the Shephelah (cf. 1 Kgs 10:27b), is not at all certain. None of the structures he allegedly built and embellished with cedar has been excavated. However, he is certainly featured in the text as Israel's first egregious exploiter of this natural resource which later generations of Israel's elite did, in fact, exploit.

The biblical text also records that in exchange for raw materials, Solomon agreed to make annual payments of large quantities of agricultural produce to Hiram (cf. 1 Kgs 5:25 and further 2 Chr 2:10). In this sovereign act, Solomon is portrayed as appropriating the future produce of the land meant for the people of Israel and offering it as collateral in exchange for building materials for state projects. The impact on Israel's economy is not mentioned, but some ecological consequences of this exchange are hinted at in the text. Apparently, the levels of produce exacted from the land so exceeded its ecological capacity that by the time construction ended both the soil and produce supply had been exhausted. Lacking the produce, Solomon repaid his debt by ceding twenty towns of the region of Galilee to the Phoenician King (1 Kgs 9:10).

13–18. Cf. further, Allen Chester Johnson, "Ancient Forests and Navies," *TransProcAmPhilolAssoc* 58 (1927): 199–209.

40. Marvin W. Mikesell, "The Deforestation of Mt. Lebanon," *Geog R.* 59 (1/1969): 1–28, here, 1.

41. Mikesell, "Deforestation," 28; cf. Further, Ellen C. Semple, "Ancient Mediterranean Forests and the Lumber Trade," *An Assoc Amer Geog* 9 (1919): 13–40.

42. Mikesell, "Deforestation," 16.

43. Nili Liphschitz and Gideon Biger, "Building in Israel Throughout the Ages," *GeoJ* 27 (4/1992): 345–52, here 352.

Solomon is also featured as a stock-piler of bronze (1 Kgs 7:47), which required a copper supply. Involvement in copper-mining would have involved Solomon and his kingdom in an industry with devastating environmental consequences.[44] Scientists studying the site where Solomon's mining operations were supposedly located have calculated that the slag from the smelting would have turned the land into a toxic wasteland, severely reducing plant productivity. Food would have had to have been brought to the mine workers from elsewhere to avert their starvation. Moreover, the health risks to this population, e.g. bioaccumulation of heavy metals and noxious gasses emitted by the smelting process, would have quickly debilitated miners, requiring a continuous exchange of personnel.[45] As past exploitation left the Lebanon highlands denuded, so now, some fifteen hundred years after mining activities have ceased at this site, the area remains a health hazard.[46]

The biblical report of Solomon's cedar acquisitions and bronze resources coupled with botanical and archeological evidence have given researchers reason to implicate the Solomon presented in the biblical text in environmental disasters. Whether they are justified in doing so depends on the question of whether, and to what degree, the story of canonical King Solomon and his reign has anything to do with the actual historical Solomon, his activities and the status of his kingdom. That question remains a matter of intense debate and cannot detain us. What is important to underscore is this: the Solomon portrayed in the text is a king who is ambitious and acquisitive, an exploiter of humans and their resources as well as natural resources. He is in pursuit of

---

44. The assumption that before the 8th c. BCE there existed no complex polities in Israel or Edom capable of industrial-scale copper mining led some researchers to date evidence of mining activity in the Negev to well after the time of Solomon, and to dismiss the account of his bronze resources as little more than exaggeration for rhetorical effect. Cf. e.g. David C. Hopkins, "The Weight of the Bronze Could Not Be Calculated: Solomon and Economic Reconstruction," in *The Age of Solomon. Studies at the Turn of the Millennium* (ed. Lowell K. Handy; Leiden: E. J. Brill, 1997), 300–11. This assumption has been challenged by the results of a recent excavation at Kirbeth en-Nahas, part of the ancient mining district of Faynan (biblical Edom), which researchers suggest are in line with the biblical claim. Cf. Thomas E. Levy et al., "High-precision radiocarbon dating and historical biblical archaeology in southern Jordan," *PNAS.* 104 (43/2008): 160–65; and further, Thomas E. Levy, et al., "Reassessing the Chronology of Biblical Edom: New Excavations and 14C Dates from Khirbat en Nahas (Jordan)," *Antiquity* 78 (2004): http://russellbadams.brinkster.net/publications/Levy%20and%20Adams%20et%20al.%20Antiquity%202004.pdf (Accessed March 3, 2010)

45. Cf. F. Brian Pyatt et al., "King Solomon's Miners–Starvation and Bioaccumulation? Environmental Archaeological Investigation in Southern Jordan," *Ecotoxicol. Environ. Saf.* 43 (3/1999): 305–08.

46. Cf. John A. Gratton et al., "A Legacy of Empires. An Exploration of the Environmental and Medical Consequences of Metal Production at Wadi Faynan, Jordan," in *Geology and Health. Closing the Gap,* ed. H. Catherine W. Skinner and Anthony R. Berger (New York, N.Y.: Oxford University Press, 2003), 99–103.

political and economic hegemony. He is willing to force people into labor to accomplish his royal designs. He has a proprietary posture toward the choice livestock and produce of others which arrives on his table through a system of state-imposed taxes. He and his court live extravagantly supported by revenue from domestic taxes and tribute from those subjugated by Solomon. He lusts after the finest natural resources and luxury items and is willing to pay whatever it takes to have what he wants: he will mortgage the agricultural produce and, if the yield fails, he will expropriate land and give it away because everything is his. Solomon's power and resources may have been much more limited than what is described. However, textually, his reign illustrates the excesses, abuse of power and socio-economic inequities associated with the monarchy. These trends would intensify under successive monarchs who reigned over Israel and Judah.

The history of the kingdoms of Israel and Judah is, with few exceptions, a litany of ineffective monarchs who abused their power and were responsible for the conditions that generated serious social inequity. Evidence points to the royal estates of the kings of Israel and Judah (cf. e.g. 2 Chron 26:10) who arrogated to themselves the right to the best grazing and farm land and its produce.[47] In doing so, they ignored traditional property rights and displaced small farmers whose lives depended on their land and its yield. Beginning in the 8th c. BCE, prophets in both Israel and Judah lamented the disappearance of the whole culture of small farming which was being replaced by centralized systems of agriculture. For Micah, this was not a welcome economic development but a deplorable state of affairs arrived at through fraud and the unjust seizure of land and property by the powerful (2:1–5). Those who managed to keep their property were burdened with taxes in the form of produce (cf. Amos 5:11; 7:1), which probably led people to over-farm to avoid having their property confiscated.[48] Judging by Isaiah's denunciation of those who consolidated confiscated properties, apparently, many small farmers lost their properties, the source of their livelihood.[49]

In brief, monarchical rule in Israel and Judah was accompanied by a set of socio-economic and political conditions which permitted the monopolization of goods and resources and the prosperity of some at the expense of others.

---

47. In her chapter entitled "Crown Agriculture in Eight Century Israel," Ellen F. Davis examines the dissolution of small farming and the responses of Amos and Hosea, cf. *Scripture, Culture and Agriculture: An Agrarian Reading of the Bible* (Cambridge: Cambridge University Press, 2009), 120–38.

48. According to Borowski, urbanism, which made its appearance with the rise of the monarchy, was facilitated by the collection of agricultural surplus as taxes. This surplus, consumed by non-productive segments of the society, (e.g. administrative personnel) also had to be stored, which required the construction of storage facilities cf. *Daily Life*, 43 and 51; Isserlin describes the relation of town/city to country as "parasitic" with the former giving little in return, cf. *Israelites*, 113.

49. Cf. Isa 5:8 and further Mic 2:2.

Despite its turbulent political history, the kingdom of Israel, with its capitol eventually established at Samaria, was fairly prosperous. Its territory included prime agricultural and grazing lands. It enjoyed international trade relations with Cyprus and Phoenicia, which supplied Israel with significant quantities of ivory, and ivory craftsmen whose work embellished royal buildings in Samaria.[50] Archeological remains of monumental structures, excavated objects carved from ivory, fine Phoenician pottery and other imported goods testify to the northern kingdom's wealth.[51] Amos and Hosea testified to its rampant social injustice, corruption and the general decadence of which the "ivory houses," beds of ivory and sumptuous palaces condemned by the prophets, were emblematic (cf. Amos 3:15; 6:4-6; 1 Kgs. 22:39). Wealth was concentrated in the hands of the elites while the economic status of the under-classes continued to deteriorate. State building projects as well as various commercial and agricultural projects were carried out by forced labor.[52]

Archaeological evidence also testifies to the emergence of an elite class in Judah by the 7th c. BCE which enjoyed great economic prosperity. This is reflected in luxury housing in Jerusalem and luxury imports, such as elephant ivory from Syria and Mesopotamia used for decorative inlay, furniture made from precious imported wood from north Syria and Lebanon and decorative shells from the Red Sea.[53] Analysis of excavated wood remains from the Negev reveals a high presence of cedar in this desert region which, according to N. Liphschitz, attests to the wealth of the regime that was able to import such expensive building material.[54]

The prophets denounced the abuses and injustices that evolved with the monarchy, which was supposed to safeguard against them. It was a common belief throughout the ancient near east that the king, who represented the deity, was charged with the prosperity and well-being of all his people, which presupposed the prevention of injustice and protection of the poor and

---

50. On the Samaria royal complex and ivories, cf. G. Barkay, "The Iron Age II–III," in *The Archaeology of Ancient Israel*, ed. Ammon Ben-Tor; trans. R. Greenberg (New Haven: Yale University Press, 1992), 302–73, esp. 319–23.

51. On the archeological evidence of monumental structures from various northern royal cities in Israel, cf. Larry G. Herr, "Archeological Sources for the History of Palestine: The Iron Age II Period: Emerging Nations," *BA* 60 (3/1997): 114–83, esp. 135–39; cf. further, David Ussishkin, "Samaria, Jezreel and Megiddo: Royal Centers of Omri and Ahab," in *Ahab Agonistes. The Rise and Fall of the Omri Dynasty*, ed. Lester Grabbe (London: T & T Clark, 2007), 293–309.

52. Lester Grabbe estimates that up to 25% of the population of the northern kingdom comprised the unpaid work-gangs forced into the state's service. Cf. "Monarchic Period" in *Anchor Bible Dictionary*, Vol. 3, ed. David Noel Freedman (New York, N. Y.: Doubleday, 1992), 563.

53. Avraham Faust and Ehud Weiss, "Judah, Philistia, and the Mediterranean World: Reconstructing the Economic System of the Seventh Century BCE," *BASOR* 338 (2005): 71-92.

54. Liphschitz, *Timber*, 122; cf. further Faust and Weiss, "Judah," 75.

vulnerable.⁵⁵ But, as L. Hoppe observed, ensuring social justice would have undermined the monarchic system since the economic support needed to maintain it depended on the social inequities and created the poverty!⁵⁶

The social and economic injustices went hand-in-hand with the disregard for the land and the environment. To pay for the luxury imports, monumental structures and lavish lifestyle of the elite classes in both Israel and Judah, a period of agricultural intensification began. The concern for ecological balance and disciplined use of the land that had characterized the settlement stage of Israel's history was trumped by economic interest and market demands.⁵⁷ The land and its resources had now come to be viewed as matter to be exploited for material gain.

As previously stated, the majority of small peasant farms were devoted to the cultivation of wheat and other grain products as well as root vegetables, all staples of the daily diet.⁵⁸ Besides providing sustenance, this agricultural mix was good for the land; root vegetables sucked up little of the soil's nutrients while grains consumed more. However, mixed subsistence cropping was not good for the elites who needed greater quantities of those commodities that brought greater profit in the exchange market.⁵⁹ As M. Chaney points out, in this period, in both Israel and Judah, there was major conflict over agricultural priorities, farming techniques and land use.⁶⁰ One side was interested in profit and indifferent to ecological concerns; the other was interested in subsistence and sustainable use of the land. The elites clearly had the upper-hand in this conflict. With greater concentration of land in their hands and the political power to squeeze non-compliant, inefficient subsistence farmers out of business through taxation, the elites were able to impose their will on small farmers whose options were limited.⁶¹ They could lose their land or align their agricultural strategies with the economic priorities of the elite and the shifted emphasis on exports

---

55. Cf. Hans Barstad, *History and the Hebrew Bible* (Forschungen zum Alten Testamentum, 61; Tübingen: Mohr Siebeck, 2008), 57–9.

56. Leslie Hoppe, *There Shall be No Poor Among You: Poverty in the Bible* (Nashville: Abingdon, 2004), 11. Cf. 1 Kgs 5:1–6.

57. The political economy of 8th century Israel and Judah and dynamics that led to agricultural intensification in this period are analyzed and presented by Marvin L. Chaney, "Bitter Bounty: The Dynamics of the Political Economy Critiqued by the Eight-Century Prophets," in *The Bible and Liberation: Political and Social Hermeneutics*, ed. Norman K. Gottwald and Richard A. Horsley (Maryknoll, N.Y.: Orbis Press, 1993), 250–63.

58. Cf. Oded Borowski, "Eat, Drink and Be Merry. The Mediterranean Diet," *JNEA* 67 (2/2004): 96–107.

59. Markets and price fluctuation were a common feature of ancient near eastern economies, cf. Morris Silver, "Karl Polyani and Markets in the Ancient Near East: The Challenge of the Evidence," *J.Econ.Hist.* 43 (4/1983): 795–829.

60. Marvin L. Chaney, "Whose Sour Grapes? The Addressees of Isaiah 5:1–7 In Light of the Political Economy," *Semeia* 87 (1999): 105–22.

61. Cf. Chaney, "Sour Grapes," 107.

and trade. On large estates, over-cultivation and monocropping, especially of grain, would have exhausted the soil's nutrients. This was done not with an eye to subsistence but to the cash-value of the crop. The growing population along with the increased demand for grain and other export produce probably explains the move into ecological frontier zones, the investment in more terrace construction and the efforts to make desert zones arable.[62] Such efforts allowed both Israel and Judah to trade on the international market. Judah participated in the Arabian grain market and exported grain to the Philistines.[63] Archaeological excavations of grain piles in the Philistine city of Ashkelon confirm the Judaean provenance of the grain.[64] Ezekiel mentions that Israel was involved in trade with the Phonenicians with whom "they trafficked in wheat" (Ezek 27:17). The prophet Amos denounced the greedy grain traffickers whose religious scruples apparently kept them from doing business on the sabbath but not from corrupt business practices once trading resumed (cf. Amos 8:4–6). Judging by Amos' comments, business as usual included the use of inaccurate measures (v. 5) and inflating volume by mixing inedible seed casing with grain (v.6). Some of these grain traders may have been acting on behalf of the crown but others may have been private dealers who were part of the emergent merchant class.

In addition to wheat, olive oil and wine were the other most valuable exchange commodities.[65] The archeological evidence from this period attests to numerous industrial-size installations that were constructed to process olives and grapes into secondary products.[66] The construction of such installations required a large labor force and the investment of significant resources. They would, of course, be unnecessary unless vast tracts of land which had previously been used for mixed agricultural purposes were devoted to the cultivation of olives and grapes. Evidence of new settlements around these oil and grape processing plants, and of royal vineyards, suggests to Chaney that this was more than a viticultural boom; it was a wholesale victimization of a vast majority of the population, many of whom were reduced to working as underpaid laborers

---

62. From the 10th to the 6th centuries, BCE, numerous run-off farms were built in the Negev. These elaborate systems explain how intensive farming was possible in an area where annual rainfall is ca. 80–100mm, cf. Michael Evenari, Leslie Shanan and Naphtali Tadmor, *The Negev. The Challenge of the Desert* (Cambridge: Harvard University Press, 1982) and further, Michael Evenari et al., "Ancient Agriculture in the Negev," *Science* 133, no. 3457 (1961): 979–96.

63. Judah's participation in the Arabic trade market is discussed in Faust and Weiss, "Judah," 71–92, here 75.

64. Cf., Faust and Weiss, "Judah," 73–75.

65. Ezek 27:17 lists oil along with wheat, honey and balm as commodities traded to Tyre. Oil was also exported to Egypt; cf. Hos 12:1.

66. According to David Eitam, olive oil was a mass production industry in both Israel and Judah from the 9th to the 7th centuries BCE; cf. "Olive Culture in Ancient Israel," http://www.gemsinisrael.com/e_article000008705.htm (Accessed Feb. 3, 2010).

on what had formerly been their own land and of which they were unjustly deprived by their new employers.[67] He states:

> To the urban elites ... the vineyards were the proud symbols of economic progress and prosperity. To the peasants whose subsistence plots had been expropriated and combined to yield the sites for these vineyards, matters looked different.[68]

With more land devoted to oil and grapes, and wheat at a premium because of its value in trade, escalating prices on essential commodities left the majority of the populations of Israel and Judah, many of whom were now landless, below subsistence levels. Moreover, agricultural intensification and monocropping, to the extent practiced, were strategies conducive to soil debilitation, not sustainable development. But this was of little importance since the goal was not food but the accumulation of wealth.

Interrupting the Monarchy

The political and social reality in both Israel and Judah further disadvantaged the poor, the peasant farmers and the laborers forced to carry out the state building projects. No benefit accrued to these people who comprised the majority of the populations of Israel and Judah. They experienced the monarchy and the new class of elites not merely as a burden but as a threat to their survival. Likewise, nothing about the new political economic reality benefitted the land and the rest of non-human creation. Increased social-economic disparity and disregard for the earth and its resources went hand-in-hand as Israel evolved from a community of settlers whose subsistence depended on respect and care for the earth and its resources, to a monarchically ruled, socially stratified society which privileged other interests.

Prophets active in the latter part of the 8th c. BCE in both Israel and Judah and those active in Judah on through its demise in the 6th c. BCE addressed this social and economic reality. They warned that without a return to covenant justice there would be no peace or security; without returning lands to their rightful owners, to be cultivated for self-sufficiency not exploited for unlimited economic gain, the ecological impact would be devastating. The exhausted earth would yield no more produce; rivers and streams would be depleted; land that was green and fertile would become barren and parched; the fish of the sea would perish; and the birds of the air would disappear. Such warnings have

---

67. Cf. Chaney, "Sour Grapes," 109.
68. Ibid. The rest of Chaney's article argues that the addressees of Isa 5:1–7, were the elites who benefitted from the vineyard industry at the expense of the poor who were forced to accommodate their economic and agricultural designs.

traditionally been understood as poetic descriptions of some future ecological devastation by which God would repay the disobedience of Israel. The idea that inducing ecological devastation, or debilitation, was a divine prerogative exercised in the face of human injustice and transgression was not exclusive to ancient Israel.[69] However, that drought, pestilence, failed crops, withered vines (cf. Joel 1:4–18) and low crop yields (cf. Hag 6:1) were attributed to God and interpreted as punishment for disobedience does not preclude that humans brought a number of these things upon themselves.[70] In light of the agricultural trends that accompanied the changed political-economic landscapes in Israel and Judah, it seems reasonable to think that some of the envisioned future environmental debilitation was actually human-made and contemporary, the result of the ecological indifference of the elite segments of the populations of Israel and Judah.

By omitting to consider a link between increased socio-economic injustice in Israel and Judah and the decline of ecological concern which led to disregard for agricultural practices that respected the land's limits and capacity, it is easy to omit concern for the environment from the list of social concerns usually associated with the prophets. That the prophets cried out on behalf of exploited humans does not preclude the possibility that they also cried out on behalf of the exploited earth. To paraphrase Laurie Braaten's question: Can we state with certainty that the prophets did not also see themselves called to be spokespersons for the Earth?[71] Did their call for a renewed social and religious consciousness not include a demand for a renewed ecological consciousness as well? It is difficult to imagine the prophets so resistant to unjust social-economic practices and yet ignorant of, or indifferent to, their concrete ecological consequences. Whether on account of an anthropocentric bias, which narrows the scope of prophetic concern to "sins" by humans against humans, or the insistence that the environment is only a recent preoccupation which should not be imposed on the prophets, ecological concern as a facet of the prophets' social concern has been overlooked.[72]

---

69. Angered by human injustice, Zeus was said to unleash violent rains until "the tilled fields of men are wasted," cf. Homer, *Iliad*, trans. A. T. Murray, rev. William F. Wyatt (Cambridge: Harvard University Press, 1999), 16, 384–92.

70. Myths concerning the earth's infertility, including the "fury of the elements" were dismissed by a first century CE agronomist who attributed infertility to ignorance and neglect of good agricultural practices, cf. Lucius Junius Moderatus Columella, *On Agriculture*, trans. and ed. Harrison Boyd Ash (Cambridge: Harvard University Press, 1941) I.3–12.

71. In his study of Joel, Laurie Braaten asks, "... since we know very little about Joel, can we state with certainty that this 'son of Petuel' did not consider himself called to be a spokesperson for Earth?" cf. "Earth Community in Joel," in *Ecological Hermeneutics*, 63–74, here 64.

72. Based on multiple sources, J. Donald Hughes shows that the ancients were what we would call "environmentally aware" and ecologically concerned. Among other things, they recognized that deforestation caused severe soil erosion, affected the water supply, and caused an

The scriptural texts inform us that the message went unheeded, that Israel failed to keep covenant justice, failed in the stewardship of the land, failed to uphold the standard of safeguard for the environment. The Israelites' assault on their own natural resources was furthered by other imperial aggressors. Assyria laid waste to the northern kingdom, burning cities and confiscating food supplies (cf. Isa 1:7). Judah fell to Babylon. Though the northern part of the kingdom of Judah escaped devastation, archaeological evidence supports the biblical testimony that Jerusalem and other important villages and cities of Judah were not spared.[73] Towns were in ruin; farm lands were turned into desert; animal life disappeared; the fields produced nothing; people were left to starve (Jer 4:23–26; 12:11; Lam 4:4–5). The assault on the land and its resources at the hands of the Babylonians furthered the ecological debilitation incurred by the agricultural strategies and socio-economic policies of the Judean elite. Judah also followed Israel in the loss of its political autonomy.[74] As kings and elites grew distant from the Source of all life who created an ecologically harmonious world so that all life would flourish (Ps 104:10–15), they grew increasingly proprietary, adopting an exploitative posture toward both human and non-human creation, which ultimately contributed to their own undoing.

Conclusion

Although we cannot be certain that ecological debilitation contributed to the downfall of the kingdoms of Israel and Judah, the foregoing investigation suggests that it was quite possible. At minimum, the evidence suggests that the ecological awareness which had characterized Israel's settlement period and was evident in the temperate use of the land, largely for subsistence purposes, was disregarded during the period of the Divided Monarchy. Agricultural practice grew increasingly oriented to the enrichment of an elite segment of the society at the expense of both the poor and the environment.

Today, global socio-economic structures continue to favor an elite class at the expense of the poor and the environment. Transnational corporations flourish on the backs of exploited workers who support various global markets

---

increase in water and air temperature. The ancients also enacted measures to protect forests and reverse the negative effects of deforestation, cf., "How the Ancients Viewed Deforestation," *JFA* 10 (4/1983): 435–45.

73. Cf. e.g. Isa 44:26; 51:3; 52:2.9; Jer 33:10; 51:24; Ezek 24:21. Why the damage inflicted by the Babylonians on Judea differed according to regions is considered by Joel Weinberg, "The Babylonian Conquest of Judah: Some Additional Remarks to a Scientific Consensus," *ZAW* 118 (2006): 597–610, esp. 603–09.

74. Few contemporary scholars now maintain that the Babylonians emptied Judah of *all* its inhabitants, bringing Judaean material culture to a complete halt; cf. the discussion in Barstad, *History and the Hebrew Bible*, 90–134 and further, Bustenay Oded, "Where is the 'Myth of the Empty Land to be Found?," in *Judah and the Judeans in the Neo-Babylonian Period* (eds. Oded Lipschits and J. Blenkinsopp; Winona Lake, IN: Eisenbrauns, 2003), 55–74.

controlled by elites sitting in boardrooms. Rarely do these profiteers see, and rarely are they held accountable for, the social and environmental costs of their policies which are motivated by concern for profit, not the livelihood of farmers or health of the consumer, much less the fragility of the environment. Mechanized and efficient production is not about the food. It is about the accumulation of wealth. Seán McDonagh offers a sobering look at the detrimental social and environmental effects of global agribusinesses which reap record profits despite the known polluting effects of oil-rich fertilizers and other chemicals, the evidence of reduced biodiversity due to monocropping, the evidence of soil debilitation, accelerated soil loss and increased desertification due to deforestation and intensive land use.[75]

Despite the evidence and warnings that past and on-going assaults on the environment are hurtling us along a trajectory toward possible environmental collapse, we continue to contribute to our own undoing. This undoing of creation is taking place in the present. It is what humans bring upon themselves when, driven by rapacious appetites for money, resources, comfort and security, they exploit with abandon the rest of creation. From the story of Israel and Judah we should learn that the rapacious can only give in to this abandon for so long before plunging themselves and the rest of creation into chaos.

---

75. Cf. Seán McDonagh, *Patenting Life? Stop! Is Corporate Greed Forcing Us to Eat Genetically Engineered Food?* (Dublin: Dominican Publications, 2003), esp. ch. 2.

3

Prophetic Imagination in the Gospel of Matthew
Michael Lodahl

> There are two basic forms of eschatology: the prophetic, which at any given moment sees every person addressed by it as endowed ... with the power to participate by his decision and deeds in the preparing of Redemption; and the apocalyptic, in which the redemptive process in all its details ... has been fixed from everlasting and for whose accomplishment human beings are only used as tools.
> — Martin Buber, *Paths in Utopia*

Even if we were to judge Martin Buber's typology of the prophetic and apocalyptic genres to be an oversimplification of complex, interwoven biblical themes, there is nonetheless undoubtedly much to learn from his model. Perhaps it would be comparable to his "I-You / I-It" typology, which he acknowledged to be an extreme bifurcation but, for that very reason, also insisted that it presented a powerful, crisis-like decision before his readers.[1]

Indeed, it is possible that the comparison does not end there. Perhaps it would not be too much to suggest that Buber's "prophetic form" of eschatology envisions God as engaging human beings and their activity in the world in a kind of "I-You" mode; in this eschatological form or genre, God truly respects and regards the creaturely realm (and, most specifically, human decision) for what it actually contributes (for both good and ill) to God's labor toward the world's redemption. This approach leaves the future open to new and unexpected twists and turns, rather than being under tight divine control. In the "I-It" mode, by the simplicity of contrast, the world and its creatures really are little, if anything, more than objects under divine manipulation: God operating relentlessly in the world's history according to an eternal, divine blueprint.

Many people both inside and outside the Christian faith assume something much nearer this I-It, apocalyptic imagination when they hear the words "prophecy" or "prophetic." Whether the source for their ideas is—to note only a few examples—Nostradamus, the Mayan calendar, Benjamin Crème's predictions about the coming Buddha Maitreya or radio preacher Harold Camping's computations about the Second Coming, many people assume that prophecy is concerned with unlocking the mysteries of some predetermined historical fate toward which the world inexorably spins. Of course, this apocalyptic imagination tends to operate on the strong assumption that the world can only get worse—a dramatic and dangerous example of self-

---

1. See Walter Kaufmann's discussion in his prologue to Buber's *I and Thou* (New York: Charles Scribner's Sons, 1970), 9–19.

fulfilling prophecy, to be sure—and that only God alone can save us from this degenerating creation.

The *prophetic* imagination envisions God, creation and human decision and responsibility in a dramatically different way from the apocalyptic. In the prophetic mode of eschatology, what human beings actually *do*—and biblically speaking particularly what *Jews* actually do—makes all the difference in the world. In this vision of God and world, God has gifted creation—and gifted human beings especially—with true agency and responsibility. If Israel is faithful to the Torah, then God will respond in blessings of land, peace and plenty; if, however, Israel forsakes the covenant and its commands, God will respond with a very different future for the covenant people. In what follows I hope to trace the logic of this prophetic imagination in a phrase from the prophet Hosea that is programmatically cited twice in Matthew's gospel: "I desire mercy, and not sacrifice."

Interestingly, in the two Matthean passages where the Hosea citation appears, the stories are common to all three synoptic gospels. Yet of these gospels, only Matthew reports in each instance that Jesus appealed to the prophetic imagination by quoting Hosea, who was ostensibly quoting God: "I desire mercy, and not sacrifice" (Hosea 6:6). The two Matthean passages in question are 9:9–13 and 12:1–8.

Matthew 9:9–13: "Go and learn what this means"

The first story is the calling of "a man named Matthew sitting at the tax collector's booth" (9:9). "In the Roman empire contracts for collecting taxes and tolls were often put out to bid. The highest bidder in turn hired local people to collect the fees,"[2] usually at toll booths where fees were collected on goods (such as fish caught in the Sea of Galilee) as they were transported out of the region. "In this system the bidder and his employees were responsible for paying the taxes to the government. But they could also try to get extra taxes from the people in order to increase their personal profit. Even if they were not skimming off the top, they were suspected of doing so … . In Judea of Jesus' time they [very likely were] … looked upon as collaborators with the Roman [occupation] and therefore as disloyal,"[3] betraying their own people. Further, the nature of this work necessitated constant contact with both Roman coinage (with its potentially idolatrous connotations) and Roman officials.

Not only were tax collectors ritually unclean, then, they were also considered cheats and, even worse, traitors. It was scandalous enough that Jesus would call one of them to become a disciple of the Messiah; even worse was the scenario

---

2. Daniel Harrington, *The Gospel of Matthew*, Vol. 1 in the Sacra Pagina Series (Collegeville, MN: Liturgical Press, 1991), 127–128.

3. Ibid., 128.

of Jesus "having dinner at Matthew's house," where "many tax collectors and 'sinners' came and ate with him and his disciples" (9:10).

We can safely assume that for most Pharisees, Jesus's actions were virtually intolerable. The Pharisees had a noble mission that, for our purposes, might be summarized briefly as the restoration of the people of Israel to true holiness. The Pharisees were essentially a lay movement dedicated to appropriating for themselves the high standards of ritual holiness associated with the Jerusalem temple and its priestly practices, and attempting to legislate those standards (as thoroughly and consistently as possible) for Jewish home and social life. To mingle with tax collectors and other non-observant Jews ("sinners") was clearly not behavior priests could engage in and remain ritually pure for Temple service; hence the Pharisees, committed to reshaping Israel into "a kingdom of priests and a holy nation" (Ex. 19:6), would not engage in such behaviors. Further, the gospels strongly suggest that at least some Pharisees were deeply displeased with Jesus doing so—presumably because of his growing popularity and, correspondingly, his potential to lead the people of Israel astray. Thus their question: "Why does your teacher eat with tax collectors and sinners?"

Jesus's reply appeals to the reality of human need: "It is not the healthy who need a doctor, but the sick." A generous reading of this text will at least leave open the possibility that Jesus perceived the Pharisees—or at least some of the Pharisees—to be "the healthy." Nonetheless, he proceeds to challenge his critics, "But go and learn what this means: 'I desire mercy, not sacrifice'" (9:12-13). "Sacrifice" evokes the whole web of meanings associated with the Temple in Jerusalem: altars, animals' spilled blood, priests, ritual purity requirements. All of it bespeaks what Marcus Borg has called "the politics of holiness": set apart space, people, animals, all kept ritually pure in order to be part of a sacrifice acceptable to the Holy One.[4]

Of course, the struggle between priestly and prophetic strands in Israelite worship and practice is nothing new or rare; Jesus could easily have offered any number of quotations from the prophets in their stinging critiques against the presumption of people who sometimes seemed to think that all God needed was another bull on the altar—that offering sacrifices was a way to buy off God, to do a kind of "religious" duty that had little to no relation to their actual everyday lives and relationships, especially to the poor.

But Jesus quoted Hosea, who quoted God, who proclaimed a clear preference for "mercy" or "compassion" toward people who need help, people on the margins, rather than the more explicitly "religious" act of offering up sacrifices. This is the first and most obvious element in the prophetic imagination. But let me briefly mention two other elements:

---

4. See Borg's insightful contrasts between the "politics of holiness" and the "politics of compassion" in *Jesus: A New Vision* (San Francisco: Harper & Row, 1987), 86–93, 131–142.

1. Jesus, quoting Hosea, says that God *desires* mercy, but the fact that Jesus is quoting this to people who, as far as Jesus is concerned, do not exemplify such mercy but instead a kind of hard-hearted superiority already means that what God *desires* is not what God is *getting*. Jesus is demonstrating mercy toward tax-collecting traitors and other assorted sinners, but apparently he is in rare company. God desires mercy and not sacrifice, but mostly God was getting—and more than likely, still is getting—ritual sacrifices rather than mercy toward the needy. The prophetic imagination lives with the tension inherent in God's desires going unfulfilled, God's will being frustrated; indeed, the prophetic imagination may even share in the divine pathos over the suffering of creation's marginalized and forgotten poor.[5] This of course is significantly different from the apocalyptic imagination that dreams of God's unilateral power being unleashed, finally, in order to *force* God's will upon recalcitrant sinners who oppress the poor.

2. Jesus calls upon his critics, and upon us, to "go and learn what this means"—to study, to wrestle with the holy Scriptures, to *learn* what kind of people God desires for us to be. Whatever the nature of God's mysterious work in the world, it is not magic. And far too often the apocalyptic imagination thrives on a strongly anticipated flourish of magic on the grandest scale. God desires mercy; God desires compassion that will energize holy kindness, hearts of flesh within and among us humans. But God apparently will not force us into it; presumably, that itself would not be the I-You way of mercy. Apparently what we most deeply need is a divine physician, not a divine warlord. There may be times when a violent warlord is what we desire: a divine master of war to destroy all evil and suffering and enforce a just and righteous world order. It may be what we desire—but perhaps it is simply not what we most deeply need.

Matthew 12:1–8: "But if you had known what this means"

In Matthew 12, we encounter another story common to all three synoptic gospels—the story of Jesus and his disciples walking through the grainfields one Sabbath day. As with the previous pericope, only Matthew reports that, in defense of his disciples' harvesting grain on the Sabbath, Jesus again quoted Hosea's line, "I desire mercy, and not sacrifice." It is this dual citation that underscores the apparent importance, for Matthew, of a kind of prophetic imagination in the ministry of Jesus.

Not at all coincidentally, Matthew is the only gospel writer who ensures that his readers appreciate that "[Jesus's] disciples were hungry." Importantly

---

5. Abraham Joshua Heschel, *The Prophets* (New York: Harper 7 Row, 1962), 233.

for Matthew, the disciples were not simply idling their way through the fields, plucking grain for want of something better to do as they traveled. "The disciples were hungry," so there is a legitimate and perhaps even pressing human need at stake. Jewish legal reasoning regarding Sabbath behavior, probably already by Jesus's time, made allowances for doing whatever necessary to save a human life: "A case of risk of life supersedes the Sabbath" (*Yoma* 8:6, Talmud). In the case of this story, however, we would rightly presume that no one was about to starve to death! Nonetheless, Matthew assures us that hunger was a live issue on this Sabbath day.

It is noteworthy, too, that the problem was not that they were picking grain that was not theirs. The Torah made allowance for just such an act of hunger relief. In Deuteronomy 23:25 we read, "When you go into your neighbor's standing grain, you may pluck the ears with your hand, but you shall not put a sickle to your neighbor's standing grain." As New Testament scholar Daniel Harrington notes, "Such humanitarian legislation was intended to sustain the needy without giving them permission to pile up supplies. There is, however, no mention of the Sabbath in these cases."[6] It was, of course, precisely this concern for upholding Sabbath observance that motivated the Pharisees' observation: "Look, your disciples are doing what is not lawful to do on the Sabbath." After all, the people of Israel were expressly commanded by God to do no labor—none whatsoever—on the Sabbath day.

In this second passage of Matthew, we read that Jesus responded, "If only you had known what this means, 'I desire mercy and not sacrifice!'" This "if only" is fascinating. I suggest that it reveals a divine yearning, perhaps Heschel's divine pathos—a longing of God for the world to be different, to be a place where compassion flows toward human suffering and need, where the hungry have plenty to eat and health care truly is provided for all. This "if only" of Jesus is essentially the same pathos he will give voice to later in this gospel when he cries out, "Jerusalem, Jerusalem, you who kill the prophets and stone those sent to it, how often did I wish to gather together your children, as a bird gathers her fledglings under wings, and you were not willing!" (23:37). Matthew's Jesus calls us to take seriously, indeed to feel, this divine pathos in the world, a divine desire for mercy that flows forth from the very heart of God the Merciful, the Compassionate.

The prophetic imagination does not envision a sweeping away of all opposition in one mighty demonstration of divine might. The prophetic imagination does envision, does experience, does express a divine yearning, a divine desire for mercy. If the apocalyptic imagination, at least as interpreted in this essay, anticipates a universal act of God that will shut down the project of human responsibility in the world, then it is erroneous and dangerous.

---

6. Harrington, 172.

It represents a longing to be relieved of responsibility for God's creation, an infantile hope to be rescued. The prophetic, instead, feels the divine compassion, testifies that God's mercy is new every morning, and calls upon each one of us to follow in mercy's wake. This is the end for which God made the world.

4

"As if We Lived in a Liberated World"[1]: The Prophetic Vision of Dorothee Soelle
Rebecca Laird

What influence does one's society and place within it have on the development of a prophetic imagination? How does one live faithfully when born in a violent world? What might be an honest and hopeful response to unimaginable suffering? The life and thought of 20th century German Protestant theologian Dorothee Soelle (1929–2003) offers a look at one woman's quest to live into these questions.

One of the stories that Soelle tells repeatedly in her books comes from the playwright Berthold Brecht's play, "Mother Courage and her Children." The play takes place in Northern Europe during the Thirty Years War (1618–1648) that pitted Protestants against Catholics and emerging nation states against the consolidated interests of Rome. The play ends in 1636 as one of Mother Courage's children, Kattrin, a young girl who cannot speak, is told "Pray, you poor creature, pray!" when soldiers lay siege to the town during the night. As all the others bend to their knees and begin to recite well-known prayers, Kattrin slips away to the rooftop of the barn and plays her drum. The sound of her drumming wakes up the sleeping town and gives them a chance to fight for their lives. Kattrin loses her life in the battle but her actions save the village. Kattrin's prayer is one of action and defiance rather than quiet acquiescence.

Soelle first told this story in 1968 when she was still simmering with anger at her own country. As a post-WWII Christian theologian, the horrors of the Holocaust were never far from her thoughts. This story offers a framework for her core theological quandary: How could her family, society and church say they prayed, like the pious villagers in Brecht's play, while the Jews were being exterminated in the death camps located not far from her childhood home? How could her family, society and church not be as dismayed as she when it became clear that the existing structures that led to educational and materialistic success and cultural acceptability (Just go to church and pray quietly? Get an education and get ahead! Don't ask too many questions about the government or military police.) also contributed to the deafening silence that allowed six million people to die? All of life Soelle seemed to be asking: Where were the rooftop drummers?

---

1. Phrase taken from the Chapter 11 title of *The Silent Cry: Mysticism and Resistance* by *Dorothee Soelle* (Minneapolis: Fortress, 2001), 191.

Analyze the Context

Soelle was born in Cologne, Germany during the rule of the Nazi Party. Her family opposed the regime and hid a Jewish friend for several weeks in 1943. Her family, however, sought to remain apolitical and urged Dorothee not to speak publically about politics and focus on her education. She dutifully and happily studied poetry, philosophy and literary criticism. She describes herself at the age of 18 in 1948 this way:

> As for me, I set out to search for my soul in the land of the Greeks. But in my studies I found nothing more than what bourgeois philology had to offer and that was too little to live on. The nihilism of the recent years left me hungry. Awakening from the liberal bourgeois world of my parents and its Christianity, I finally began to look for another philosophy of life. I studied theology in order to get at the truth that had been kept from me long enough. Slowly a radical Christianity began to nest in me.[2]

She hungered for more than culturally acceptable mores and piety. The "radical Christianity" that took root compelled her to scrutinize Christian complicity in social oppression and violence and to evaluate her faith, not on creedal understandings, but on how Christian faith compels its followers to hold onto a hopeful future while resisting violence, speaking out and standing with those who suffer.

Sarah K. Pinnock summarizes that "Dorothee Soelle's writing is driven by an urgent need to respond to her concrete situation socially, politically and religiously. She presents a prophetic vision of faith in response to moral apathy, secular indifference to the church and the many injustices of history."[3] Soelle's acute awareness of the society into which she was born led her to contextual thinking. All of her writing—her theological volumes, autobiographical writing and poetry—and her living were done remembering the ashes of Auschwitz. She never allowed herself to wander far from the question that outraged her: How could good, Bach-listening, family-loving people turn a deaf ear and hold their tongues as fellow citizens were gassed due to differences in religion, race and lifestyle? How could she live out her faith and call others to join in ways that did not keep silent when whole groups of people were oppressed? Her rootedness in her own context—not one she chose but one she was born into—made her theology both political and poetic. She believed each person had to see how one's life was inextricably woven into one's culture and society. There was no such

---

2. Soelle, *Against the Wind*. (Minneapolis: Fortress, 1999), 13.
3. Sara Pinnock, "Introduction" in *The Theology of Dorothee Soelle*. (Harrisburg: Trinity Press, 2003), 14

thing as an individual who stands totally outside of the social environment. The interrelationships between people, groups and communities give an individual his or her uniqueness and sense of call to act on behalf of others. As an educated German of the 20th century, she took seriously the responsibility and call to act as Kattrin did—to point out those who sought to do harm and find the right music and instrument to both warn of danger and sing of hope.

Once Soelle recognized that political passivity and the highly-personalized piety of good but silent people had been contributing factors to the horrors of the Holocaust, she knew that the backdrop of her life and society could not nor should not be forgotten. She would think and write about God all of her life and she remained convinced that political passivity in an age of genocide was a sin greater than any individual breach of private morality. Silence that led to the death of others was serious sin.

Live out God

Nearer the end of her long life, after years of involvement in protest movements and political action in many corners of Latin and South America, Soelle revisited Kattrin's story in her writing. She still resisted the passivity of private prayers and preferred active prayers that place the one praying into direct solidarity with those who suffer. Yet she writes: "When I think on this today, living in a post-Christian world, I ask myself something else. Would Kattrin have beaten her drum if others had not prayed? If she had not learned to pray? If she had not grown up in a world of prayer? Do drumming and praying belong together as praying and doing justice do in Dietrich Bonheoffer? Is this contradiction really an either/or?"[4] She began to appreciate the affirmative aspects of her Christianized culture while she continued to resist the structures that continued to demand silence.

Soelle came to describe prophetic action, which she would often term "resistance", as linked with the life-nourishing prayer that she called "mysticism." These responses were not to be mutually exclusive. Indeed she came to believe that mysticism (interior encounter that feeds what is most human in us) is political and that resistance (actions that call oppressive structures and systems to account) is a kind of "embodied mysticism." In her understanding the soul that is united to God (mystical union) begins to see with God's wide open eyes. And when one sees what God sees one prays by seeking the liberation of those who suffer. She writes, "To use 'God's senses' does not mean simply turning inward but becoming free for a different way of living life: See what God sees! Hear what God hears! Laugh where God laughs! Cry where God cries!"[5]

---

4. Soelle, "The Guarantor of Poor People's Rights," in *The Theology of Dorothee Soelle,* Sara Pinnock, ed., 25.
5. Soelle, *The Silent Cry,* 293.

Kattrin, who drummed to save the life of those under threat, illustrates this embodied mysticism. Soelle had come to distrust much of ritual prayer as she found beseeching the "far-off" God to intervene and save millions from the gas chamber untenable. That God did not act and turned those who prayed into passive people who turned away hoping an external force would step in to stop evil. Soelle came to see Jesus as God's representative in the world. According to Dianne Oliver, Soelle called "for a sharing of dependence and responsibility between God and humanity. We are dependent on Christ representing us to God, but we are also responsible to represent God in the world."[6] Soelle posited that Christ stood in for us and inched open the door holding it ajar so that we could come and represent God, too, in our relationships to one another.

Sarah Pinnock writes, "To articulate faith in God theologically, the proper question [for Soelle] is not 'Do you believe in God?' as if God is an object to be known but 'Do you live out God.'"[7] Living out God—representing God, seeking ongoing redemption in history—is to follow Jesus, to be with him, as a part of the continuing incarnation of God in the world.

This concern for an embodied, this-worldly active spirituality that is able to enrich life in community fills Soelle's final book, *The Silent Cry*. She reflects on years spent traveling to Latin America, especially to Nicaragua where she joined with communities struggling for basic survival. She concluded that "the soul that is united with God sees the world with God's eyes. That soul, like God, sees what is otherwise rendered invisible and irrelevant. It hears the whimpering of starving children and does not let itself be diverted from real misery, becoming one with God in perceiving and understanding as well as acting. ... It is a mysticism of wide open eyes."[8]

Once one begins to see with open eyes and observes the suffering of the world, how will one respond? In *Against the Wind*, Soelle's memoir, she describes meeting Dorothy Day, founder of the Catholic Worker Movement, who was a remarkable pacifist and activist for the poor. Day is remembered for her hospitality toward the unemployed workers of New York City. What Soelle found so fascinating about Day is that she never gave up her commitment for the poor but sometimes cried for days overwhelmed by the struggle of the poor for food and dignity. This gift of tears was an example of the embodied mysticism. There is much sorrow on the way to ultimate liberation. One must honestly lament and mourn the situation of the poor as a part of living out God in the world. Soelle writes:

---

6. Dianne L. Oliver, "Christ in the World" in *The Theology of Dorothee Soelle*, 111.

7. Sarah Pinnock, "A Postmodern Response to Suffering after Auschwitz" in *The Theology of Dorothee Soelle*, 134.

8. Soelle, *The Silent Cry*, 284.

What I learned from this remarkable woman [Day] is that spirituality is a movement of the spirit where separation between inward and outward—is done away with. In spirituality what is inward is to become outward, visible and audible. When we learn to share pain and join with others, everyday life is hallowed, because our desires and fears begin to radiate in it. Our lives and experiences are not casual items to be discarded but treasures worthy of being remembered and reflected upon.[9]

To live fully rooted in the world with all of its trouble is to recognize one's need for God. It leads to a "hermeneutic of hunger" that place where we so hunger for bread, or dignity or meaning—depending on the poverty of our context—that we must plumb our stories and prayers and ideas of God anew to find something that can sustain life and hope. Soelle taught people in both Germany and Latin America to "read the Bible, learn to lament, see images of resurrection, search the Scriptures and traditions for help in the midst of distress that comes from hungering for God."[10] She wrote, "If we don't find an answer, we cling to those parts of the tradition that speaks to us in our despair."[11] For Soelle, this method of reading the Bible paralleled faithful living. Live and read with your eyes open, cry if you must, live in solidarity with those who suffer, search the scriptures and daily life for signs of hope, crumbs of bread, and when you can't find much hope, grab hold to what can sustain in life and in death.

Soelle tells a simple story from 1984 when she and others were involved in a blockade to protest the installation of a missile base in Mutlangen, Germany. It was raining and the protesters were huddled under a tarp when a middle-aged woman on a bike rode up to offer them hot tea. The woman supported the peace activities but could not join them for fear of losing her job. Soelle recalls the woman said, "But since I favor more practical measures anyway, I brought you tea." This simple statement became for Soelle an example of "all-sharing" which she understood as a characteristic of God and consequently God's people. She asks, "How shall I express the fact that the poor woman's tea in that rainy night in Mutlangen was 'all sharing.'"[12] This story exemplified for Soelle what is sacred in life. In a simple human sharing of tea in the rain, she, like the woman who gave her last copper coins in the treasury (Mark 12:41–44) spoke in the language of hope.

---

9. Soelle, *Against the Wind*, 83.
10. Luise Schottroff, "Come, Read with My Eyes," in *The Theology of Dorothee Soelle*, 45.
11. Ibid., 51. Schottroff quoting Soelle, *On Earth as in Heaven*, xi.
12. Soelle, *Dorothee Soelle: Essential Writings* (Modern Spiritual Masters Series), (Maryknoll, NY: Orbis), 219–20.

Embed the Vision of a New World in Your Hands

Dorothee Soelle died in 2003 and at the Worship Service of Mourning and Thanksgiving for her life the Lutheran bishop of Nordelbien, The Right Reverend Baerbel von Wartenberg-Potter, preached these words:

> A new heaven and a new earth is what the seer John describes in the great vision of the book of Revelation. It is a new earth, differently constituted than the one we are accustomed to, with a different way of living and thinking, a new way of acting and sharing. It is the newness in accordance to Christ that will make the earth into a new creation for all living beings. Dorothee's vision was shaped fundamentally by this vision, and she tirelessly guided us along this path. ... Our old earth is terribly drenched in blood, torn by war, and damaged by dying forests and withering fields. ... On this earth, the unheeded cries of children, whose mothers have no bread to give them, die inaudibly. ... [Soelle] did not only work for a new heaven and a new earth. She also sang, wrote poetry, loved, and laughed and assembled people together. What she strove for was not some *fata morgana*, some mirage from beyond; rather it was to concretely embed this vision in our hearts and hands.[13]

Soelle did not wait for a new heaven in some immaterial future; she wanted it to be "on earth as it is in heaven." She understood the way to bring heaven to this earth was by "embedding this vision" in her daily life and in her social interactions. She taught, raised children, protested, networked and in her writings sought to find a language for God that would join God's actions with here-and-now resistance. She offered active prayers and shared goods with those she knew who suffered. She wrestled with images, language and classical theology and sought ingredients of hope wherever she found them, even in the cupboards of literature, music, self-reflection or scripture. This wide-angle harvesting of ideas was criticized both by church and academy. She was never fully embraced by either institution. Yet, she consciously chose to follow Dietrich Bonheoffer's instance on the "radical this-worldliness of Christianity."[14] Her prophetic vision of the world was not otherworldly or utopian. She did not look for God on high. She looked for God in this world, in the ordinary people and places where praying and drumming, shedding tears and sharing tea all take place and are signs of people representing Jesus and living out God together on the way to a new world with a different way of living.

---

13. Von Wartenberg-Potter, "Funeral Sermon," in *Theology of Dorothee Soelle*, viii.
14. Soelle, *Against the Wind*, 91.

Soelle summarizes her response to the question of how might we live out of prophetic vision in the midst of life with all of its joys and great sorrows:

> How can we sing the Lord's song in a strange land? By an exodus from the Egypt of capitalism, by taking others' and our own pain seriously, and by manifesting at every level of our lives the wholeness that has become real for us in Christ. We manifest this wholeness physically and psychically, rationally and spiritually, in our toils for justice and a life that is worthy of human beings. We also show it in our laments about the defeats, in the experience of liberation.[15]

To live out God is to celebrate freedom, dignity and hope in the midst of daily life, together, right here and right now.

---

15. Soelle, *Against the Wind*, 85.

Part II: Open our Eyes, Open our Ears

Mark H. Mann

I was a college student the first time I spent a significant amount of time outside of the United States, working with other American college students on a summer ministry team traveling in the United Kingdom and Ireland. As is no doubt typical of youth encountering another culture for the first time, we spent a great deal of time noting the many differences between American and British culture. For example, although the Brits and Irish spoke the same language that we did, they said and did many things differently, and we observed it all, especially the fact that they, as we so often jokingly say, drove on the "*wrong* side of the road." Now compared to traveling to India or Russia, we had it easy in Britain and Ireland, where the people spoke the same language as us and share a very similar culture with Americans. My brother, who has worked with a church and international development agency in Kosovo, had a much more challenging cultural situation. Kosovars speak an entirely different language from Americans and, among the more notable and interesting differences, shake their heads to indicate "Yes" and nod to indicate "No."

It is when confronting cultural differences such as these for the first time that we begin to realize the contingency of our own culture's practices as well as what sociologists of religion refer to as the "taken-for-grantedness" of our social reality.[1] What this means is that there is no absolutely correct way, for instance, to say yes or no, much less a correct side of the road on which to drive. Instead, these are simply practices that our cultures have developed over time, which for those embedded in a particular culture have simply come to be taken for granted as a true and right part of the world—as true and right as the fact that the sky is "up" and on a cloudless day is "blue." That is, we don't think about nodding to say "yes" or even consider that we might instead shake our head to indicate the same if we had grown up in a culture that does. We simply do these things without thinking about them.

What these rather mundane examples are meant to illustrate is first of all that many, if not most, of the practices we perform as human beings are those that are taken for granted and therefore completely invisible to us. They are like the air that we breathe—so much a part of our normal day-in-day-out lives that we are completely unaware of them unless something like encountering a culture that does things differently brings into our awareness the fact that things might be, and in fact often are, different. This is perhaps best exemplified in the

---

1. Peter L. Berger, *The Sacred Canopy: Elements of a Sociological Theory of Religion* (Anchor Books, 1990).

way that indicating a simple "yes" or "no" can be done in countless ways in many different cultures.

And this brings us to the second implication we might draw from the fact that much of our so-called reality is socially constructed—its sheer relativity. That is, not only are there countless ways to say "yes," but there is also no absolutely correct way to do so. Within a particular culture, of course, there is. For me to say "Da" or "Ja" or "Si" or "Oui" will indicate an affirmative response to a Russian, German, Spaniard, or Parisian, respectively, but not to an American who has had no encounter with those languages and cultures. And for me to use one of these words to such an American, I would NOT have said "yes" correctly because for that person the right way to say yes is to say "Yes." This is why Americans often say, for instance, that the British drive on the "wrong" side of the road. It's not that there is some rational or absolute reason why one should drive on the right side versus the left, but that they don't do it in a way that is right within our culture. The problem, of course, is that if we have had little experience with multicultural settings, we might have absolutized our culture's practices and therefore honestly think that other ways of doing things are in a real sense wrong.

When serving as a missionary in Russia in the early 1990s, I experienced this problem quite often among the various university students on short term mission trips for whom I served as host. From them I would often hear complaints about how Russians "did things wrong," when in fact what those Russians were doing was simply different or expressed some value that Russians hold that Americans do not.

The point I wish to make here is not to advocate cultural relativism. Quite the contrary: as a Christian I do believe in absolute truths and values and hold God's self-revelation in the person of Jesus Christ to be the standard against which we should judge all truth and all values. Rather, my point is that there is a great deal of the cultural world that we as Christians inhabit that is completely invisible to us but which needs to be made visible because, held up to the light of the person, life and teachings of Christ, it is shown to be deeply sinful. And this is what having our eyes and ears opened by the prophetic imagination is all about: bringing the people of God to see how many of our taken-for-granted beliefs and practices either have nothing to do with, or are even counter to, the will and purposes of God.

This will sound odd to some, particularly those who think of sin only in terms of individual attitudes or practices, which has been a particular temptation for Christians in the highly individualized West. But all we need to consider is the practice of slavery to see how sin can also become embedded in cultural assumptions and practices. Slavery was a taken-for-granted and therefore "invisible" part of life in southern American states in the early 1800s. Otherwise moral, upright and deeply committed Christians had no problem justifying and supporting the practice, and hundreds of thousands were even willing to give up their lives defending it. And it was not just individuals who practiced slavery, but entire cultural and governmental systems that supported and maintained it. In fact, due to the systemic nature of evil, even those who spoke out strongly against slavery nevertheless helped to bolster slavery insofar as they benefited from slavery and helped fill the pockets of slave owners through buying cheap cotton, tobacco and sugar produced on Southern plantations.

Such was the sinful situation in ancient Israel that God called the ancient prophets to speak against. Practices of idolatry, infidelity to the covenant, oppression of the poor, the widow and the orphan had become so commonplace and taken-for-granted that the people of Israel were completely unable to see how evil they had become or to hear God's call to righteousness, mercy and justice. This, then, was one of the chief roles of prophets like Amos, Hosea and Joel: to confront the people of Israel with their sins, to help them see how deeply their lives and society had become infected by sin, to open their eyes to the many explicit and implicit ways that they, as individuals and as a people, had forsaken their covenant with God.

Such was also the case during the time of Jesus, but perhaps in even more insidious ways. Jesus, for Christians the great prophet *par excellance*, faced a situation in many ways far more complex than the ancient prophets of Israel. Not only was he faced with speaking to those who needed to be called into covenant relation with God, but also those who were actively seeking to be faithful to the covenant, but in sinful ways. I mean, of course, the Pharisees, whose chief goal was to be prophetically faithful to the covenant, but whose attitudes, teachings and practices nevertheless exhibited deep infidelity and sinfulness. Like the ancient prophets, the Pharisees saw as their vocation calling the people of Israel to be faithful to the commands of God, as expressed especially in the Mosaic law. But in doing this they had come to focus their attention on the letter of the law, completely forgetting the spirit of love at its core, and thereby hypocritically piling a burden upon the common people that even they, the Pharisees themselves, were unable to bear. The prophetic challenge that Jesus faced, then, was helping the Pharisees to see the way that their good intentions were being undermined by another kind of idolatry: works righteousness. Sadly, the biblical record only notes two Pharisees whose eyes and ears were opened by the prophetic Word of God: Nicodemus and Saul/Paul.

This is often the way that sin works. It becomes embedded in various cultural and personal attitudes and practices and is therefore completely invisible even to those particularly concerned with living righteous, Godly lives. This is generally what Walter Brueggemann is talking about in *The Prophetic Imagination* when referring to the "royal consciousness," Of course, in calling this kind of embeddedness in sin "royal" Brueggemann has also highlighted the ways in which social systems and power function in the formation of the cultural world we often take for granted. It is those in power who play the largest part in defining and forming the world that we inhabit, and often in ways that support the maintenance of the status quo and their own position of power, authority and wealth within it. This is, of course, not always intentional. But even those with the best of intentions can still perpetrate sin when failing to recognize its embeddedness in the structures and subtleties of cultural life. Indeed, so hidden can such sin be that even those being victimized by it most profoundly may unwittingly contribute to its perpetuation.

And this is why prophets tend *not* to be popular people. They tell us things that we do not want to hear and bring to our attention things that we do not want to see. For starters, we do not tend to enjoy being told that our way of doing or seeing things is wrong, or at least not necessarily right. Social scientists call this experience "culture shock"—the pain of having the social reality we tend to take for granted constantly challenged. But beyond that, we are even less likely to enjoy having our world and our particular participation in it being called sinful. If this claim is true, it means that we are in some sense culpable for the evil perpetrated, not to mention that we need to make changes in our lives. And this is why, in the end, the first step in the nurturing the prophetic imagination is having our eyes and our ears opened. It is painful, but change—and we are ever being called by God to change and to grow as God's holy people—will never come until first we have come to an awareness that much of our taken-for-granted world is sinful. The church, the Body of Christ, is called to be a people set apart for God, but insofar as we have come to take for granted aspects of the royal consciousness of *our* world we are not fulfilling God's call to holiness, righteousness and justice. As painful as it may be, we need to have our eyes and our ears opened once again to the voice of God and pray for the strength and wisdom to be led forth in truth.

In varying ways, the following four chapters each explore the pervasiveness of the royal consciousness and the many challenges of having our eyes and ears opened to the prophetic call of God. The first is a sermon presented as a keynote address at our conference by theologian and sociologist Michael Eric Dyson, which looks at the role of the prophetic through the vocation and struggles of the prophet Elijah. Dyson focuses in his sermon especially on the extent to which a true prophet must always speak from a position of marginalization—as one outside of but speaking into and against positions and systems of embedded power—affirming that prophets must always be critical of those in power in order not to surrender their own prophetic voices to the wiles and temptations of the royal consciousness. Through this sermon one hears echoes of Dyson's own experience as a kind of prophet of the American black church (he is a also an ordained Baptist preacher). Prior to the 2008 presidential election, Dyson was a close confidant and advisor of then-candidate Barack Obama, but has since found himself one of the most outspoken critics of President Obama (who now embodies the royal consciousness of American culture, for good or for ill), especially in relation to blacks and the poor and, not surprisingly, completely distanced from his former friend. Dyson posits the role of the prophet, therefore, as one that must ever be pulling back from power, and speaking from the critical margins of society, and especially in solidarity with the poor and oppressed. Dyson also sounds a hopeful note, in the end. The role of the prophet can lead to deep loneliness and isolation, but prophets must always remember that they are not alone. Ultimately, as the story of Elijah powerfully conveys, they serve God, and God has set aside and is ready to lift up thousands of others who have not bowed their knees to Ba'al—the veritable "god" of the royal consciousness.

Similarly, in Jacquelyn Winston's "Assassin of Prophetic Imagination" we find an historical account of the demise of the prophetic imagination in the Christian church. According to Winston, this unfortunate occurrence can be traced to the conversion of the Roman Emperor Constantine in the early 4th century and the subsequent transformation of the church from a body of persecuted martyrs to persons of wealth, power and social position. Winston then explores the way that the royal consciousness of 4th century rhetorical strategies became used by Christians to argue against and essentially objectify and marginalize others. Sadly, Winston finds, such strategies continue to be used by Christians in the American church today, with persons from various political persuasions committing public acts of rhetorical violence against brothers and sisters in Christ simply because of differences in political commitment.

In "Appropriating the Prophetic Visions of Du Bois and Thurman," Karen D. Crozier explores the ways in which the royal consciousness of racist attitudes have been embedded in American culture throughout its history. Du Bois, through his idea of "double consciousness" in his seminal *Souls of Black Folk* is shown as the first to prophetically call into question ways in which such consciousness had been appropriated by black persons with devastating spiritual, social and political consequences for black Americans. Crozier then looks to Howard Thurman, one of the great theologians and preachers of the 20th century, as one who has helped black Americans to move beyond the problem that Du Bois identified by drawing upon the "authentic realism" found in Jesus' teachings about the kingdom of Heaven.

Rounding out this section are two chapters that look at what it might mean for us to have our eyes opened to the problematic complexities and injustices of the global economy. In the first, Lee Van Ham, long-time proponent of Jubilee Economics, argues that the recent economic crisis has revealed various problematic assumptions that underlie current United States and world-wide economic practices that *should* but have *not* been questioned by those seeking to address the crisis. He then goes on to identify ways in which these assumptions have taken on the kind of status that central theological beliefs hold within religious traditions, that they are "idols" at whose feet we worship, but which need to be shattered if we are going to see the fulfillment of the prophetic vision for peace and justice embodied in the Hebrew prophets and life and teachings of Jesus.

Picking up on these themes, in what is perhaps the most disheartening of essays in this section, Orlando R. Serrano, Jr., provides a close analysis of practices related to Fair Trade Coffee production. Fair Trade practices have been touted by many as an answer to systemic injustice in the production and trade of coffee, sugar and many other similar commodities. However, Serrano lifts the veil around Fair Trade, revealing the deep ways in which Fair Trade still assumes dehumanizing and oppressive economic ideologies and practices. In the end, Serrano offers creative alternatives based upon Jesus' teachings about the Kingdom of God and early Christian communal teachings and practices. While this certainly should be read, then, as hopeful, Serrano's analysis ultimately also points to the tremendous challenges faced by those who wish to nurture the prophetic imagination in our world today. Indeed, truly unmasking the evil of the royal consciousness requires continually unpacking and unmasking the many layers of systemic sin and constant vigilance. Indeed, the work of nurturing the prophetic imagination will never be done so long as our Lord tarries!

5

It's Hard Out Here for a PIMP (a Prophet who Imagines Moral Possibilities)

Michael Eric Dyson

It is an honor to be here today at Point Loma to have this opportunity to chat with you a bit about some important things, and, as I'm wont to say in my tradition, what the Lord has laid on my heart. I want to thank Drs. Nelson and Mann for their gracious hospitality and for their brilliant leadership here at this institution and of course over this conference and Dr. Carr for the gracious introduction.

Now I ain't got but thirty minutes. I am a Baptist preacher. Usually I introduce myself in thirty minutes, then start preaching. But Bart Ehrman, who has gained quite a bit of notice lately as a biblical scholar and who has deconstructed some of the beliefs about scriptures, argues that we can't assume that people have a certain level of biblical literacy anymore, because we're living in a different era. He didn't say we're living in a postmodern era where we have really challenged the stability of certain understandings of the Word. So with that in mind, I want to take a bit of time to read from the nineteenth chapter of I Kings, in the Hebrew Bible, what we call the Old Testament:

> [1] Now Ahab told Jezebel everything Elijah had done and how he had killed all the prophets with the sword. [2] So Jezebel sent a messenger to Elijah to say, "May the gods deal with me, be it ever so severely, if by this time tomorrow I do not make your life like that of one of them."
> [3] Elijah was afraid and ran for his life. When he came to Beersheba in Judah, he left his servant there, [4] while he himself went a day's journey into the desert. He came to a broom tree, sat down under it and prayed that he might die. "I have had enough, LORD," he said. "Take my life; I am no better than my ancestors." [5] Then he lay down under the tree and fell asleep.
> All at once an angel touched him and said, "Get up and eat." [6] He looked around, and there by his head was a cake of bread baked over hot coals, and a jar of water. He ate and drank and then lay down again.
> [7] The angel of the LORD came back a second time and touched him and said, "Get up and eat, for the journey is too much for you." [8] So he got up and ate and drank. Strengthened by that food, he traveled forty days and forty nights until he reached Horeb, the mountain of God.
> [9] There he went into a cave and spent the night. And the word of the LORD came to him: "What are you doing here, Elijah?"

¹⁰ He replied, "I have been very zealous for the LORD God Almighty. The Israelites have rejected your covenant, broken down your altars, and put your prophets to death with the sword. I am the only one left, and now they are trying to kill me too."

¹¹ The LORD said, "Go out and stand on the mountain in the presence of the LORD, for the LORD is about to pass by." Then a great and powerful wind tore the mountains apart and shattered the rocks before the LORD, but the LORD was not in the wind. After the wind there was an earthquake, but the LORD was not in the earthquake. ¹² After the earthquake came a fire, but the LORD was not in the fire. And after the fire came a gentle whisper. ¹³ When Elijah heard it, he pulled his cloak over his face and went out and stood at the mouth of the cave. Then a voice said to him, "What are you doing here, Elijah?"

¹⁴ He replied, "I have been very zealous for the LORD God Almighty. The Israelites have rejected your covenant, broken down your altars, and put your prophets to death with the sword. I am the only one left, and now they are trying to kill me too."

¹⁵ The LORD said to him, "Go back the way you came, and go to the Desert of Damascus. When you get there, anoint Hazael king over Aram. ¹⁶ Also, anoint Jehu son of Nimshi king over Israel, and anoint Elisha son of Shaphat from Abel Meholah to succeed you as prophet. ¹⁷ Jehu will put to death any who escape the sword of Hazael, and Elisha will put to death any who escape the sword of Jehu. ¹⁸ Yet I reserve seven thousand in Israel—all whose knees have not bowed down to Baal and all whose mouths have not kissed him."

Excuse me for that rather lengthy reading of the Scripture. The great southern historian C. Van Wilpert says a title is a contract between an author or a speaker and his or her audience. So I want to reflect on "It's Hard Out Here for a P.I.M.P." Now in my mind, P.I.M.P. is not pimp. It's an acronym. P.I.M.P.: A Prophet who Imagines Moral Possibilities. Elijah has been doing battle with the forces, as he sees them, of evil. The people of Israel have been seduced by a god who has not made them but is purely of their making, a god foreign to their tradition, bowing their knees down to Baal. And it has been horrible for those who are the faithful, because they have been slaughtered. And Elijah has been sent a death threat by Jezebel, who says, "I'm making it my intention and my greatest duty to make sure that by this time tomorrow you are dead. And like those other prophets, you too will die." And Elijah is afraid for his life. People think that prophets are built of steel, that they have bulletproof hearts.

To engage in an act of prophecy is not simply trying to predict the future—that's not even what biblical prophecy ultimately is about. If you try to have a one-to-one correlation between what some prophet said and what God subsequently did, you'd be hard-pressed to see the level of fulfillment really be extraordinary. But what is more important about prophecy is to get deep into the mind and imagination of God—to have the audacity to risk the belief that God somehow communicates to human beings and that you can tap into the imagination of God or you can be overrun by the imagination of God. You can be hit like a Mack truck by God's will, by God's desire, by the energy and imagination of God's mind. That's a rather, if you will, not humble, not characteristically gentle, but that's a rather—some would argue—arrogant way to assume that one can exist in life. That you can actually know the mind of God. That you can feel the pulse of God. That you can be driven by God. After all, in the name of that vision, many people have done evil and desperate things; many people thinking they have served God have murdered and created mayhem. And so Elijah, feeling that he is in the grip of God's imagination, knowing that he has been pushed forward by what he feels God wants him to do, runs for his life, because now he's been threatened.

Prophets are often a threat to the social and civil order. Prophets are not simply there to make people feel good. Prophets often don't make kings feel very good. In fact, prophets are the ones saying, you know, "You da man." But "you da man" like you're the man who's messing up. You're the man who's engaged in all kinds of nefarious activities. You are the man who's contradicting your very principles. Remember Nathan going to King David, saying that very thing. Once you were the apple of God's eye and you were riding high, and now because of your own particular lust and the consumption of desires that have not been disciplined, you are messing up big time and contradicting your very principles. And so, you da man all right, but not "You da man." No, no, no—you da man. No, no, no—you're the man. Not that kind of celebratory back-slapping celebration, but it is a challenge to those who are in power, if we are really prophetic, if we really have the imagination of God at stake.

God often opposes those who are in power, and, ironically enough, the biblical record tells us time and time again that God is responsible for getting people in power, but people who are in power tend to forget what they are in power for. Folk get elected, selected, and then they tend to forget what they were there for—what they were sent for—because the voices around them begin to squeeze out that divine anointment and possibility. A host of people who are advisors begin to crowd out the ability of this particular prophet or this anointed leader to hear the voice of God. And it's difficult, and none of us need be arrogant about it, because all of us are tempted by the traps of life. All of us are seduced by power. All of us are seduced by influence. You don't know until your name is up in lights. You don't know until people bow down in your presence.

You don't know until they acclaim you as a great singer or great entertainer or great thinker. You don't know that temptation until then.

And so here it is that Elijah is running for his life, because the prophetic imagination often runs counter to what the world of power wants. And as a result, there's a conflict, and the person who pays the price is often the prophet. And so now Elijah is running for his life, and he comes to the mouth of a cave and the angel speaks to him, asking, "What are you doing here?" He says, "Look, it is enough oh Lord, now take away my life." I've read to you from the New International Version, but the King James Version says, "It is enough oh Lord, now take away my life for I am not better than my fathers." He said, they've beat up on the prophets, they've murdered them, they've thrown down your altars, they bow their knees to a foreign god; they are no longer listening to the prophetic narrative that I have enunciated. Just take my life; it's over. It's a wrap. It's done. I don't want to live anymore.

It's hard out here for a prophet who imagines moral possibilities because you're often thinking, Dad gum, I'm just trying to do the right thing. How come folk can't hear me? How come they just can't do what I tell them to do because God has inspired me to say what I'm saying? Because perhaps one of the reasons people can't hear a prophet is because they don't want to hear the truth about their circumstances or situations. And so it is difficult for us to hear, so sometimes we turn to entertainers or we turn to artists, we turn to visual artists and artists of the word. Because we can't sometimes take the truth from prophets who stand to proclaim the Word. Now sometimes a prophet is a bit arrogant or self-important, confident beyond any measure of reasonable expectation. You know, when you got the Word of God, you figure that you're the dude, you're the one who's walking around, you're the woman. Look, I got the Word of the Lord, step off. You know I'm that person.

And yet what Elijah discovers is that it's hard out here for a prophet, because prophets are often alienated from the structures of society that would give them commendation. It doesn't celebrate what they do; they don't get the national awards to celebrate their prophetic integrity or imagination. They are often running counter to the prevailing logic of the times, or what Eric Hoffer used to call the "temper" of the times. And so now it is not a comfortable position, and it ain't well paid. Ain't a long line of people signing up to be no prophet. The job description is awful tough. You don't have much money, not much social acclaim; you may die in the process. I think I am going to be a nurse practitioner, thank you very much. And so, the long line of prophets diminishes or is diminished, is eroded, is lessened, because the demands are so high. And those who are called to such a duty often find themselves in direct contradiction to the society around them, and that leads to depression and grief.

Martin Luther King, Jr. was a deeply depressed human being. Why? Because he was called by God to speak a word of prophecy to an era that didn't want to hear it. Now that we celebrate Martin Luther King, Jr.'s birthday as a national holiday, it is hard for you to imagine that it was hard for Martin Luther King, Jr. But here was a man who for the last three years of his life was persona non grata. He could hardly get a speaking engagement to speak at universities. No American publisher wanted to publish his book. His own staff spoke out against him or disagreed with him. His own organization initially said, when he spoke out against the war in Vietnam, "That represents Dr. King; that doesn't represent the board of the Southern Christian Leadership Conference." And then when he spoke out against the war in Vietnam a year or two later, Whitney Young, who was then the head of the National Urban League, and Roy Wilkins, who was head of the National Association for the Advancement of Colored People, said, "You're wrong, you're problematic, to break precedent. The man in power, Lyndon Baines Johnson, has done more to help black people then any recent president, and here you are speaking out against him, here you are taking a stand against him. It will lead to grief!"

It leads to depression. King was deeply depressed, not because he wasn't sure of his vocation, though he tried to figure it out. He said, "Maybe I need to go back to teaching. Maybe I need to retire and give up this prophetic vocation. Maybe I need to stop staying on the road 360-some-odd days a year. Giving something like 380 speeches a year. Never at home, the children don't even know me; my wife is a stranger to me. My home will not even receive me gladly." You can romanticize what it means to be a prophet, but to pay the price for that prophecy is another thing, and often the price of prophecy is grief and suffering and depression. And so Elijah is there like Martin Luther King, Jr. was there, Martin Luther King, Jr. wondering what would be his end. It got so tough at the end that he could never stand to be in a room that had windows. Because he was wondering, "Is it going to be now that I will be murdered? Some bullet will come crashing through the window?" He was very uncomfortable. This man was not even forty-years-old. When they did an autopsy on his body, they said he had a heart of a sixty-five-year-old man. Distress was too deep; the pain was too penetrating and poignant. The depression was so profound.

It's hard out here for a prophet who imagines moral possibilities that are against the era in which we live and against the logic of those who are in power. Prophets would rather be on the payroll, paid, supplemented, stipends, foundation grants. Prophets would rather live in nice homes and drive nice cars, this prosperity gospel that has choked Christian belief in the last fifteen to twenty years. But it's just a recycling of what happened. Even the great Harry Emerson Fosdick was victim to some of this stuff back in the '30s. You think about the fact of this—the more things change, the more they stay the same. People think that God is about cosigning your home, God is about getting a better car, driving a nice car. Trying to live in a nice crib. Ain't nobody mad about that. But the point is, don't worship at the altar of materialism, because it blocks prophetic enunciation. It makes you more comfortable in the world in which you're trying to deliver judgment and have analysis, and you become compromised with the trinkets of power, with the seductions of access, with the powerful poignancy of influence. Name in lights, on books, on marquees and you become quiet, compromise what you want to say.

And so Dr. King was depressed because he was in the land of grief, because he was grieving and lamenting the steep decline of the American moral imagination and that America was in the grip of a notion called white supremacy. That some people believe that just because they were of one race, they were better than others. That they were superior, that they were more intelligent and more likely to be the recipient of God's favor. King said that I don't even know that god. The God I worship is a God of love that believes in justice, and justice is what we do when we think about love. As I've often tried to say, "Justice is what love sounds like when it speaks in public." And so, we've got to figure out a way to love people in public spaces that allows justice to roll down like waters and righteousness like a mighty stream, King said, and for that, the head of the F.B.I.—or at least his second in command—said that King was the most dangerous leader in America. For that, for the desire to not have one person drink at a white water fountain and another person drink at a black water fountain, he was considered to be a threat to American society. Because he wanted white children and black children to go to the same school, he was seen as a threat to America. And so he was deeply and profoundly grieving and depressed; the mortality descended upon him with rushing fervor.

And like Elijah, he withdrew as well, as Elijah withdraws and says, "Lord it's enough to take away my life; they've killed your prophets, torn down your altars, they've bowed at another god." And God led Elijah to get something to eat. Because you've got to feed the prophetic imagination, but you've got to feed the prophetic body as well. That means sometimes there's a relationship between your nervous system and folk who get on your nerves. If you're not healthy, if you're not in your right mind, you're not in the mind to hear the word of God or even to put on the mind of God, the imagination of God. There is a strict relationship between physical resource and physical stability, and material resource and hearing the godly imagination. That's why some people who are subject to poverty, that's why some people who are viciously relegated to the periphery of American society, that's why some people who go to schools where they don't have any resources, books that are second- and third-hand, pages ripped out, their bathrooms don't even work, their toilets are in disrepair, their teachers are living in overcrowded rooms—and those kids are acting up because they didn't even eat breakfast that morning. Lead paint and asbestos is their common companion. And then we wonder why those children have attention deficit disorders. We wonder why they can't pay attention in a significant fashion. Their stomachs are grumbling. They are physically malnourished, they can't even hear or consume the mental nourishment because they have been psychologically depleted and physically assaulted.

God says to Elijah, "You can't even understand what prophetic poignancy you posses. You can't even understand the great imagination because you are tired, worn out, worn down." And so even though he is grieved and depressed, God wants to speak to him. God wants to lift him up. But God can only do that by feeding the prophetic imagination, by feeding the prophetic body. That's why some people who try to get into this abstract spirituality that enunciates and articulates this vast notion of God being some spiritual being and we are all floating on high are not relevant. If your God ain't got nothin' to do with the redistribution of wealth and trying to get people paid right and at a decent wage, if your God ain't got nothin' to do with folk having their bellies filled because they are hungry, if your God ain't got nothin' to do with trying to help folk out of the misery they're in—then, that God is not relevant. That God is not of much use to those of us who are struggling down here on the ground.

Levinas, the great philosopher, said that some try to see God *sub specie aeternitatis*, that we see God from above and the eternal perspective. But I'm with the Wes Montgomery crowd. That's a jazz musician. Down here on the ground. You all don't know nothin' about that. You're all into Jay-Z and Britney Spears. I ain't mad at none of them. Taylor Swift. Or Kanye. Now this ain't got nothin' to do with my sermon this morning, but I got to defend Kanye just a little bit up here today. I'm talking about prophets and how tough it is. It's hard to be a prophet. I ain't saying Kanye was no prophet. He didn't intend nothing edifying. But he was mad, because he had this stupid notion that people who got awards should actually deserve them. We ain't sayin' Taylor Swift ain't cool. We ain't saying that Taylor Swift ain't got no skills. But Taylor Swift on Video of the Year, up against oh-oh, oh-oh, come on:

> All my single ladies, All my single ladies,
> All my single ladies, All my single ladies,
> Oh, oh, oh, oh, oh, oh
> Come on, come on.

So Kanye seizes the microphone. It was rude, it was ridiculous, like prophets often are. You don't want to live next door to no prophet—they're ridiculous people. They don't brush their teeth, they don't shave, they don't sometimes put on their proper adornment. But boy, when that word comes out of them, it's ridiculous and cantankerous. And so Kanye seizes the microphone and he starts to speak, and people are pissed. How dare he? How many young black and Latino and first nation people are Taylor Swifted every day? Except they don't even get a chance to get the microphone to speak back. And, guess what, I bet you Chuck Berry was watching, saying, "Do it!" Chuck Berry was going, "Where were you when Elvis was getting my awards?" Huh? I bet you Little Richard was saying, "Do that!" Shut up, give me my Grammy. Whhhh! Cause Little Richard said, "Pat Boone got my award!"

So Kanye wasn't intentionally engaging in a prophetic act. But the consequences were prophetic because what it did was try to compensate for the denial of legitimate and authentic recognition of black artistry in the world, where their superior achievements were not recognized. Now, that don't mean then that Taylor Swift ain't got no skills. What it means is that sometimes we are not sensitive to other children who have been Taylor Swifted. Those who are denied opportunity, but don't have amplification from the same tribe that dissed them. Beyoncé gave her the microphone later. But many people of the same tribe who have dissed the others have not allowed them to amplify their pain and misery.

And so if I were to link that back into this (rather suspiciously): Elijah is out there saying it's enough, cancel tomorrow, it's done, it's a wrap. We try to pass over the mournful passages of our souls, the dark night of the soul. Because when you are a prophet, sometimes that darkness must be calculated as the price to be paid in order for the advance to go forth, and sometimes to your own detriment you are a vehicle for a transcendent blessing. But the problem is that you just don't want to just get trapped there. Sometimes cynicism is the luxury of those who have the time to think and calculate, but those whose backs are against the wall got to stand up.

And so God says to Elijah, "What are you doing here?" He says, "Look, I'm representing you. I know you know. Don't tell me you, you too? I'm here because they've messed up." He says, get something to eat. You're tired, you're weary, your nervous system is painfully overwrought. Howard Thurman, the great prophet, said, "We must yield the nerve center of our consent to God." That means at the center of your soul, like Dag Hammarskjold, the great U.N. secretary, said: "There must be a 'yes', even in the midst of 'no.'" Even in the midst of denial, even in the midst of lapsed opportunity, even when you think everybody else is gone and you the only one left.

And he says to God, "I'm the only one left." Be careful when you telling God that you are the only one, 'cause God be making more that look just like you. Right? Remember that Bill Cosby used to have that thing with the children—"I'll get rid of you and make another one that looks just like you." Oh, parents are terrorists, aren't we? You're telling God you the only one left? Slow down! Is God still God? Part of the prophetic imagination is to imagine that you got a successor and some company. And so sometimes the temptation is to believe that we're the only one. I'm the only Michael Eric Dyson. Well hope I am, but I ain't the only one. I'm the only Desmond Tutu, I am the only Martin Luther King, Jr. and I'm the only Stanley Hauerwas, I'm the only Katongole, I'm the only Mann, I'm the only Nelson. You are, but you ain't the only one that God sent. You're not the only one with the Word. God said there are 7,000 others who have not bowed their knees to Baal. They have not been seduced. You just don't know them.

And so what you have to do is not to imagine you are the only one left, because when you think that you are the only one, you start making mistakes. You are on the court and think that you are only one that can shoot, and you are trying to toss up threes, and here is a dude under that basket who can dunk it if you just pass him the ball. Man! And so you're not the only one. There's a team, but sometimes that team is invisible. So you have to use your prophetic imagination to organize a colloquia, a congregation of fellow sufferers and servants who are here to do God's work, and never have the audacious assumption in the negative sense to assume that you are the only one. God says to him, "You're tired, and because you're tired and your nervous system is overwrought, you don't understand that there are others out here who are working in different venues." Remember Jesus later said, "I got sheep you know not of." There are other folk working out here. You think that your church is the only one, your denomination's the only one, you think your religion is the only one. You think your way of knowing God is the only way. You ain't the only one. You're not the only person, you're not the only people, and Elijah was especially distraught because he says, I thought I was better than those white supremacists who trained me. Thought I was better than those crackers and rednecks that I left behind. Those were the real racists. But I am pure. I am part of the Y Generation. I listen to Jay-Z. I listen to Snoop Dogg:

> Follow me, follow me, follow me, follow me, but don't lose your grip
> Nine-trizzay's the yizzear for me to mess up
> And I ain't holdin' notin' back
> And brother I got twenty on the gansta' sack
> I said a Rat-tat-tat-tat
> Right . . .
> Falling back on at it
> With a heck-a-fie gansta lean
> And funky-on-the mike like a old batch o' collard greens
> It's the capital S, oh yes, the fresh N double O P

D O double G Y D O double G ya' see
Showin' much flex when it's time to wreck a mic'
Pimpin' what and clockin' a grip like my name was Dolomite.
Yeah.

Well. I got black friends. I know a couple of Negroes, some Native Americans, and some Asian brothers and sisters. I'm down. I'm cool. I eat at Mexican restaurants. I go to concerts that feature diversity. I am cool. I am not like my ancestors. Then you discover that I'm no better than them. Why? Because some of them did the best they knew how, their moral intestines gutted by blinding bigotry. And we think we're better, and yet here we are living in a so-called post-racial era. And we still live in abject poverty and misery. And if you push even enlightened young white brothers and sisters hard enough, how much are we willing to admit that our privilege rests upon the denial of opportunity for so many others?

I am not better than my fathers. That recognition will make it difficult for you to even deliver your prophecy, because if I am no better, then I might as well end it ... No! 'Cause ain't nobody perfect, and ain't nobody got the ultimate truth, but you are humble enough to admit that just like your mothers and fathers you have your impediments and obstacles, then that opens a pathway for divine revelation! And so God says to Elijah, He says, "Check out the seven other thousand who ain't bent their knees to Baal. Go anoint another king to take over them that's messing up, then anoint your successor, who is going to be the prophet after you. Cause you ain't the only one."

It's hard out here for a prophet if you think that you the only one. This is a long-distance race. You got to pass the baton on. You think Jordan is great, but then comes Kobe Bryant. Okay, Lebron James too. You think you're FloJo, and then comes somebody else—started to say Marion Jones, but that would be difficult right now. Wilma Rudolph before them all. You think that you're the only one, that you're the zenith, you're the high point, you're the apotheosis? You are the prophetic imagination, you are the cat's pajamas from God? You are not the only one, and it's hard sometimes, and we get stuck in grief. And we must go through grief; you cannot avoid it. But what ultimately saves you, even in the midst of your grief, is to recognize that you have a community of co-aspirants who desire the same thing you do, but you must imagine their existence in order for your own to be made more worthy. And for you to become an ultimate instrument of God, you must imagine that there are others who possess an equal measure of God's grace.

And as I end, that's why it's so important even as a prophet not to assume that your way is the only way. Howard Thurman said, "You can go to the Atlantic Ocean, you can dip your glass in the Atlantic Ocean. It may be full of the Atlantic Ocean, but it ain't all the Atlantic Ocean." Sometimes we're depressed and grieved because we're trying to do it all by ourselves, thinking our way is the only way. I deal with my conservative brothers and sisters all the time and they are so sometimes mind-numbingly self-righteous and self-assured and confident that they have God's word and they know what the deal is, and they're against abortion—they are pro-life, but they ain't pro-livin'. I ain't mad. Choose your moral position; I respect you; but don't assume you got the only way. Don't assume you the only one. Why do you assume that because you live in Montana, Idaho, you got God's number on speed dial? And you assume that those poor black and brown and red and yellow people who are beyond the pale—literally—of your imagination are somehow not as blessed by God. You must realize you are not the only one.

And so it's hard out here for a prophet who fails to recognize you are in a great community with a great cloud of witnesses. And as I end then, you must recognize, no matter where you are, no matter what generation you're in, no matter what kind of music moves you, no matter what kind of spirituality that you have, it's not the only one. It's not the only way. It's not the only path. And the God we worship is bigger and more powerful and calls us to a prophetic vocation and to imagine others who are there with us, who can check us, who can challenge us, and who may ultimately change us.

God bless you.

6

The Assassin of Prophetic Imagination: Imperialistic Rhetoric in Ancient Rome and Contemporary America
Jacquelyn Winston

Introduction

The gospel call to sacrificial surrender and neighborly love was replaced with the strident voices of power when Constantine became the first Christian emperor of the Roman Empire in the fourth century. The merger of church and state which occurred under his reign is often referred to as "Constantinianism," although the culprit is neither Constantine nor his conversion, but rather the seductive allure of power which led the imperial church to trade its prophetic imagination and voice for an imperial one which was used to justify Crusades, heresy inquisitions and multiple "just" wars in the name of God. The imperial church's ascent to power was facilitated by its ability to access the language of power which was viewed as culturally normative. The trappings of empire embodied in social class, taught in elite Roman educational venues and reinforced by social practices, was conveyed by coded rhetoric designed to garner legitimacy for successful communicators who could portray themselves as authentic cultural agents and guardians of Roman Christian values.

When faced with the dramatic demands for change in light of their new status as the imperial church, the Constantinian church adopted the established language and social roles of the Roman elite without recognizing the potential dangers. By adopting the language of empire, the fourth-century church substituted the clarion call of the prophet in its experiences of martyrdom for the unyielding destructiveness of social, religious and military triumphalism.

In a similar fashion, the modern Christian church faces an equal threat to its own prophetic voice when it enlists the language of power to substitute for sacrificial service. After years of being deeply enmeshed in strategic positions of political influence in America, a sudden loss of political power has led some Christians to resort to the use of polarizing stereotypical language in an attempt to recapture political hegemony. Rather than reasoned political debate, these Christians use demonizing language to portray their opponents as foreign, dangerous and evil, much like the rhetoric of empire used by the fourth-century imperial church. Walter Brueggeman's "royal consciousness" is at work in these discursive exercises, not to directly silence the opponents of the church, but instead to create a cacophonous din which drowns out other voices, portraying them as a threat to foundational Christian beliefs. In the past and in the present, when the church uses words as weapons, the result is the loss of the church's prophetic proclamation and identity as an alternative *polis*.

The Prophetic Proclamation and Its Imperial Counterpart

The herald of the kingdom of God, the prophet John the Baptist, declared the words of Isaiah in anticipation of the coming messiah: "Prepare the way of the Lord, make his paths straight. Every valley shall be filled, and every mountain and hill shall be made low, and the crooked shall be made straight, and the rough ways made smooth; and all flesh shall see the salvation of God" (Luke 3:4–6). John the Baptist followed this announcement with a sharp redress of the Jewish people who sought baptism to cleanse their sins, but failed to act justly. They mistakenly thought that they could separate their ritual acts of worship towards God from their treatment of their fellow humans. The core of the gospel reinforces our mutual responsibilities to link worship of God with love of our neighbor. This perspective underscores the messages of countless prophets and is the spark which enlivens the prophetic imagination.

At the inauguration of his earthly ministry, Jesus' prophetic proclamation also repeated the words of Isaiah: "The Spirit of the Lord is upon me, because he has anointed me to bring good news to the poor. He has sent me to proclaim release to the captives and recovery of sight to the blind, to let the oppressed go free, to proclaim the year of the Lord's favor" (Luke 4:18). Jesus was able to preach these words of freedom to the poor and oppressed remnant of Israel struggling under Roman oppression because he had first resisted the seduction of imperial power offered to him by Satan in the wilderness (Luke 4:1–13; cf. Mt. 4). In addition to being offered control of the kingdoms of the world, Jesus was tempted by Satan to place his physical needs ahead of the purposes of God. Jesus' response is telling: He recognized that divine words are the antidote to incessant human cravings and the need to control. With his statement, "One does not live by bread alone, but by every word that comes from the mouth of God," he demonstrated the power of words as instruments of life (Mt. 4:4). His proclamation of the divine message and adherence to the sacrificial task which God the Father entrusted to him not only opened the door of salvation for many, it also established a pattern for the way that his church was to embrace its dual tasks as prophet and *polis*.

As the early church underwent persecutions, from the crucifixion of Jesus to the martyrdoms of Stephen, Ignatius, Perpetua and countless other followers of Christ, martyrologies established the essential character of the early church as a community of sacrificial servants whose acts of self-surrender began long before their ultimate triumph over death through death. Their lives exemplified service and the seeking of justice. Even opponents of the early Christians admitted that their service towards the poor and disadvantaged was an admirable quality to be imitated.¹

Like the Old Testament prophets, who often sacrificed their lives to communicate their divinely inspired messages, Christian martyrs exemplified their beliefs through their deaths. This is not to say that martyrs' deaths proved the rightness of their own beliefs in an instrumental fashion. Instead, as Chris Huebner has expressed:

> [T]he martyr is not one who dies for or because of her beliefs. Rather, the death of the martyr is ... the expression of belief itself. Martyrdom does not arise out of a feeling of control over death. Rather, it is ... an expression of a way of life that gives up the assumption of being in control.²

According to Huebner, martyrdom engenders domains of knowledge that reveal new concepts by viewing martyrdom as an embodied social practice.

This approach to martyrdom as a practice which gave rise to new arenas of knowledge stands in stark contrast to the discursive practices of fourth-century imperial church leaders. The imperial church fathers were also concerned with knowledge and power, but their goal was to establish epistemic legitimacy in *this* world, not embrace the sense of otherness and vulnerability suggested by martyrdom.³ The conditions of their situation changed dramatically under the rule of Constantine. No longer faced with the threat of martyrdom, they met an even more dangerous foe—social and religious legitimacy and the seduction of political power. And just as martyrdom was an embodied practice of worship which revealed the alternative way of the kingdom of God, so the fourth-century role of friend of the emperor drastically altered the worship and ways of being in the imperial church. No longer pariahs, Christian bishops became imperial counselors, diplomats and kingmakers.⁴

---

1. Aristides, *Apology* 15.277 in *The Ante-Nicene Fathers, Vol. X*, trans. D. M. Kay, edited by Allan Menzies (Grand Rapids, MI: Eerdmans Publishing Company, 1979), 277; Emperor Julian, *Ep.* 22.429 (LCL III:69), *Fragment of a Letter to a Priest* 305 (LCL II:337) in *The Works of the Emperor Julian*, vols. 1–3. Trans. by Wilmer Cave France Wright (Loeb Classical Library. Cambridge, Mass: Harvard University Press, 1962).

2. Chris K. Huebner, "The Agony of Truth: Martyrdom, Violence, and Christian Ways of Knowing," in *A Precarious Peace: Yoderian Explorations on Theology, Knowledge, and Identity.* (Scottdale, PA: Herald Press, 2006), 137.

3. Huebner, "The Agony of Truth," 139.

4. No bishop more clearly exemplified this transition to imperial power than Ambrose of Milan. His *De officiis* was modeled on the work of the same name by Cicero in which Ambrose carved a new elite—the Christian clergy. Among the many studies on the politicization of episcopal power in the fourth century, see Neil McLynn, "Ambrose of Milan: Church and Court in a Christian Capital," *The Transformation of the Classical Heritage*, (Berkeley: University of

The transition from martyr to powerbroker for the imperial church was facilitated by the adoption of discursive practices, and ways of being and thinking which were common to the Roman elite. Educated in the same schools with similar rhetorical and philosophical strategies, the imperial bishops adopted the social persona of the Roman patrician to establish their legitimacy.[5] The competitive arena for legitimacy was not in the amphitheatre with the lions or the executioner, but rather in church councils and in theological writings which identified the parameters of theological truth, along with its orthodox purveyors. No longer the "other" of the Roman Empire, imperial church fathers drew the boundaries of acceptable doctrine as well as acceptable persons.

One important way that this was achieved was through the use of physiognomic characterization. Physiognomy was an ancient pseudo-science which posited the view that moral character could be discerned by reading the signs of a person's body.[6] In reality, physiognomic rhetoric was less the science of body language as it was depicted, and more of a bruising rhetorical strategy designed to portray one's opponent as "other" by building on social prejudices and stereotypes.[7] A declamatory strategy learned in schools of rhetoric as part of the status formation and education of Roman elite men, physiognomic invective stereotyped one's opponent by portraying them as effeminate (gender physiognomy), foreign (geographic physiognomy), or bestial (zoological physiognomy). Although Christians were the objects of physiognomic stereotyping in the second and third centuries by Roman writers,

---

California Press, 1994), 22; Ivor J. Davidson, "Social Construction and the Rhetoric of Ecclesial Presence: Ambrose's Milan," in *Studia Patristica*, papers presented at the thirteenth International Conference on Patristic Studies held in Oxford, 1999, ed. M. F. Miles and E. J. Yarnold, (Leuven: Peeters, 2001) 37: 385–93.

5. The Cappadocian fathers (Gregory Nazianzen, Basil of Caesarea and Gregory of Nyssa) were educated with the pagan Emperor Julian, and like Ambrose and Eusebius of Nicomedia, shared a similar pattern of rhetorical education and elite social formation based on status competition and imperial patronage.

6. The Greek word *physiognomonein* meant to judge a person's character from their physical appearance. Physiognomy was an ancient discursive strategy pervasive in public speech in ancient Greece and Rome from the 4th c. BCE to the 4th c. CE with periodic revivals in the 16th and 18th centuries. Elizabeth Evans identified the 4th c. CE as a heightened period of its use in oral and literary discourse, *Physiognomics in the Ancient World*, Transactions of the American Philosophical Society, vol. 59, part 5 (Philadelphia: 1969): 5. Although used by Christian writers such as Tertullian to a minimal degree prior to the 4th c., physiognomic characterization proliferated in imperial Christian discourse as suggested by Ambrose's statement that "the movement of the body is a sort of voice of the soul" in *De Officiis* 1.71; NPNF2 v. 10:1.18.71 (In *A Select Library of Nicene and Post-Nicene Fathers of the Christian Church*, Second Series, vol. 10, edited by Philip Schaff and Henry Wace [Grand Rapids, Michigan: W.B. Eerdmans, 1954], 71).

7. Maud W. Gleason, *Making Men: Sophists and Self-Presentation in Ancient Rome* (Princeton, NJ: Princeton University Press, 1995); Tamsyn Barton, *Power and Knowledge: Astrology, Physiognomics, and Medicine under the Roman Empire* (Ann Arbor: University of Michigan Press, 1994).

when they became the dominant power, they resorted to physiognomy as a way of distancing themselves from their opponents. In the competition for power between rivals debating Trinitarian doctrine and its competing view, Arianism, quite often those calling themselves orthodox portrayed their opponents as bestial, foreign or effeminate. So, when Bishop Ambrose described his Arian opponents as having gestures that were unseemly, particularly a manner of walking that exuded arrogance and fickleness (and by inference effeminacy since women were portrayed in Roman society as emotionally unreliable), he built his argument upon cultural expectations that there was an appropriate way for a man to walk.[8] Thus, his Arian opponents were ostracized for their unacceptable physical mannerisms which were used as proof that their theological beliefs were equally abhorrent. Ambrose's tactic is reminiscent of the rhetoric used by former California Governor Schwarzenegger when he battled with his state's legislature and called his opponents "girly men."[9] Schwarzenegger's rhetoric inferred that his opponents were weak and cowardly, unwilling or unable to exercise moral courage on behalf of the people of California. His rhetorical strategy used embedded social stereotypes about strength and masculinity to ridicule his opponents.

The writings of the imperial church fathers of the fourth century are replete with physiognomic characterizations designed to create a legitimate orthodox church at the center of Roman society and a rejected, supposedly deviant heretical "other." Instead of insuring theological faithfulness to the teachings of Jesus, physiognomic characterization marginalized orthodox opponents, while simultaneously blinding those who used it to their own propaganda. Thus, the conquest was bilateral—while gaining access to imperial power, the church also unconsciously inculcated many of the values, ways of thinking and practices of empire. The "otherness of the church" which characterized the church of the martyrs became triumphalism. Physiognomic rhetoric, a practice purported to reveal the truth, in reality *created* socially accepted truths on the basis of criteria other than theological knowledge. The voice of the prophet announcing the kingdom of God by serving the poor and disenfranchised gave way to the voice of imperial power justifying the right to control lives in the here and now. And as often happens, once embedded in Christian thought and practice, these ways of power and control became normative.

The subsequent centuries are dotted with repeated examples of ecclesial triumphalism accompanied by stereotypical rhetoric used to justify the

---

8. Ambrose, *De Officiis* 1.72; NPNF2 v. 10:1.18.72. The use of the word "man" is intentional here to convey the Roman penchant for male dominance.

9. John Broder, "Schwarzenegger Calls Budget Opponents 'Girlie-Men,'" *New York Times*, July 19, 2004, http://www.nytimes.com/2004/07/19/us/schwarzenegger-calls-budget-opponents-girlie-men.html.

church's authority.[10] Even in the present American church, where a supposed wall of separation exists between church and state, recent social debates reveal continued attempts by segments of the church to legitimize its views and power by the use of stereotypical language and imagery. For instance, in recent healthcare debates, signs and words have depicted President Barack Obama as Hitler or a communist, and aspects of his program as sponsoring "death panels." These are not simply advertising gimmicks designed to sell a product. They are rhetorical strategies which draw upon a deep well of fear and hate from America's historical past. They connect embedded social fears about loss of control with the uncertain economic conditions of the present and project an even more uncertain future. And like physiognomic rhetoric, they superimpose negative stereotypes upon the physical bearing of their subject to create an "other."

Two types of ancient physiognomic invective are being replicated in contemporary attempts to portray President Obama as outside of mainstream American values—geographic and zoological physiognomy. In ancient geographic physiognomy, the ethnicity and ethnic features were accentuated to reinforce foreignness or strange origins. By depicting the opponent as strange and foreign, the rhetoric played on ethnocentric fears, suggesting that this strange foreigner would destroy the nation's way of life. Similarly, modern "birther" arguments infer that President Obama's supposed Kenyan birth disqualifies him from being president, and therefore his presidency is illegitimate.

Ancient zoological physiognomy portrayed the orator's opponent as inhuman or bestial. Therefore, if the subjects were inhuman, not only were they dangerous like a wild animal, they were clearly inferior, lacking human intelligence. An image circulated by supporters of the "birther" movement portrayed President Obama as a baby monkey surrounded by two older monkeys with the caption "Now you know why no birth certificate."[11] A Republican Party Central Committee member from Orange County, California who circulated this picture in an email is a retired Christian book publisher. Some of her supporters felt that too much was made of her joke, but the defense of this "joke" demonstrates ignorance of America's racist heritage and specific historical depictions of black men as apes.

The "death panels" and the "birther" controversy, and the marginalizing rhetoric upon which they are built, mimic themes in D.W. Griffith's 1915 film, *Birth of a Nation*. Set in the reconstructionist South, the film portrays a fictional post Civil War town experiencing a second devastation of its way of life when

---

10. The speech of Pope Urban II at the Council of Clermont in 1095 calling for the First Crusade is one such example. Robert Van Voorst, ed. *Readings in Christianity, 2nd ed.*, (Belmont, CA: Wadsworth Publishers, 2001), 120–121.

11. R. Scott Moxley, "Racist Orange County Republican Email: President Obama and his Parents are Apes," *Orange County Register*, April 20, 2011, http://blogs.ocweekly.com/navelgazing/2011/04/racist_orange_county_republica.php.

former black slaves are allowed to rule. Social anarchy ensues and order is only restored when the film's hero, the Klansman, dons his white sheet to prevent the destruction of cherished white traditions. This "fear of a black man" is an engrained but often unarticulated fear with a long history in the United States. So, the "birther" movement which questions Mr. Obama's right to serve as president due to his supposed foreign birth, and pictures of President Obama depicting him as an African witch doctor or monkey each link social stereotypes and fears with words and images of him as "other." [12]

Of course, it is important to recognize that these stereotypical depictions are not advanced by the Christian church as if it were a monolithic institution with a single point of view. However, extremely visible in both the rhetoric and images have been individuals and leaders identified as far right politically who also posit their views as integrally linked to their Christian faith. Stereotypical rhetoric has been used to depict political opponents as "other" with many Christians injudiciously accepting the destructive language and the inferred conclusions of the stereotypes without recognizing the violence that such attitudes perpetrate upon their own Christian faith.

Equally detrimental to Christian faith and witness has been the rhetoric used by some Christians to explain certain cataclysmic events and personal tragedies as evidence of divine wrath. The assertion of Rev. Pat Robertson that the 2010 Haitian earthquake was caused by God's wrath because the Haitian people made a "deal with the devil" when they overthrew their French rulers to achieve independence builds on racial stereotypes but does not apply a similar standard to the American quest for independence.[13] Similarly, the rhetoric and signs displayed by Christians protesting at the funeral of Cpl. Matthew Snyder attributed his death in Iraq to God's judgment against the U.S.'s tolerance of

---

12. One of many groups using stereotypical rhetoric and images that is also connected to conservative Christian groups is The American Grand Jury, founded by Bob Campbell. It claims to be a grassroots organization designed to advance the cause of removing President Obama from his supposedly illegitimately obtained leadership of the country. Toward this end, the organization is planning a 20-state tour to deliver legal statements to various state capitals, culminating in a "trial" of Obama for treason at ATLAH World Missionary Church in New York City. http://americangrandjury.org/obama-kenya-birth-registration-dr-orly-taitz. Zachary Roth, "Conservative Activitist Forwards Racist Pic Showing Obama as Witch Doctor." TPM Muckraker, July 23, 2009, http://tpmmuckraker.talkingpointsmemo.com/2009/07/conservative_activist_forwards_racist_pic_showing.php?ref=fpa. An advertising campaign started by a church sold T-shirts and bumper stickers urging people to pray for Mr. Obama, referencing Ps. 109:8 that "his days be few and another take his office," and the following verse asking that his children be orphans. http://gawker.com/5407568/christian-conservatives-praying-for-god-to-kill-obama.

13. In addition to the imperialistic bias of Robertson's views, there were many historical inaccuracies in his pronouncement; see Robert Marquand, "Pat Robertson Haiti comments: French view theory with disbelief," *The Christian Science Monitor*, January 14, 2010, http://www.csmonitor.com/World/Europe/2010/0114/Pat-Robertson-Haiti-comments-French-view-theory-with-disbelief.

gays.[14] This inauspicious combining of Christian theodicy with political and social rhetoric is a feeble attempt to control an uncontrollable environment and to explain the unexplainable. In other words, it seeks simplistic, stereotypical answers to account for present ills. And, like the fourth-century church fathers who stereotyped the heretical "other" to create the boundaries of legitimate and illegitimate faith and establish their theopolitical power, modern heresiologists use cultural and religious stereotypes to secure their ideological authority in the face of waning political power. This suggests that many modern Christian conservatives who use President Obama as the scapegoat do so by accepting the conclusions of these stereotypes—that he is to blame for the present ills of America because he is foreign or inhuman, and does not cherish true American values.[15] When reasoned to their logical conclusion, the conjectures seem ridiculous, yet the underlying mistrust and hatred which the stereotypes engender persists, in spite of proof that they are false. But the result of such a rhetorical program is that its users attempt to gain power while losing their spiritual souls. The church of the martyrs recognized its responsibility to serve the poor and to proclaim the message of the kingdom of God that Jesus announced at his inauguration because its identity was based on worship of God and service to the poor, not the need for power.

The church as a prophetic voice clearly has a message for the world, but the content of that message cannot be legislated by self-interest. It must be the same message that Jesus preached —to serve those who are broken and bruised, to proclaim the now, but not yet of the kingdom of God, and to acknowledge the Great Reversal of Jesus' message—that the first shall be last and the last first. As Stanley Hauerwas and William Willimon describe it, the confessing church is not a synthesis of two extreme views of the church's responsibility that either attempt to glorify God by humanizing social structures or convert individuals while ignoring the church's social obligations and the politics of Jesus. Instead, the confessing church is an alternative *polis* whose overriding task is to worship Christ in all things by being the community of the cross.[16] They further explain that the cross is a sign of what happens when God's account of reality is taken more seriously than Caesar's.[17]

The prophetic voice of the church is only possible as long as its prophetic imagination remains vibrant, stoked by holy flames of worship that gain their

---

14. Bill Mears, "Justices to hear case over protests at military funerals," *CNN*, March 9, 2010, http://www.cnn.com/2010/POLITICS/03/08/homosexuality.protest/index.html.

15. Some have gone so far as to claim that President Obama is the anti-Christ. Daniel Wallace, "Is Obama the Anti-Christ," *Christian Post*, August 20, 2009. http://www.christianpost.com/news/is-obama-the-antichrist-40392/.

16. Stanley Hauerwas and William H. Willimon. *Resident Aliens* (Nashville, TN: Abingdon Press, 1989), 44–47.

17. Ibid., 47.

meaning from the Divine Savior. When the voice of Caesar and an imperial agenda become the puppetmaster of Christian rhetoric, the church runs the risk of losing its prophetic voice and being strangled to death by the strings being pulled "tightly" around its neck.

Appropriating the Prophetic Visions of Du Bois and Thurman: Considerations for the Academy
Karen D. Crozier

Introduction

The African American prophetic tradition includes critiques of various forms of institutional, structural and societal injustice and oppression. In the 1800s the prophetic witness of Gabriel Prosser, Denmark Vessey and Nat Turner organized and mobilized many enslaved Africans to revolt against the evils of slavery.[1] Moreover, African American "sheroes" have played invaluable leadership and prophetic roles in the struggle for racial uplift and empowerment. Ranging from such notables as Sojourner Truth, Harriet Tubman, Anna Julia Cooper, Maria Stewart, Ida B. Wells, Mary McCleod Bethune, Nannie H. Burroughs and Fannie Lou Hamer, these women dared to imagine a world that affirmed their humanity.[2] Like their male counterparts, Black females have labored as agents in the church and in society to envision a world free from the terrors of racism and social oppression.

Unlike the women and men previously mentioned, W. E. B. Du Bois (1868–1963) is considered a scholar-activist who described Black life in a way that spoke critically and cosmologically in his prophetic double-consciousness theory and ethic. After being the first Black person to receive a doctoral degree from Harvard, Du Bois published his now classic text *The Souls of Black Folk* (1903) which categorically affirmed the humanity and divinity of the enslaved, displaced African. Moreover, Du Bois' multidisciplinary theory and praxis helped to open the eyes of a generation of scholars across various disciplines, including theologian Howard Thurman (1899–1981) and sociologist of religion C. Eric Lincoln (1924–2000).[3]

---

1. Gayraud Wilmore, *Black Religion and Black Radicalism: An Interpretation of the Religious History of Afro-American People*. 2nd ed, Revised and enlarged (Maryknoll, NY: Orbis Books, 1983).
2. Katie G. Cannon, *Black Womanist Ethics*. American Academy of Religion Academy Series, no. 60. (Atlanta: Scholars Press, 1988) and *Katie's Canon: Womanism and the Soul of the Black Community* (New York: Continuum Publishing Company, 1995); Evelyn Brooks Higginbotham, *Righteous Discontent: The Women's Movement in the Black Baptist Church*, 1880–1920 (Cambridge, MA: Harvard University Press, 1993); Marcia Y. Riggs, ed., *Can I Get a Witness? Prophetic Religious Voices of African American Women: An Anthology* (Maryknoll, NY: Orbis Books, 1997); Cheryl Townsend-Gilkes, ed., *If It Wasn't for the Women: Black Women's Experience and Womanist Culture in Church and Community* (Maryknoll, NY: Orbis Books, 2001); Delores S. Williams, *Sisters in the Wilderness: The Challenge of Womanist God-Talk* (Maryknoll, NY: Orbis Books, 1993).
3. Dolan Hubbard, ed., *The Souls of Black Folk: One Hundred Years Later.* (Columbia, MO:

In this chapter we argue that Du Bois's prophetic vision, found within his double-consciousness theory, is transracial yet it takes seriously the psychosocial complexity and impact of racism and symbolic whiteness without reifying the scientific fallacy of race. Du Bois' vision is, first, discussed in the context of Lincoln and Mamiya's landmark study, *The Black Church in the African American Experience* (1990).[4] Next, an extensive discussion of Thurman's reinterpretation of the religion of Jesus is provided that offers Christian spiritual and religious resources to engage the contemporary manifestations of racism and white supremacy. Then, Du Bois and Thurman are synchronized to accentuate integral facets of a prophetic response within and beyond racial identity politics. Our hope is to nurture, inspire and engage present and future generations of scholar-activists who prophetically denounce the evils of the legacy of slavery, colonialism, Jim Crowism and new contemporary manifestations thereof while also announcing life, and an unequivocal surrender to GOD whom we experience as the Creator and Sustainer of life.

Du Bois' Influence on Lincoln and Mamiya

C. Eric Lincoln and Lawrence H. Mamiya's *The Black Church in the African American Experience* is an extensive, comprehensive sociological analysis of the most stable, independent institution in African American culture. They provided the field of sociology of religion with a sound, robust sociological framework to interpret the phenomenon of African American religious experience. In their privileging of Black experience through religiosity, they unveiled the distinctive characteristics of the sacred and potent institution known as the Black Church. Furthermore, they debunked the myth of cultural bankruptcy of African American religion, or mere borrowing from White, Euro-American Christianity. Standing on the shoulders of Du Bois, they contend:

> The dialectical model of the Black Church is reflective of W. E. B. Du Bois's phenomenology of consciousness, his poetic articulation of "double-consciousness" as summarizing both the plight and potential of the African and Euro-American heritage of black people; "two struggling souls within one dark body." Du Bois did not provide any final resolution of this double-consciousness, but he did recognize the need for complete freedom for African Americans in order that their human potentials could be fully realized.[5]

The University of Missouri Press, 2003); Reiland Rabaka, *Du Bois's Dialectics: Black Radical Politics and the Reconstruction of Critical Social Theory* (Lanham, MD: The Rowman & Littlefield Publishing Group, Inc., 2010).

4. C. Eric Lincoln, and Lawrence Mamiya, *The Black Church in the African American Experience* (Durham, NC: Duke University Press, 1990).

5. Ibid., 16.

Lincoln and Mamiya's appropriation of the double-consciousness for the Black Church exposes the negative, oppressive conditions of Black life while also exploring the redemptive possibilities that are unique to this religious institution. However, we contend Du Bois does provide a resolution within his double-consciousness theoretical paradigm. Du Bois' double-consciousness theory points to a way beyond the dialectic or two-ness that entails a synthesis of sorts. Moreover, this synthesis includes the healing and participation of both the oppressed and oppressor in addressing "the problem of the color line" towards the humanizing of one and all. In short, in carefully examining Du Bois's double-consciousness theory, we find that there exists an inherent spirituality, one that refuses to acquiesce to racial injustice and oppression while simultaneously being aware of and asserting one's humanity.

Many are familiar with Du Bois' poignant articulation of the two souls within the dark body of the African American because it has been cited on numerous occasions. For those who have not seen or heard of Du Bois' analysis of the hybrid and liminal existence of African Americans, here it is:

> After the Egyptian and Indian, the Greek and Roman, the Teuton and Mongolian, the Negro is a sort of seventh son, born with a veil, and gifted with second-sight in this American world—a world which yields him no true self-consciousness, but only lets him see himself through the revelation of the other world. It is a peculiar sensation, this double-consciousness, this sense of always looking at one's self through the eyes of others, of measuring one's soul by the tape of a world that looks on in amused contempt and pity. One ever feels his twoness—an American, a Negro; two souls, two thoughts, two unreconciled strivings; two warring ideals in one dark body, whose dogged strength alone keeps it from being torn asunder.[6]

In his description, identity crisis and conflict abound as Du Bois names the struggle of the Black soul to affirm her humanity in the midst of the hostile, disdainful gaze of and by White counterparts. However, ironically, Du Bois also points to the stamina, the fortitude of the Negro as she is cognizant of her hybridity while maintaining a sense of unity. In this vein, Du Bois intimates that the duality within African American life and experience does not necessarily qualify as a psychological pathology. The fact that one is able to recognize one's humanity on one hand, and the constant attack of one's humanity on the other hand, makes an emphatic statement for life. One is not torn apart by mere acknowledgement of one's reality of having to negotiate and navigate

---

6. W. E. B. Du Bois, *The Souls of Black Folk* (Chicago: A. C. McClurg & Co., 1903), 2–3.

dehumanizing forces, powers and practices. For Du Bois, as will be presented more clearly later, this recognition is the path to becoming more fully human.

Interestingly, Du Bois mentions the two-ness experienced by African Americans as being two different trajectories with no hope of reconciliation. This observation suggests that Du Bois does not see a resolution beyond this conflict and crisis. However, he later shares his hope of moving beyond the contradiction of two-ness when he asserts:

> The history of the American Negro is the history of this strife (the double-consciousness),—this longing to attain self-conscious manhood, to merge his double self into a better and truer self. In this merging he wishes neither of the older selves to be lost. He would not Africanize America, for America has too much to teach the world and Africa. He would not bleach his Negro soul in a flood of white Americanism, for he knows that the Negro blood has a message for the world. He simply wishes to make it possible for a man to be both a Negro and an American, without being cursed and spit upon by his fellows, without having the doors of Opportunity closed roughly in his face.[7]

In this less familiar quote of Du Bois, some could argue that it is the precursor to Martin Luther King's integrationalist, political ideology with the theological vision of the Beloved Community. More specifically, connections can be made to the excerpt from King's "I Have a Dream" speech that refers to being judged by the content of one's character and not the color of one's skin. While there may be some correlations, what Du Bois says sixty years earlier is that one's humanity or sense of self is inextricably grounded in culture, national origin and reality, and not necessarily race. In short, where King may have inadvertently decontextualized persons of a darker-hued skin, Du Bois does just the opposite. Notice how Du Bois discusses the American Negro as one who possesses a soul that was perceived to be exclusive to Euro-American Christianity in *Souls*.[8] Moreover, the American Negro, according to Du Bois, sees the value of America in spite of its atrocious practices of colonization, slavery and segregation. This ability to see the beauty within speaks to a strong sense of culture already present within the American Negro. In other words, self-identifying as both American and Negro with the potential to Africanize America (but resisting the temptation to do so) clearly identifies the American Negro as a civilized being with a past, present and hope for a nonracialized future.

---

7. Ibid., 3.

8. Edward J. Blum, *W. E. B. Du Bois: American Prophet*. (Pennsylvania: University of Pennsylvania Press, 2007), 13, 15.

On another level of contextualization, Du Bois discourages the American Negro from self-abnegation or the erasure of one's Negro soul. He is convinced that both Africa and America have something of substance to offer, and American Negroes can more readily contribute to civilization if psycho-social barriers are removed to allow greater access for them to do so.

Du Bois' vision of becoming more fully human presupposes both an awareness of and yet a nonconforming to the White gaze.[9] As Eugene Wolfenstein points out in employing Ange-Marie Hancock's reference to Hannah Arendt's notion of the "conscious pariah," "such individuals, aware of their outcast status, simultaneously base themselves in it and struggle against the exclusions that define it."[10] For Wolfenstein, Du Bois is one who is keenly aware of his outside status as a "conscious pariah," and thereby works to negate the status of the negation. In short, for Du Bois, the double-consciousness or twoness is both a problem and potential solution.[11] The dark soul must carry the burden of the misrecognition of self in order to become a truer, integrated self. If not, the problem of the color line maintains its destructive power over racialized bodies, souls and relations.

This Du Boisean way of transcending the problem of the color line is not an easy psycho-social task. On one hand, it assumes that the problem of the color line is not necessarily a static or fixed problem. The manifestations and social constructions of race during Du Bois' time are similar to, yet different from, today's. Therefore, the challenges of being aware of the changing complexity, construction and manifestation of race today requires a persevering spirit and experience of healing to remain engaged in negating the negation. On the other hand, it implies that there is no such thing as ontological Blackness or Whiteness or Redness or Yellowness or Brownness. Racial pride that reifies a scientific fallacy must be relinquished in favor of an ontology that grounds and affirms everyone's humanity. Like Du Bois, Howard Thurman points the way to a psycho-social and spiritual ontology that assists in the recovery of one's humanity for those who seek to acknowledge and transcend the problem of the color line.

Thurman's Spirituality of Resistance

Where Du Bois places emphasis on negating the negation, Thurman draws attention to the analysis and development of an interiority of the disinherited person that facilitates in helping her to determine her destiny even in the midst of multiple levels of oppression and displacement.[12] Examining one's attitude

---

9. Eugene Victor Wolfenstein, *A Gift of the Spirit: Reading* The Souls of Black Folk. (Ithaca, NY: Cornell University Press, 2007). 12, 25.

10. Ibid., xi.

11. Ibid., 23–26.

12. Howard Thurman, *Jesus and the Disinherited*. (Nashville, TN: Abindgon Press, 1949,

towards the oppressor is essential for Thurman. If one does not deal properly with this question, or until one does, "he cannot inform his environment with reference to his own life, whatever may be his preparation or pretensions."[13] This notion of being acted upon while simultaneously acting on and in one's milieu is reminiscent of Du Bois' struggle of becoming a truer self. Thurman unequivocally asserts that the denial of either the oppressor or one's oppression renders the disinherited to a perpetual state of subjugation and non self-actualization.

In drawing on the religion of Jesus, Thurman notes how Jesus, a member of a disinherited group under Roman domination, "recognized fully that out of the heart are the issues of life and that no external force, however great and overwhelming, can at long last destroy a people if it does not first win the victory of the spirit against them."[14] Thurman raises two significant points with this declarative insight. First, the heart as the reservoir of ultimate meaning constituting one's center and sense of self does not have to acquiesce to the stultifying realities of political and social disenfranchisement and humiliation. Second, this constitutive element of the humanity of the disinherited must express itself in a way that does not internalize the values of the oppressive domination system. Hence, twin hallmarks of Thurman's interpretation of the religion of Jesus are resistance to the devastating blows of social oppression and externalization of one's humanity.

Resistance for Thurman is "the physical, overt expression of an inner attitude."[15] Although he articulates the role of armed resistance in the psyche of the disinherited and during Jesus' day as a form of resistance, he asserts that this was not the way of Jesus. Instead, in the midst of his people experiencing suffering, domination and humiliation under the Roman imperial regime, Jesus proclaims that "the Kingdom of Heaven is in us."[16] This is no sign of naiveté or a private religious remedy for coping with existential questions of life and death. Rather, it represents what Thurman calls an "authentic realism."[17] In essence, Jesus was clear that the assertion of the kingdom as a form of resistance was the first step to protecting one's inner life because internal landscapes and capacities, and not merely external forces, determines one's destiny. Within first century Palestine, says Thurman, "it seems clear that Jesus understood the anatomy of the relationship between his people and the Romans, and he interpreted that relationship against the background of the profoundest ethical insight of his

---

reprint, Richmond, IN: Friends United Press, 1981).
   13. Ibid., 23.
   14. Ibid., 21.
   15. Ibid., 26.
   16. Ibid., 27.
   17. Ibid., 28.

own religious faith as he had found it in the heart of the prophets of Israel."[18] In this vein, Jesus points the way beyond racial degradation and dehumanization. Thus we find Du Bois' deep yearnings of becoming an integrated, truer self articulated in Thurman's recovery and reinterpretation of Jesus as one who exemplifies an ethic both within and beyond a dialectical of inherited and disinherited, oppressed and oppressor.

In a persuasive and provocative manner, Thurman asserts:

> The basic fact is that Christianity as it was born in the mind of this Jewish teacher and thinker appears as a technique of survival for the oppressed. That it became, through the intervening years, a religion of the powerful and dominant, used sometimes as an instrument of oppression, must not tempt us into believing that it was thus in the mind and life of Jesus. "In him was life; and the life was the light of men." Wherever his spirit appears, the oppressed gather fresh courage; for he announced the good news that fear, hypocrisy and hatred, the three hounds of hell that track the trail of the disinherited, need have no dominion over them.[19]

Jesus proposed values and an ensuing ethic that did not comply with the rules, borders and orders of the domination system. In many instances, he was an outlaw to unjust laws that negated life for him and the masses of his people. He consistently crossed gender, ethnic, class, ability and age lines, and other barriers that challenged the status quo. Consequently, he was able to project a deeper vision of human relations that invited the disinherited to participate as social agents and determiners of their destinies. As actors according to values of a different realm than Caesar's—the kingdom of God—they disrupted the death-dealing blows inflicted by the Roman Empire.

The concept of the kingdom of God has many different theological connotations. Thurman's interpretation of the phrase within the religion of Jesus carries the meaning of the presence and power of God abiding within persons that contributed to the development of their interior structures to engage the world as subjects. Sociologists James Bryant and Paget Henry refer to Thurman's notion of the inner presence as "*a priori* residue of God-meaning"[20] that is integral to helping one find one's ground of being in the Source of being. Hence, for Thurman, there is something of God in every person. Furthermore,

---

18. Ibid., 28.
19. Ibid., 29.
20. James Bryant, and Paget Henry, "From the Pattern to Being: Africana Phenomenology and Howard Thurman," *6th Annual Phenomenology Roundtable Meeting* (Temple University, June 2006), 6.

it was this constituting self and God relationship that represented "the ultimate key to a full and unshakable experience of oneself as a human."[21]

Jesus, according to Thurman, "projected a dream, the logic of which would give to all the needful security"[22] in the midst of civil insecurity and Roman domination. In short, Jesus' individual ethical engagement had social implications for both the disinherited and inherited. Jesus challenged them to adhere to the following ethical imperatives:

> You must abandon your fear of each other and fear only God. You must not indulge in any deception or dishonesty, even to save your lives. Your words must be Yea—Nay; anything else is evil. Hatred is destructive to hated and hater alike. Love your enemy, that you may be children of your Father who is in heaven.[23]

The nature of the relationship between Roman and Jew would be transformed as the Jewish masses began to act accordingly. The power to heal and be healed rested first and foremost within the disinherited.

Here, in Thurman's interpretation and appropriation of Jesus' life and teachings, one sees the integration of spiritual matters with pressing social and existential issues. The kingdom of God as an internal spiritual presence is employed to address issues concerning life and death. For Thurman, like Du Bois, it was the problem of race. There was no bifurcation between the sacred and secular. Hence, when Thurman was advised by his white male professor in seminary not to concern himself with the transitory nature of social ills because his creative energy and brilliance could be far better spent on universal matters of the human spirit, Thurman "pondered the meaning of his words, and wondered what kind of response [Thurman] could make to this man who did not know that a man and his black skin must face the 'timeless issues of the human spirit' together."[24]

Thurman engaged the spiritual and social by nurturing a self amid the brutal forces of segregation, and the sad reality of American Christianity had become *raced* instead of Christianizing race.[25] Furthermore, as Bryant and Henry note, "he focused his religious praxis on attempts at creating integrated sacred canopies in which ritually produced experiences of oneness in the Spirit would lift individuals beyond the socially inherited differences."[26]

---

21. Ibid.
22. Thurman, *Jesus and the Disinherited*, 35.
23. Ibid.
24. Howard Thurman, *With Head and Heart: The Autobiography of Howard Thurman* (New York: Harcourt Brace & Company, 1979), 60.
25. Bryant and Henry, "From Pattern to Being," 2.
26. Ibid., 3–4.

Learning from Du Bois and Thurman: Coping, Creating and Self-Constituting

This brief overview of Du Bois and Thurman does not do justice to their work and contribution. Nevertheless, what they exposed in their response to being racialized is a key to informing and nurturing a prophetic imagination at the intersection of race, religion and spirituality. We will review their contribution in this section in the context of psychological and sociological strategies in response to race.

Du Bois described the problem of the color-line at the beginning of the twentieth century in a way that asserted the humanity and cosmological worldview of emancipated Africans in the U.S.[27] In declaring that Black folks had souls with access into the metaphysical world the same as their White counterparts, Du Bois entered a discourse to which he had not been invited. In the process, he unveiled physical and metaphysical realities and possibilities by explicating "the spiritual world in which ten thousand thousand Americans live and strive."[28] The descriptive eloquence with which he spoke of sorrow and pain, hope and healing assisted in the reconstituting of the Black self in engaging the problem of the color-line. The depth and breadth of his insight suggests that the *Souls of Black Folk* is both autobiographical and sociological.[29]

In his phenomenological description of Black life, Du Bois encouraged his African American readers to bear the burden of the double-consciousness. According to Wolfenstein, "he surrenders neither side of his cultural identity, but rather engages in the struggle to lift the Veil that renders them contradictory—to solve through social and political action the problem of the color-line."[30] Here, Wolfenstein follows Du Bois' capitalization of the term "Veil" and understands Du Bois to be using it to refer to "the barrier of stereotypical beliefs and oppressive practices that splits or dirempts the historical and social space of African American life."[31] If the "Veil" is understood accordingly alongside Du Bois' desire to retain both cultural identities, it is safe to say that there is no inherent contradiction between African and American cultural identities and expressions. Moreover, such two-ness, duality, or hybridity was not the psychological pathology, but rather the establishment of the Veil—the horizontal and invisible line of demarcation that rendered Black Africans in the U.S. as inferior while severely limiting their access to becoming more fully human. Those who construct and abide by the scientific and social fallacy reify the ideology of White supremacy, and thereby fall prey to the illusion. Du Bois projected a new vision of what constitutes being and becoming human

---

27. Blum, *Du Bois: American Prophet*.
28. Du Bois, *The Souls of Black Folk*, xxxi.
29. Wolfenstein, *A Gift of the Spirit*.
30. Ibid., 9.
31. Ibid., 8.

that could not be accomplished unless one bore the burden of the double-consciousness towards cultural integration, and the removal of the Veil.

For many, the burden of the double-consciousness may seem too much to bear, or may seem illogical. What good outcomes or affirming coping behaviors can emerge from such a stance? The other two alternatives, assimilation and radical isolation, are deemed by Du Bois to be insufficient in addressing the problem of the color-line.[32] The former ethical response to the reality of the veil suppressed one's Negro self to survive on the unfortunate terms of White supremacy, and the latter emerged as a result of "playing the game" according to the rules but still finding oneself excluded and dismissed. According to Du Bois, feelings of anger, bitterness and rage brewed within these dark souls that could easily lead to violent retaliation and the expression of revolt or revenge.[33] Denouncing both revolt and revenge and the insufficiency of these ethical responses in addressing the problem of the color-line, Du Bois challenged African Americans towards a more peaceful, protracted response in hopes of contributing to the symbolic death of the Veil.

The suffering that ensues as a result of either resisting or acquiescing to the problem of race is no small thing. In an endeavor to put the Veil to rest, the symbolic death of the Black cultural self must be resurrected and healed. Thurman, in *The Luminous Darkness: A Personal Interpretation of the Anatomy of Segregation and the Ground of Hope*, poignantly described the nature of what we call symbolic death in this lengthy quote:

> The real evil of segregation is the imposition of self-rejection! It settles upon the individual a status which announces to all and sundry that he is of limited worth as a human being. It rings him round with a circle of shame and humiliation. It binds his children with a climate of no-accountness as a part of their earliest experience of the self. Thus it renders them cripples, often for the length and breadth of their days. And for this there is no forgiveness, only atonement. And only God can judge of what that atonement consists. What does it mean to grow up with a cheap self-estimate? There is a sentence I copied many years ago, the source of which I have forgotten: "We were despised so long at last we despised ourselves."[34]

Falling prey to the internalization of systemic degradation is tragic yet extremely difficult to avoid. The victim becomes the victimizer that perpetuates the

---

32. Du Bois, *The Souls of Black Folk*, 143–145.
33. Ibid., 144–145.
34. Howard Thurman, *The Luminous Darkness: A Personal Interpretation of the Anatomy of Segregation and the Ground of Hope* (New York: Harper & Row Publishers, 1965), 24.

reification of the Veil. Yet, for Thurman, in the religion of Jesus, there is a ground of hope.

As stated above, Thurman challenged the disinherited to explore their attitudes towards the oppressor. Implementing a pre-Freirean dialogical pedagogical process, Thurman problematized the problem of the color line in *Jesus and the Disinherited*. This was significant, because it allowed space for a critical analysis of available options in response to the oppressor. African Americans were invited to view themselves as actors, as participants with an interior instead of being merely objectified as encoded objects. Although the violent force of oppression loomed large, it was neither the final nor sole predictor of one's destiny. There was an option of "a more excellent way."

One particular implication of Thurman's spirituality of resistance was that once the disinherited responded according to oppressive structures and systems, the inherited would also have an opportunity to experience their humanity. As King proclaimed, "Human salvation lies in the hands of the creatively maladjusted."[35] Thurman, too, understood Jesus to be creatively maladjusted to the Roman Empire, and therefore able to externalize something from deep within that disrupted the unhealthy, dehumanizing oppressed-oppressor dialectic. In the moments and movements of disorientation, the oppressors are exposed and thereby challenged either to resist the privileged position that is based on a scientific fallacy or continue to acquiesce to the socially constructed reality.

On many levels, Thurman redeemed Christianity in the U.S. for those who had ears to hear, eyes to see and courage to walk as Jesus walked. The colonizing, segregating, lynching and disenfranchising practices of those who claimed Jesus as the Christ presented a religion that had no apparent "good news" for the socially marginalized. Bryant and Henry assert that "Thurman saw the Christian canopy as a severely damaged one that was incapable of giving to its members (particular its black members) the unshakable experiences of themselves as human beings."[36] Thus, when asked by a gentleman from India, who believed Thurman to be a traitor to all dark-skinned people of the earth, about his visit as a delegate in the name of Christianity, he responded: "I think the religion of Jesus in its true genius offers me a promising way to work through the conflicts of a disordered world."[37] Thurman continued by stating, "I make a careful distinction between Christianity and the religion of Jesus. . . . From my investigation and study, the religion of Jesus projected a creative solution to

---

35. Martin Luther King, Jr., "Transformed Nonconformist," *Strength to Love*. (Philadelphia: Fortress Press 1963/1981), 27–28.
36. Bryant and Henry, "From Pattern to Being," 2.
37. Thurman, *With Head and Heart*, 114.

the pressing problem of survival for the minority of which He was a part in the Greco-Roman world."[38]

Unfortunately, Thurman believed that many Christians in the U.S. had betrayed Jesus. The recovery of the religion of Jesus enabled Thurman, and those Civil Rights leaders in the 1960s that he mentored, to participate in the Spirit of a movement that empowered and affirmed, transformed and inspired. Non-violent resistance as a continuity of the religion of Jesus and restoration of institutional Christianity provided a balm for the socially, politically and economically disinherited, and thereby challenged the inherited to relinquish power that dehumanized both self and others.

Thurman, like Du Bois, envisioned a world where racial politics do not hold sway over human relations and development. As each became increasingly aware of this painful reality, they found creative responses to retain and affirm his identity as human first and foremost. Second, cultural integration for Du Bois and spiritual oneness for Thurman through non-violent resistance constituted the core of their ethical aims. Third, both men saw within and beyond the Veil, and therefore attempted to live out in the mundane what they had experienced as seers or prophets. Though it is commonly known of Thurman's training and identity as a mystic,[39] recent works on Du Bois have acknowledged his prophetic and spiritual insight as well.[40] In the end, the dialectical tension concerning race was seen as a contradiction to be resolved, or an injustice to be removed, but never as one to be eternally embraced.

Conclusion

Du Bois and Thurman will remain as pivotal prophetic visionaries whether or not the problem of the color line persists. Their rich, theoretical praxes found creative, redemptive responses that point beyond the debilitating effects of the ever changing concept of race. For those of us who choose life instead of death, hope instead of despair, wholeness instead of fragmentation and community instead of alienation, may we continue to announce a new way of being human within and beyond racial identity politics, and invite others to do the same.

---

38. Ibid.

39. See ibid., and Luther E. Smith, *Howard Thurman: The Mystic as Prophet* (Washington, D.C.: University Press of America, 1981).

40. See, for instance, Blum, *Du Bois: American Prophet*, 2007; and Wolfenstein, *A Gift of the Spirit*, 2007.

8

Unmasking the Gods of the Marketplace: God's Economy as a Counter to the Religious Functions of Prevailing Economic Models
Lee Van Ham

Is there such a thing as God's Economy? I believe there is an economic model that can rightly be called "God's Economy," though it also goes by many other names. I say this knowing that, inevitably, putting God's name in front of anything, even a church, will likely reflect poorly on God sooner or later. But even with that risk, when an economic model lives and thrives within Creation's ongoing processes, it does so through designing economic structures that mimic Creation's ways. And that, I contend, rightly bears the name "God's Economy."[1] Such a Creation-rooted economy exists. It has a life-sustaining track record over millennia. During that time it has not existed as an unchanging, single form, but has had the adaptability of the evolutionary process itself. It is also the best economic model for correcting our current economic, ecological and spiritual crises.

God's Economy contrasts sharply with the prevailing neo-liberal global economy that is structured by publicly-traded, global corporations, financial institutions and the governments that serve them. God's Economy also differs from the primary economic and business curricula in universities—including faith-based ones. This is a serious omission in faith-based curricula.

The economic orthodoxy that continues to reign, despite its flagrant failures, regards what I am calling God's Economy as heterodox economics—and that's if they are kind. "Heterodox," in this case, simply means any economic model or ideas that do not fit the reigning economic orthodoxy. Despite such marginalization, varieties of heterodox economics are being practiced and taught by many. God's Economy, economically heterodox and thoroughly biblical, is both prophetic and imaginative, very much in keeping with Walter Brueggemann's claims in his book, *The Prophetic Imagination*.[2] God's Economy criticizes what Brueggemann calls the "royal consciousness" and its economics of empire. The threat to royal consciousness which God's Economy brings is not

---

1. Until I read the book by Ross and Gloria Kinsler, *God's Economy: Biblical Studies from Latin America* (Orbis Books, 2005), I thought calling an economy "God's Economy" was too bold. Gradually I became convinced that my own lack of boldness kept me blind to the economic model inherent in creation and affirmed in Scripture. I am grateful to their daring title and what it has helped me to see.

2. Walter Brueggemann, *The Prophetic Imagination*, 2nd edition (Minneapolis: Augsburg Fortress Press, 2001).

only in what it denounces, but what it models: a superior alternative economy rooted in a deep connection and covenant with Creation and Creator.

I turn now to two ways that prophetic imagination impacts economics. First, prophetic imagination sees through the illusions of the reigning economic model. Second, it sees how economies function as religion, thus opening them to both economic and theological assessment.

Prophetic Imagination in Economics: Sees Through Illusions of the Reigning Economic Model

During the four years of my life in a Christian college and then four more in three graduate schools, plus 32 years pastoring in Christian congregations, I was neither taught, nor did I teach, that there is an economic model that can bear the name "God's Economy." During those years I was well aware that the Bible had lots to say about money. But to speak of God's Economy is different than talking about our relationship with money or financial stewardship. Those are personal; God's Economy is systemic. It has structures. God's Economy is a paradigm, a worldview. In this economic model, God is not only an ethicist who guides us in making just and moral economic choices, but an economist who prefers one economic model to another. God the economist has embedded an economic model in the processes of Creation, and those who practice God's Economy create and use structures that mimic that model.[3] Those structures differ from ones used by the reigning economists, bankers and Wall Street institutions who regard most of the structures of God's Economy as so insignificant that they see no relevance or use for them. Or, if they do have regard for these structures, they intend to override them. In this harsh context, God's Economy is a prophetic economics because it resists what is and offers a robust, threatening alternative.

God's Economy is like a set of lenses. Look through them and we see the world differently. It is helpful to remember that an infrequently used word for "prophet" is "seer." Like an artist, a prophet sees images that others have not seen. The heterodoxy of God's Economy prophetically saw critical flaws in the reigning economic model as that model rose to unparalleled dominance worldwide from 1980 to 2008. During that time, economic rules and guidelines, once thought essential, were brushed away like mosquitoes on a summer day. The very people and institutions whom we trusted to see economic reality, and who asked us to trust them to see clearly, were themselves caught up in illusions. Bubbles, repackaging mortgages and derivatives created complexities that were not even well understood by their creators, let alone their handlers or consumers. These products escaped oversight, but rewarded their handlers with fat incomes. Wealth was being created, they said.

---

3. Douglas M. Meeks, *God, the Economist: The Doctrine of God and Political Economy* (Minneapolis: Augsburg/Fortress Press, 1989).

But in 2008 these illusions were shown to be exactly what they were. Often, when our illusions shatter, our eyes are opened to a different worldview. But, in this case, the blind leaders clung to their illusions. The system had to be saved, they argued. Far from changing their worldview, they refused to see anything wrong with their wealth creation innovations. Since then, their losses have been socialized, while their profits continue to be privatized. They are now even bigger than they were when they were too big to fail, and have, so far, avoided any significant reigning in or regulation.

Nonetheless, the cataracts have been healed among many elsewhere. Re-thinking economic models is gaining traction. It is the right moment for all using the lens of God's Economy to say how we see different realities converging. The failures of the corporate-led economy continues, and in some areas crescendoes. Wealth is being redistributed from the masses to the few. Creation cries through an asthmatic atmosphere and with a polluted bloodstream, longing for the change. Spiritually, people manifest symptoms of epidemic anxiety and insecurity, experiencing profound disconnection from Creation. Many feel forced to make decisions within an economic model increasingly at odds with their deepest values.

In this acute dysfunction and disorder, the lens of God's Economy opens eyes to the healing and hope of an economic model that shapes the common good. Such sufficiency for all of Creation's inhabitants is possible because God's Economy, copying Creation, shares Earth's bounteous provision according to structures that assure enough for all. When it comes to the common good, God's Economy has a successful track record. It continually updates itself, and is being reborn into new structures for this time.

The company of people who see that we must modify our economic model includes those who have won the Nobel Prize in economics: Amartya Sen, Joseph Stiglitz, Paul Krugman and Elinor Ostrom. Thousands of congregations, campuses and groups could join the eloquent work of these highly regarded economic voices. But as of this moment, we do not have those "thousands" who know God's Economy well enough to live it or teach it. Still, if we will embrace God's Economy, we can move rapidly to increase its practice, both in the operations of the institutions to which we belong and as contemporary discipleship in our personal and collective lives.

It is the right moment for seeing—to see clearly what we mean when we speak of God's Economy. It is the right moment because the failures of corporate-led economies are not only continuing, but in some areas crescendoing. It is the right moment because God's Economy is an ancient economy reborn into new structures for this time. It is the right moment because God's Economy is an economy for the common good, in which all of Creation lives in the abundance of enough for all, instead of wealth for a few and scarcity for the masses. It is the right moment because Creation herself cries with longing for the change.

In addition to seeing through the illusions of the prevailing economic model, the lens of prophetic imagination also reveals how an economy functions as religion.

Prophetic Imagination in Economics: Sees the Religious Function of Economies

One of the major benefits of God's Economy is that it immediately sees a connection between spirituality and economics. It uses the word "economy" according to its original meaning. "Economy" derives from the Greek word *oikonomia*, which means to manage the household of the planet according to the creational order. In this way of seeing economics, spiritual criteria spring into relevance for assessing how an economy is doing. The important economic indicators are no longer only whether there is growth or whether the stock market indices are going up or down. Now we also ask such different questions as, "Is the economy expressing the values of the created order? Does the value of the vast work of caring show in its indicators? And, can it value economically what gives meaning to life?"

Connections between economics and spirituality can feel jarring to all who see no connection between spirituality and the Federal Reserve, the World Bank, *The Wall Street Journal*, the supermarket, the shopping mall, or their credit cards. But using different optics, the connection is vivid. All who have a capacity for prophetic imagination have repeatedly pointed out that economics is filled with religious functions. It competes with deity because it functions with its own deity.

Showing his own capacities as a seer, Jesus opened eyes to the religious function of economics with his words, "Either we serve God or Mammon" (Matt 6:24). Since he spoke those words, the religious function of economics has taken a quantum leap through modern globalization, expanding into a world religion. Religious leaders of all faiths who see this, have begun to convene interfaith conversations to speak out about what they see, critiquing this new configuration of economic religion.[4] They are speaking up about where global

---

4. See as one example the work of Kairos Europa, http://www.kairoseuropa.de/fix/english.html, which expresses the work of Ulrich Duchrow, University of Heidelberg, Germany, and others. Also, within Christian ecumenics, discussions have produced reports on how economic religion is being used by today's empire. Two examples can be found on the websites of the World Alliance of Reformed Churches, "Covenanting for Justice in the Economy and Earth Project," 2004, http://warc.jalb.de/, and the World Council of Churches, "Alternative Globalization Addressing People and Earth," February 2, 2006, http://www.oikoumene.org/en/resources/documents/assembly/porto-alegre-2006/3-preparatory-and-background-documents/alternative-globalization-addressing-people-and-earth-agape.html.

economic religion disregards Creation and Creator; they also see an alternative, and describe the structures of an economy whose religious orientation fits within the creational order. Prophetic imagination, then, is generating many seers who evaluate corporate-led globalization not only as economics, but also for its capacities as religion.

In November, 2009, the CEO of Goldman Sachs, Lloyd Blankfein, told an interviewer that Goldman Sachs was doing God's work.[5] This example of connecting economic policies with deity led Dean Baker, co-director of the Center for Economic and Policy Research, to say, "It's probably best to leave the gods out of discussions of economic policy."[6] But my quarrel with the Goldman Sachs CEO is not that he connected deity and economics. I too see a connection. But I disagree vigorously with his theology. Goldman Sachs is doing God's work only when "God" refers to the deity served in the religion of the global economy. But change the economic model to God's Economy, and then the god served by Goldman Sachs is not the Creator-God at all, but Mammon.

Increasing Our Skills as Seers: Seeing the Religious Functions of Today's Global Economic Model

By looking at today's global economy using the lens of religion, we practice our skills at seeing the religious functions of this economy. Different people see different connections between economics and spirituality. Those different perspectives add to the profoundly important picture we get when we observe how the economy functions as religion. Describing the economy using the categories of religion reveals how our economic choices are spiritual choices as well. Any tendency to treat the economic-spirituality connection as mere curiosity misses the worship that economic models are given. The devotion can be fanatical. Devoted disciples of an economic model argue for it with passion and practice it with steadfast commitment. Many people with souls, hearts, minds and strength deeply related to the God of all Creation can testify to the tension they feel working in a world in which The Market trumps the God to whom they desire to give primary allegiance.

What follows is my own work-to-date as a seer, looking at how the economy functions as religion and how it has become the world's most expansive religion. The more clearly we see the global economy in religious perspective, the more we see how God's Economy is a real contrast to it in both its economic and religious capacities.[7]

---

5. John Aldridge, "I'm Doing 'God's Work'. Meet Me. Goldman-Sachs," *The Sunday Times* (November 8, 2009), http://www.timesonline.co.uk/tol/news/world/us_and.

6. Dean Baker, "Walking Away from Negative Equity," *The Guardian/UK* (February 1, 2010).

7. I was introduced to seeing the economy as religion by Barry Shelley, a political economist

God and the Pantheon of Deities: The Market is the supreme deity, a modern Zeus. Mount Wall Street is today's Mount Olympus. Traits of The Market deity include having sovereign, unfettered and omnipotence in power. The Market, with its mysterious, "invisible hand," knows most and best, approaching omniscience. The logic of the Market has reasons of its own. It is self-regulating and knows what is good. When The Market expands, it is embodied as a Bull deity, a golden calf to dance around; but when The Market contracts, it behaves in the minds of investors like an untamed Bear. Best to leave her bearish ways alone.

Another deity of the pantheon, Mammon, is wealth—especially accumulated wealth. Devotion to Mammon extolls maximizing profit and accumulating without limits; it is an addictive devotion to "More!" without any sense of "Enough." Publicly-traded corporations have a legal responsibility to their shareholders to serve Mammon. It is within the global activities of The Market where Mammon's worshippers are blessed or chastised.

Other important deities in the pantheon include Growth, Progress, Profit, Productivity, Consumption, Technology and War. Divinity in economic religion is revealed through the great devotion these are given, with little, if any, questioning. All are regarded as good, necessary, or both. All stir deeply the human spirit. We project upon them our own soul desires for more, better and triumph. As a result, they have a spirit to them and a life of their own.

The Fall: When people yield to the temptation to outsmart The Market, believing to know more than The Market, they Fall into sin. Instead of trusting The Market, they doubt it. Regulating The Market is an example of not trusting The Market. Intervening in market logic with regulations is to play god. Countries who regulate too much, or refuse to open their economy to the rich nations that design the global economy, suffer economic hardship for their heresy. Conversely, economic success results from following orthodox market logic. The rich countries rightfully have the authority to arrange the rules for global economic engagement. Their righteousness is conferred by The Market and is displayed by their wealth.

Sin: When we yield to the temptation to regulate The Market's freedom and sovereignty, we sin. Disobeying The Market has consequences. It triggers economic hardship and loss—the curse of falling from the Edenic state of trust and harmony. Sin leads to social marginalization, even banishment from the community of the faithful. Putting faith in any thing other than The Market is heresy. The rich, righteous people and countries deservedly make the rules for how others can participate in the religion of The Market. Poor people and

---

with theological training. I heard his presentation in July, 2004, at a gathering of the Sabbath Economics Collaborative in Boston, and have continued since to look at the prevailing economic model as a powerful, functioning religion.

poor countries do not have that right because of their tendency to stray and habitually sin.

Salvation: The path of salvation is wealth accumulation. Without accumulating enough to participate in The Market's activities, one is doomed. To follow any path other than wealth accumulation is heresy, and inevitably, means falling into sin. We testify to our salvation through our assets such as car, home, smart phone, clothing, up-to-date technologies, where we travel, vacation, eat out, and with whom also bear witness to being saved. But the path is an anxious one because, unless we have accumulated a lot, working for more is unending. Even after we have been to the altar and been saved, the feelings of insufficiency return. Salvation is an unending quest heavy in effort, light in grace.

Creation: The evolutionary processes of creation reached their climax with the advent of the human being. Humans are the apex, and all of creation is there to serve humans. Whatever parts of creation do not serve The Market and its corporations have little value. "Usefulness" is the operative word. No matter how beautiful a natural setting may be, unless it can be developed, mined or somehow improved for human use, it has no value. Rock formations are just rocks unless they contain seams of coal or hold uranium, copper, oil, natural gas or gold. The wildness of nature is a foe unless it can be tamed for use by humans. Conservation of nature and species is handled through parks, preserves and other protected areas so that the rest is freed for development and use by the agencies of The Market. The legacy of human civilization is one of progress, improving what nature has given us. The Market makes Earth's story secondary and subservient to the ascent of humans and the advance of human history.

Human Nature and Individual Worth: The Market teaches that it is our nature as humans to rationally seek the highest value for the lowest cost. Also, that we seek convenience and self-improvement above all else. Our capacities to care, share and cooperate are trumped by our greed, selfishness and competitiveness. In fact, what appears to many as greed is actually acting in self-interest. The Market works with self-interest to bring forth salvation and human welfare, thus transforming greed and acquisitiveness into virtues.

The worth of individuals is pervasively assessed by the symbols of wealth accumulation that they can display. Self-worth intertwines with net worth and can be determined by it. In the case of accidental death, families can be compensated according to the worth of the deceased calculated by some formula such as what their earning capacity would have been over their lifetime.

Priesthood and Clergy: The chair of the Federal Reserve Bank is The Market religion's high priest. Heads of the World Bank, International Monetary Fund, Treasury Department and large banks are leading clerics. They interpret to others the mysterious hand of The Market and other economic mysteries. They decide on what theology of The Market, Mammon and other deities fits the orthodox creed of the present and what does not. They, along with the Security and Exchange Commission's regulatory role with Wall Street traders and fund managers, determine what is right and wrong practice for the priesthood, as well as the staff they oversee throughout the economy.

Temples, Shrines, and Places of Worship: Insurance company towers, banks pointing skyward and corporate headquarters are inhabited by the priests and staff of market religion. Among the most hallowed shrines are Wall Street, the Federal Reserve Bank, the World Bank and the International Monetary Fund. Close behind are the financial and corporate institutions who have achieved the status of too-big-to-fail—a status of accumulated wealth, power and control that assures their salvation no matter their mistakes. Grace is highly operative at this level. Their functions are holy to The Market—so sacred in the marketplace that governments step up to insure their continuing security. They have achieved the eternal life given by The Market. The priesthood and staff of treasury departments and governments, joined by the teaching ministry of corporate media, explain to citizens that redistributing some of their financial assets to these sacred economic players is a reasonable sacrifice they need to make to the economy. The market religion's staff responsible for laws gets in step with the financial priesthood and offers a concurring vote to further curry the worship of the citizenry. Citizens are assured that The Market will bless them for it; dissent would encounter the wrath of The Market. Blocking the return to the holy path of increasing wealth as measured by stock exchanges, Gross Domestic Product and the global economy is a serious transgression.

Worship and Ritual: Humans are defined first and foremost as consumers. No other ability, interest or desire that we have is regarded as important as our desire to buy—ostensibly to improve our lives. Furthermore, our consuming happens according to our innate rational selves: we buy the best quality at the lowest price. The ritual of finding bargains is core to our worship activity in the marketplace. To miss a bargain or pay more than someone else did evokes shame. The exchange of money for a product makes tangible our connection with The Market gods. It is almost to touch them.

The products available for purchase are the result of human and corporate processes that take nature's wild capital, extract it as cheaply as possible and transform it into commodities for sale. It is market religion's sacred, sacramental and transformative process by which the natural world is reshaped for the holy use of accumulating wealth.

Sacrificial worship, including human sacrifice, factors large in worshipping the deities in the pantheon of the global economy. Most notably, the deity War, which is the protector of the powers that roam Earth seeking resources and markets, demands the sacrifice of able-bodied men and women. Though controversial, human sacrifice continues to be part of the religion of The Market.

Missionaries and Evangelism: Adherents of The Market sell its beliefs and benefits worldwide. The World Bank, International Monetary Fund, other global financial institutions and global corporate chains all go into all the world to proclaim their gospel and make disciples. They train their personnel in the good news that is to be proclaimed. They commission advertisers to put the good news into symbols, sound-bytes and irresistible invitations to join in market religion's way of salvation. They promise that dedication to The Market will satisfy the deep human longings to improve life, add to self-worth and be fulfilled. The governments of the U.S. and other wealthy nations exert enormous coercion on poorer nation-states to convert, especially if they are strategic in location or abundant in resources. This zealous missionary activity is expressed by the word "globalization."

Religious Education and Faith-Based Higher Learning: Managers of corporations, economists, financial advisors, business school faculty, owners of businesses and business media are a massive faculty of education and advanced learning in the religion of The Market. Advertisers join in through mass media instruction of the creed of The Market's religion. The training and indoctrination by advertisers is psychologically well-researched. They know exactly how to engage the conscious and unconscious desires of consumers. No expense is spared in producing curriculum; testimonials reinforce their instruction in the catechism of The Market.

Spiritual Practice or Discipleship: Faithfulness in discipleship focuses in producing, consuming and disposing of old items for what is newer. The deity Productivity demands long work hours, low-wage workers, child labor, or even slave labor. The deity Consumption demands as much spending as possible. Going into debt and using all one's credit proves one's degree of discipleship and spiritual advancement. Staying alert to fashion and purchasing the latest is another trait of a good disciple. Spiritual growth and maturity are shown when our lifestyles and workplaces express the fullness of The Market consciousness. We are known by the fruit we bear.

Entrepreneurs school themselves thoroughly in market logic and mystery, hoping to succeed as they translate their concept and business plan into the marketplace. They may seek the blessing of capital investors willing to join them in the risk of their adventure in market discipleship. Their faith, often a life and death choice financially, is an expression of their devotion.

The moral quality of discipleship is determined by how well a behavior advances the activity of the marketplace. Behavior that adds to the activity of the deity Growth is deemed virtuous even if natural capital such as air, water, or top soil are diminished in the process. The stock exchanges and Gross Domestic

Product determine whether or not the Growth is well pleased with us. Our discipleship is only as moral as its ability to please Growth.

Financial Stewardship and Charity: The people and countries held in the clutches of sin may be recipients of specially designated charitable funds. In times of disaster, charity gets triggered by compassion among the rich, righteous people and nations. But at other times charity is no more than a by-product of decisions whose real purpose is to achieve some advantage or recognition being sought by the market worshippers making the donation. To give away too much is sinning because it reduces one's capacity to participate more fully in The Market religion. As such, it deprives one of contributing to the greatest good. Good financial stewardship involves investing as much capital as possible for the greatest return. Such investment is more important than charitable donations in measuring-up as faithful stewards.

Theological Spectrum: Is there another way of salvation for Earth and her inhabitants other than the religion of The Market? Market fundamentalists say, "No, there is no other way than the current global economy. Alternative religious paths are," they insist, "deceivers and not to be trusted." Other voices express some flexibility in how The Market behaves. They see The Market tolerating variation and alternatives as long as The Market and its pantheon are supreme.

Conclusion

Seeing the religious dimensions and functions of economics empowers us. We see that it is not necessary to be a chief economist to belong in a conversation about economics any more than economists or business people need to be theologians or spiritual directors to engage in religious theology and spirituality. Sooner or later we all do both. By increasing our capacity to speak religiously about economics, we increase the contribution we can make to transforming our world toward God's Economy.

That said, to frame an economic model as "God's Economy" is most likely not the best way to communicate with non-religious groups about alternative or heterodox economics. Other frames, such as economic democracy, caring economics, the economics of commonwealth, ecological economics and solidarity economics, to offer only some names, will likely serve better. So, though I believe there is an economic model that is rightly called "God's Economy," I doubt the value of calling any model of economics "God's Economy" in public discourse. The words we choose need to help communicate a message of urgent importance in this moment. We need economic conversion, and, if it happens, it will also be a religious event whether or not everyone recognizes it as such.[8]

---

8. Economist Herman Daly and theologian John Cobb emphasize that the large-scale economic conversion now needed, if it happens, will not be only an economic event, but most especially a religious event. They make this point in their co-authored book, *For the Common*

Casting our lot with economic heterodoxy requires a certain irreverent boldness—all the more so because the reigning orthodox paradigm produces enormous profits for corporations and banks, as well as ridiculous incomes for CEOs and others working in the financial sector of the economy. But irreverent, bold disobedience to orthodox economic practices is an inescapable choice for prophetic minds and hearts engaged in the drama of planet Earth. The species, rain forests and atmosphere plead with us to disobey the economic orthodoxy of the past century. All of creation groans. Yet, the mighty influence of global corporations, through whom the current orthodoxy is institutionalized, continues to demand that scientific data necessitating a new paradigm be minimized. The drama heightens. All who see what the corporations do not see, or do not want to see, can expect to receive the consequences and repression that the orthodox know well how to administer.

The most pervasive world religion that human civilization has known is the current global economy. Defined by corporate-led globalization, this religion proceeds with enormous financial resources. It has an evangelistic fervor that rivals and exceeds any missionary effort of Christians or any other world religion. Countering it requires not only knowledge, but imagination. Indeed, it is the willingness to use imagination that opens the door to the new paradigm. Walk through that door and all the data—what the orthodox examine and what they ignore—looks different. Crossing that threshold takes us into prophetic imagination and the heterodox economic wisdom of God's Economy.

My hope is that God's Economy will be far more consciously owned in the conversations and curricula of congregations and faith-based campuses. Just as congregations, faith-based institutions and interfaith groups energized the Civil Rights Movement of the 1960s, so today, in this economic and ecological moment, the opportunity exists for congregations to energize a great awakening and widespread spiritual conversion to an economic model that is aligned with God's evolutionary Creation.

Good: Redirecting the Economy toward Community, the Environment, and a Sustainable Future (East Sussex, UK: Beacon Press 1991), 381ff.

9

Seeing Beyond the Economy of Appearances: Fair Trade as Phantasm of Justice
Orlando R. Serrano, Jr.

Introduction

The purposes of this paper are to understand one of the ways the hegemony of capitalist space is maintained, remind us of the urgency with which we need to dismantle it, and share a few notes on how the Christian tradition can contribute to this work of abolition. Over the next few pages, I will work through a fair trade coffee global commodity chain (GCC) between Nicaragua and the U.S. Currently, fair trade is being touted as a way to redistribute wealth and alleviate the disparities between consumers and producers in particular places connected across space by GCCs. It is not my intent to criticize the people who depend on this (or any) chain for their livelihoods, but to think critically about the work fair trade does to foreclose on apertures to alternative and equitable world-making practices. That is my larger concern: making an-other world that has room for many worlds. My focus on spatiality is important because it is actually a focus on ways of being; who/what we are is in large part dependent on where we are.[1] Starting at the site of production, continuing through the fair trade system, and finishing at a retail site this essay outlines how fair trade functions to make repartitioned geographies common sense and reinforce capitalist hegemony. I follow this with some thoughts on space/space-time and the political import of recognizing and mobilizing both parts of space-making; of recognizing and mobilizing both parts of world-making. Lastly, I will share a few notes on how the Christian tradition and those who count themselves within it can and should participate in the unruly task of destroying in order to create.

The Fair Trade Global Commodity Chain

Copa Viva estate is located in Nicaragua's northern coffee growing region. It is 500 acres in size. According to Martha, internal auditor in charge of

---

1. I understand that where we are not can also define who we are. i.e., stateless peoples, maroons and refugees. However, these subject positions are defined by negation. Two points here. First, I think it politically necessary to work toward making a world in which lifeways are defined by what one is as opposed to what one is not. Second, though maroon societies (communities formed by escaped slaves in the Americas) are a very material/radical practice of freedom in our world, the logic of capital is such that these ways of being together are always within the reach of it. See Arturo Escobar, *Territories of Difference: Place, Movement, Life,* (Durham: Duke University Press, 2008).

certification programs, the estate permanently employs 200 workers and adds another 150 during the harvest season. The estate's geography itself—the physical and material ground—is the result of multiple travels stretched over decades and oceans. *Coffea Arabica* is native to what is now known as Ethiopia. From there, it spread to the Asian Pacific, the Central and Southern Américas and Southeast Asia via capitalist enterprises that doubled as colonial endeavors.[2] In the 19th century, the coffee industry began to take hold in the Central and Southern Américas. By introducing coffee to these lands and peoples, producers began processes of un-making and re-making places that included appropriation of communal lands, enclosing large parcels, eliminating biodiversity, creating forced labor and altering the landscape.[3] Before the creation of large coffee estates, this region of Nicaragua consisted mostly of subsistence plots and farmers.[4] In a very literal way, by remaking the land the people who lived on it previously became different: they ceased being subsistence farmers and peasants and morphed into wage laborers and (semi)proletarians. One can see here why where we are matters, and how location is an ideological and material construct: the idea of communal land holding constructs/is constructed by shared earth; the idea of private property constructs/is constructed by individual owners.[5]

Doña Helena purchased Copa Viva in the 1970s. The daughter of German migrants, her family has worked with coffee in Nicaragua for three generations. Recently, she began transforming the estate from one that is traditional and mono-crop to one that is organic, sustainable and biodiverse. Currently, close to 300 acres are used to grow organic coffee that is sold at fair trade price, or a guaranteed $1.26 per pound of green beans. The extra money helps Doña Helena provide on-site housing, three meals a day for employees, schooling for the workers' children and a clinic. Partly because of her own view on how to

---

2. It is important to understand the dual capitalist and colonial functions of entities like the Dutch India Trading Company, the British West Indian Trading Company and the Virginia Trading Company in order to keep at the forefront the fact that capital*ism* and colonial*ism*—ongoing processes—depend on each other.

3. See Julie Charlip, "So That the Land Takes on Value: Coffee and Land in Carazo, Nicaragua," *Latin American Perspectives* 26, no. 1 (1999): 92–105; John Crawford, "History of Coffee," *Journal of the Statistical Society of London* 14, no. 1 (1989): 50–58; and Robert Rice, "A Place Unbecoming: The Coffee Farm in Latin America," *Geographical Review* 89, no. 1 (1999): 554–579.

4. Charlip, "So That the Land Takes on Value"; Rice, "A Place Unbecoming."

5. It should also be noted that private property is also dependent on the category of trespasser and vice versa. Henri Nouwen illustrates: if private ownership is not our primary method around which social organization occurs, then people cannot trespass, or steal, or be criminal; see "Only in God," *Show Me the Way: Daily Lenten Readings* (New York: The Crossroad Publishing Company, 2001), 26–28. This completely alters our relationship with our neighbors. Although there are examples from without the Christian tradition that argue this point—and are mentioned in this paper—I call on Nouwen here to register both a more Catholic and organic canon of Christian thought.

operate a coffee estate, and partly in order to survive, Copa Viva is becoming a different kind of capitalist place, but a capitalist place nonetheless. Poignantly, this is occurring not because of how it is being re-made by altered agricultural practices, but because of the system it is called into being by and is dependent on.

At this juncture, a brief history of the fair trade system is useful. It was conceived at the Bretton Woods Conference of 1944 as a network that would serve as the infrastructure for an alternative trading organization to the international regime composed of the World Trade Organization, International Monetary Fund and World Bank.[6] However, throughout the 1980s the fair trade system changed its focus from being outside the dominant marketplace to gaining greater access to it. Fair Trade Labeling Organizations International (FLO) became a clearinghouse for labeling initiatives such as TransFair, the organization that labels most products in the U.S. These initiatives serve as certifiers for corporations willing to meet—or able to feign the appearance of meeting—FLO's fair trade criteria, thereby opening up the dominant market for more fair trade producers. That fair trade changed in focus during the 1980s is not surprising. It was in fact during this time that—led in large part by Margaret Thatcher and Ronald Reagan—neoliberalism starting unfixing capital: from particular territories, from under regulatory bodies, from bargaining agreements with labor, from contracts that limited imports. One of these contracts was the International Coffee Agreement (ICA). First signed in 1962, the ICA put a floor on the price for green coffee in addition to setting import quotas. When the U.S. declined to renew its membership in 1989, the agreement lost its force and prices plummeted.[7] It is in this context that fair trade began to grow *as a niche part of the dominant capitalist market*.

One of the aims of the fair trade system is to make visible the links between consumers and producers.[8] What actually happens is multiple obfuscations of the processes by which surplus value is made and appropriated. Pick up a package of TransFair certified coffee and it will read something like this: "By choosing Fair Trade Coffees you are supporting economic independence for coffee farming families, and getting a great cup o' joe to boot." The text aims to demonstrate that because it is the second most exported commodity by countries in the industrializing world, "For every daily coffee drinker in the U.S.,

---

6. Gavin Fridell, "Fair Trade and Neoliberalism: Assessing Emerging Perspectives," *Latin American Perspectives* 33, no. 8 (2006): 8–28.

7. As the largest purchaser of green coffee, the U.S. heavily impacts the international trade in coffee. Without the participation of the U.S., the impact the ICA has on the industry that unions have in "right to work" states: virtually none.

8. Fridell, "Fair Trade and Neoliberalism;" Julie Guthman, "The Polanyian Way? Voluntary Food Labels as Neoliberal Self Governance," *Antipode* 39, no. 3 (2007): 456–478; Peter Leigh Taylor, Douglas Murray, and Laura Raynolds, "Keeping Trade Fair: Governance Challenges in the Fair Trade Coffee Initiative," *Sustainable Development* 13 (2005): 199–208.

there is one worker elsewhere in the world who depends on coffee for his or her livelihood."[9] As the connection between consumers and growers is made explicit and visible, the rest of the commodity chain is rendered invisible; a large bulk of the people and labor that animate the chain, as well as the proto-capital that is accumulating unevenly along it are fetishized, hidden. Or, more accurately, they are *re*fetishized. The transporters, dockworkers, certifying organizations, grocery store workers, baristas and—most importantly—roasters and traders are discursively erased from the purview of the consumer. The erasure of the roasters and traders is key because most of the value and money in the chain accumulates at these sites.[10] Although some money is redistributed at one point in the commodity chain—the production end—this is not necessarily occurring anywhere else. Stated differently, the uneven development that defines capitalism and capitalist geography is obscured, but does not disappear.

Refetishization occurs in a more problematic way at the site of retail in that it leads to the further naturalization and entrenchment of capitalist space by masking itself as change. The label found on all TransFair certified products is private property that realizes its value at the moment of purchase. The label (Fig. 1) stands in for a set of approved labor practices and enforceable standards of behavior the owner of the label must meet in order to maintain ownership.[11]

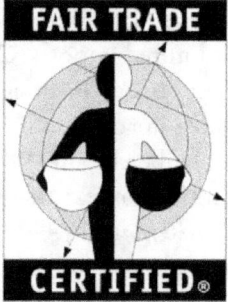

Figure 1. Fair Trade Certified, TransFair USA

The broker of the label, TransFair, reinforces the property characteristics of the label by setting parameters of proper use including size, placement, proper angle and acceptable alterations.[12] The figure standing in a way that suggests protection against would be trespassers is used without irony. The labor, negotiations, standards and rules wrapped up in the label that is bought and sold are not all that is exchanged. It could be argued that what is being purchased

---

9. TransFair USA, "Fast Facts: Fair Trade Certified Specialty Coffee," (2007): http://transfairusa.org/pdfs/fastfacts_coffee.pdf.

10. René Mendoza Vidaurre, *La Paradoja del Café: El Gran Negocio Mundial y La Peor Crisis Campesina* (Managua, Nicaragua: Instituto de Investigación y Desarollo Nitlipán-UCA, 2002).

11. Guthman, "The Polanyian Way?", 457.

12. TransFair, *Fast Facts,* op cit.

at the register along with coffee are ethics and political action. Julie Guthman notes a problematic political rationality that labels produce is that "putting a monetary value on ethical proclivities is even thinkable, as if 'doing good' is one more thing to be bought and sold."[13] Furthermore, by locating the sites at which 'doing good' occurs and change originates from in the global north the peoples of the Central and Southern Américas are organized at the lower end of a regional hierarchy. This is no minor act of positioning. It replicates colonial paternalism and perpetuates the myth of diffusionism: the peoples of Western and Central Europe are the makers and movers of history.[14] Having begun at a site of production and worked through the fair trade system, we now arrive at a site of retail and a final location in this particular GCC: Whole Foods Market.

Based out of Austin, Texas, Whole Foods is the largest organic grocery store in the U.S. It achieved this status by purchasing Wild Oats in 2007 after a bit of back and forth with the Federal Trade Commission.[15] Although Whole Foods' profit margin has increased due in large part to the wallets of a clientele that buys into the image of a grocery store that takes care of its workers and producers, the company's politics and practices are decidedly anti-union and anti-labor. Employees of Whole Foods who earn the least do so at what the general public would consider a living wage—on average $13.15 per hour. In addition to this relatively high wage, workers are also compensated with health insurance and retirement benefits.[16] However, wages have remained the same for the past two decades, turnover occurs at a rate of 25% per year, and most employees work no more than four years.[17]

Over the past seven years, Whole Foods has acted against unions and organized labor on several occasions.[18] In the interest of time, I will briefly

---

13. Guthman, "The Polanyian Way?", 473.

14. James Blaut, *The Colonizer's Model of the World: Geographical Diffusionism and Eurocentric History* (New York: Guilford Press, 1993).

15. Matthew Blake, "Whole Foods CEO Sows Wild Oats," *The Nation* (accessed 10 October 2009): http://www.thenation.com/doc/20070919/blake.

16. Blake, "Whole Foods CEO Sows Wild Oats." A small side-note here: One should note that coercion does not always occur at gunpoint; 401(k)s work too.

17. John Harkinson, "Are Starbucks and Whole Foods Union Busters?" *Mother Jones* (2009): http://motherjones.com/politics/2009/04/are-starbucks-and-whole-foods-unionbusting; and Sharon Smith, "What Smells at Whole Foods?" *The Socialist Worker* (2009): http://socialistworker.org/2009/05/07/smells-at-whole-foods.

18. Most recently—and perhaps most famously—Whole Foods CEO John Mackey published an opinion piece in the *Wall Street Journal* in which he wrote, "Many promoters of health-care reform believe that people have an intrinsic ethical right to health care—to equal access to doctors, medicines and hospitals. While all of us empathize with those who are sick, how can we say that all people have more of an intrinsic right to health care than they have to food or shelter? Health care is a service that we all need, but just like food and shelter it is best provided through voluntary and mutually beneficial market exchanges. A careful reading of both the Declaration of Independence and the Constitution will not reveal any intrinsic right to health

summarize two instances. In 2002, workers at the Madison, Wisconsin store successfully unionized. However, both the local store and the corporation refused to recognize the employees' affiliation with the United Food and Commercial Workers (UFCW) local chapter. According to one of the women who helped organize the campaign, management scheduled and rescheduled bargaining agreement meetings for over a year. Even as these "scheduling conflicts" kept on happening, CEO John Mackey flew to the store to hand out pamphlets titled "Beyond Unions" to the employees. Eventually, due to both the protracted nature of the contract "talks" and the usual high employee turnover rate the union disbanded.[19] The company managed to break up the first—and only—organized store. One of Mackey's publicly stated goals for 2013 was still on track to be accomplished: remain 100% union free.[20]

In March 2010, Whole Foods teamed up with Costco and Starbucks to launch the Committee for a Level Playing Field for Union Elections. The three companies put together this coalition to defeat what they feel is a threat: the Employee Free Choice Act (EFCA). One of President Obama's perceived priorities, the EFCA would change current workplace organizing efforts by altering the way unions are recognized. Instead of requiring a majority in a secret ballot before forming a union, employees would be able to form a union by simply collecting a majority of signed pledge cards. Opponents of the act argue that pro-union workers could use coercive measures to acquire the necessary cards and that the lack of anonymity would expose employees against organizing to danger.[21] Proponents of the act argue that the secret ballots are not very secret and easy to manipulate. The point here is not whether or not unions are the answer for mitigating exploitative relationships between management and labor; much has been written on the discriminatory, racist, xenophobic and sexist politics of many a union.[22] The point is that unions challenge a key principal of liberal and neo-liberal ideology that drives capitalism as an

---

care, food or shelter. That's because there isn't any. This "right" has never existed in America," "The Whole Foods Alternative to Obamacare: Eight Things We Can Do to Improve Health Care Without Adding to the Deficit," *Wall Street Journal* (2009): http://online.wsj.com/article/SB10 001424052970204251404574342170072865070.html.

19. Blake, "Whole Foods CEO Sows Wild Oats"; Harkinson, "Are Starbucks and Whole Foods Union Busters?"; Smith, "What Smells at Whole Foods?"

20. Harkinson, "Are Starbucks and Whole Foods Union Busters?"

21. Blake, "Whole Foods CEO Sows Wild Oats"; Harkinson, "Are Starbucks and Whole Foods Union Busters?"; Annie Shattuck and Zoe Brent, "Calling Out Whole Foods: Whole Foods Quietly Cutting Employee Free Choice," *Food First: Institute for Food and Development Policy* (2009): http://www.foodfirst.org/en/node/2547; Smith, "What Smells at Whole Foods?"

22. See Aviva Chomsky, *Linked Labor History: New England, Colombia, and the Making of a Global Working Class* (Durham: Duke University Press, 2008); Dana Frank, *Buy American: The Untold Story of Economic Nationalism* (Boston: Beacon Press, 2000) and *Bananeras* (Boston: South End Press, 2008); and Colleen Lye, *America's Asia: Racial Form and American Literature, 1893–1945* (Berkeley: University of California Press, 2004).

economic system and then produces and occupies space in particular ways: the unfettered and self-determining individual is the scale from which to organize the world and that s/he must be protected at all costs. Or, to borrow Margaret Thatcher's words, "there is no such thing as a society, only individual men and women."[23] The building block for capitalist space is the materialization of this idea: private property, where private property is the extra-corporal physical manifestation of modern liberal individual subjectivity. This is why private property is so vehemently defended. As the second largest union-free food retailer behind only Wal-Mart, Whole Foods'—in spite of its employee-friendly image—anti-union activities reify the primacy of the individual worker over a collective of workers, the private over the common, as the scale from which to organize the world.

Fair Trade as Hegemonic Capitalist Space

The fair trade system helps to maintain the hegemony of a capitalist space by giving the appearance of change in the practice of reform as well. Once again, we must understand reform for what it is here, not a revolutionary practice as much as a permutation/recalibration of what is already in place.[24] Geographer Doreen Massey argues that Space—a product made by both humans and non-humans—consists of both space and time. Another way to say this is that Space is the result of a particular articulation of topography and temporality.[25] Massey opens Space up by theorizing it as a location of possibility and multiplicity: the topographic and temporal combinations are exponential. In the context of this paper, capitalist Space consists of a topography structured around "the market" articulated with a modern liberal temporal location.[26]

Topographic change is what makes the fair trade system so dangerous to alternative spatial orders and world-making projects. It is in fact a way in which

---

23. Found in David Harvey, *A Brief History of Neoliberalism* (Oxford: Oxford University Press, 2005), 23.

24. Another way to understand this is to conceptualize reform as crisis management. It is a response to outcry from the people regarding a specific issue. One need only look to our current moment of health care and financial reform to see that nothing is changing.

25. Doreen Massey, *For Space* (London: SAGE Publications, 2005).

26. Note: In the same way that one does not need to be white to be a white supremacist, one does not need to be a practicing capitalist to be located with a liberal temporal logic (D. Rodriguez, 2008). For example, the Sandinista Revolution was an anti-capitalist movement that operated within a liberal temporal logic and teleology predicated on a Marxist universal end to history and the need to cultivate a liberal citizenry. See Maria Josefina Saldaña-Portillo, *The Revolutionary Imagination in Americas and the Age of Development* (Durham: Duke University Press, 2003). Thinking about the multi-dimensionality of space/space-time requires pluriplanal and pluritopic imaginings that push the Cartesian quadrant to the point of irrelevancy due to its inability to delineate them. See Massey, *For Space*; also Walter Mignolo, *Local Histories/Global Designs: Coloniality, Subaltern Knowledges, and Border Thinking* (Princeton: Princeton University Press, 2000) and *The Idea of Latin America* (Malden: Blackwell Publishing, 2005).

capitalist spatial order maintains hegemony. Hegemony is defined here as a tenuous moment of stasis in the making and distribution of power attained by both coercive and consensual actions, and maintained by an unevenly structured articulation of differences.[27] It is crucial to make clear the neutral fact of unequal power where power is the ability to get persons to be or do something they would not be or do on their own. It is when unequal power exploits difference to the threshold of fatality or beyond that it ceases to be neutral and indeed becomes an instrument for premature death.[28] In other words, how unequal power is coupled with difference, or combination of differences, and to what ends is what makes it productive or destructive. The hegemony of capitalist space needs to be undone precisely because it has historically depended and presently depends on the coupling of power and difference along multiple axes—race, ethnicity, gender, sexuality, class—to destructive ends. The fair trade system results in the appearance of retailers such as Whole Foods that sell TransFair products, that pay their employees only marginally better than other stores, and farms like Copa Viva that provide housing, schooling and medical care. These new topographies make capitalism seem qualitatively benign and in doing so manufacture a kind of consent.

The fixity of capitalism's temporal location adds force to the idea that the system can fix itself and is indeed improving. Capitalism is animated in large part by modern liberal thought that has at its core the ideal of the unfettered individual. Two additional tenets of modern liberal ideology are a belief in its own universal applicability, most often violently practiced as imperialism and/or colonialism, and the unidirectionality of history. These two combine to become a coercive narrative of universal human progress and history. Thatcher once again provides the perfect sound byte for the neo-liberal iteration. Regarding

---

27. My theorization of hegemony is developed by drawing on the work of several scholars. See Ruth Wilson Gilmore, "Fatal Couplings of Power and Difference: Notes on Racism and Geography," *The Professional Geographer* 54, no. 1 (2002): 15–24 and *Golden Gulag: Prisons, Surplus, Crisis, and Opposition in Globalizing California* (Berkeley: University of California Press, 2007); Antonio Gramsci, *The Antonio Gramsci Reader: Selected Writings 1916–1935*, edited by George Forgacs (New York: New York University Press, 2000); Stuart Hall, "Race, Articulation, and Societies Structured in Dominance," in *Sociological Theories: Race and Colonialism* (Paris: UNESCO, 1980); and "Gramsci's Relevance for the Study of Race and Ethnicity," *Journal of Communication Inquiry* 10, no. 2 (1986): 5–27; and "Race, Culture, and Communications," *Rethinking MARXISM* 5, no. 1 (1992): 10–18; and Laura Pulido, *Environmentalism and Economic Justice: Two Chicano Struggles in the Southwest* (Tuscon: University of Arizona Press, 1996) and *Black, Brown, Yellow, and Left: Radical Activism in Los Angeles* (Berkeley: University of California Press, 2006).

28. Gilmore, "Fatal Couplings of Power and Difference," 16, 22; and Hall, "Race, Culture, and Communications," 17. The life and teachings of Jesus Christ embody and pass on the ways unequal power can operate differently, to life-affirming and sustaining ends: the last shall be first, the meek shall inherit the earth, the master will be the servant.

the increase in free trade and rolling back of welfare measures she famously said, "there is no alternative."[29]

Attempts to create apertures to hegemonies otherwise must be concerned not only with pointing out that there are alternatives all around us.[30] This can have the adverse effect of making capitalist spatiality seem less destructive and fatal. What is required is a systematic unmaking of capitalist Space by dismantling its topography and temporality while simultaneously creating alternative terrains and points of departure.[31] A substantial part of the problem with establishing, producing and inhabiting more equitable space is that the temporal aspect needs to change. What this means is that to imagine other ways to produce variegated space with multiple trajectories, one cannot begin from a modern liberal location. Ideologies originating from this temporal location and the material practices they engender saturate and limit our imagination.

Postscript: Turning Our Eyes Elsewhere

To borrow from and re-phrase Walter Brueggemann, modern liberal ideology and material practices are our current world's royal consciousness. We in the Christian tradition can have an important role and function in dismantling capitalist Space. It is up to us to turn our eyes elsewhere for just practices of living in the world and with each other. It is up to us to refuse fair trade as consolation for inequity, to look beyond it. When we turn to the life of Christ and the Christian tradition we see glimpses of what God's kingdom looks like and the material practices necessary to bring it forth. Stated otherwise, we have the methods to create apertures to another world. In so doing, we can participate alongside other anti-systemic movements aimed at undoing this particular spatial order and fulfill our charge to call the hegemonic powers that depend on death to reproduce themselves *ad infinitum* to account. We need to dis-articulate ourselves from modern liberal thought, practice and history, then find a place within the margins and alongside those situate. In this way we can keep our eyes fixed on the kingdom of God and be who we are called to be. The following are practical ways to do just this:

- We must not participate in the machinations of imperial state building that appear in multiple guises. A distinctly modern invention, the state demands our lives in order to replenish and reproduce itself.[32] Quite

---

29. Quoted in Harvey, *A Brief History of Neoliberalism*, 40.
30. J.K. Gibson-Graham, *The End of Capitalism (As We Knew It)* (Minneapolis: University of Minnesota Press, 1996).
31. Giovanni Arrighi, Terence K. Hopkins and Immanuel Wallerstein argue that it is not enough to be against a particular structure, one has to be simultaneously for another. See *Anti-Systemic Movements* (London: Verso Books, 1989).
32. Carolyn Marvin and David W. Ingle, *Blood Sacrifice and the Nation: Totem Rituals and*

to the contrary of much mainstream writing, the nation-state is still powerful and still the apparatus necessary to re-regulate policies and bend them toward the will of multi-national corporations. Our lives are claimed by another Reality. Let us move and find our being in this Being's imagination (Acts 17:28).[33]

- We must disavow the modern liberal ideology and material practice of organizing the world from the starting point of the unfettered individual. When the individual is the starting point for making our world, the purpose of society is to protect her and her property. Let us instead reclaim our Christian tradition of starting from the common, from the social as the building block for our world (Acts 2:43-47).
- Let us practice forgiveness materially: economically, territorially and socially. After all, we have been taught to pray for our debts to be forgiven in the manner we forgive the debts of others (Matthew 6:9-13).
- We must call out the lie buried in the social construction of scarcity predicated on the faulty logic of classical economic theory uncritically founded on the idea of infinite accumulation. This is not to deny the material fact of food insecurity in Haiti, Nicaragua, Fresno, Nogales and Appalachia. It is to deny the myth of scarcity: we have enough resources in the world for people to not live on the threshold of death if we do not allow the uneven allocation of food to continue (Matthew 25:31-46; John 21:15-19).
- Let us practice our non-modern location and trajectory in the everyday through observation of the church calendar and lectionary. Re-orienting our year to both end and begin with the Reign of Christ the King, and the rest of our days to the rhythms of Advent, Lent, Easter, Pentecost and Ordinary Time is a practical way to live in another time, to walk in another place.

Lastly, we must look not only at our past trajectory, but to our future as well. We are limited in topographic possibilities in the sense that all we have is a physical world. However, we can leave from different places—material, historical and ideological; head in different directions—multiple forms of social dependence and reproduction; and get there at different times—variegated historical trajectories. All of this requires disarticulating the coercive universalizing temporal aspect of capitalist space from its topographic counterpart: working toward multiple developmentalisms and historicities in spite of one world.

---

the American Flag (Cambridge: Cambridge University Press, 1999).

33. William T. Cavanaugh, *Torture and Eucharist: Theology, Politics, and the Body of Christ* (Malden: Blackwell Publishing, 1998).

Part III: Refuse To Be Consoled

Jamie Gates

When I landed in Cape Town, South Africa in September of 1999 for a year's worth of ethnographic field research, I already had a decade's worth of having my eyes opened to the injustices of the world and my ears opened to the cries of those who suffer. Having grown up in South Africa during some of the most violent years of Apartheid, I had to come to terms with how even people who called themselves Christians were complicit in the suffering of others. Studying church history at seminary opened my eyes to the slaughter of innocents in the name of Christ during the Crusades, the exploitation of the poor by the indulgences of the Papacy, the Christian justifications for the trans-Atlantic slave trade, the complicated role that missionaries played in opening up Africa to colonial and commercial exploitation, the active and complicit role the church played in US segregation, eugenics and white supremacy, the silence of much of the church during the Nazi Holocaust, the complicity of evangelical Christians in supporting exploitative US foreign policies toward Central and South America, the active role that Christians played in the 1994 genocide in Rwanda, etc. I had to personally come to terms with the ways in which Apartheid was preached from the pulpits in South Africa, or not spoken about at all. The deafening silence of the church in the face of great suffering was as painful and indicting as active participation in it.

I had returned to South Africa to study race relations in the new "Rainbow Nation." A growing cynicism in the church's willingness to address the suffering of others led me in other directions for my doctoral research. I was three weeks into my field research in the Western Cape coast fishing communities when I received a distressing international call from my mother: "Jamie, Heather is in the intensive care unit; she has cancer of the blood." My twenty-four-year-old sister, about to complete her Master's in Public Health from Boston University, all but engaged to a wonderful young man, an exciting life ahead of her, had collapsed in the emergency room and was diagnosed with an advanced stage of Acute Myelogenous Leukemia (AML). Eleven days after this phone call, my family and I arrived in Boston to find Heather in a deep coma. She died two days later, thirteen days from the time the family found out about the disease.

Never before had my family and I experienced such deep pain and loss.

And never before had I experienced so directly the power of God in a people who walk in solidarity with those who suffer.

The church gathered in deep grief around my family; over 1,100 people came to Heather's funeral from all over the world. A fellow missionary kid,

Christie Stotler, drove with me as we took Heather's car and possessions what seemed like a million miles from her apartment in Boston to my parent's home in Vineland, NJ. I remember vividly the silent tears of my former professor Jan Lanham from Eastern Nazarene College. I happened to see her through the tinted window of the car as we drove off to the grave site. She hadn't even made her presence known during the funeral; she just stood with us in solidarity. Gifts of support poured in to cover all of our travel expenses, funeral expenses and burial expenses. A young woman in my father's church, Tammie Vaughan, purchased my family's plane tickets from and back to South Africa out of a settlement she had recently received from a debilitating car accident. Food was dropped off at the house for weeks. Letters and phone calls came in for months. For years people cared for and often carried my family in our grief. When I eventually returned to South Africa to complete my dissertation fieldwork, it was a brother in Christ, Quinton Williams, who mourned with me for a year. Quinton had just three years prior lost his mother, father, brother and sister in a terrible automobile accident. We mourned together; we continue to mourn together.

Our family's suffering was real and deep as we mourned Heather's death, but it pales in comparison to much of the suffering and loss we can name throughout history. All families lose loved ones. But this experience of suffering and the presence of the Body of Christ in that suffering awakened me to a way of being in the world that witnessed to the best of what is possible when the church is being faithful to its prophetic calling. I began to search for other places throughout history where the church was present with those who were suffering. Haven't the People of God at their best been a people like this? Hasn't there always been at least a remnant, a portion of those who call themselves Christian, who have learned to lament, who, like Rachel weeping for her children, "refuse to be consoled?"

Emmanuel Katongole makes a case in this section of the book that lament is the form and shape of the prophetic imagination. He sees it as the task of the church to build up local communities of memory and lament, a people who, in the words of Jeremiah, "refuse to be consoled." Katongole encourages us not to shy away from the painful memories of the past. He encourages the church not to shy away from confessing complicity in the suffering of the world. Once our ears are opened to the cries of those who suffer, and our eyes are opened to our own complicity in their suffering, the imagination nurtured by the prophetic voices of our faith drive us first to confession, to contrition and to lament. Father Katongole calls us to be disciples of the Jesus who, when drops of anguished blood ran down his face in the Garden of Gethsemane, pleaded for his disciples to bide with him but one hour.

In exploring just what leads to Christian complicity and silence in the face of great suffering, we turn to Kathleen Norris and her work on one of the great temptations of our time (and perhaps of all time): acedia. "I think of acedia as the spiritual aspect of sloth. The word literally means not-caring, or being unable to care, and ultimately, being unable to care that you can't care. Acedia is spiritual morphine, but it does more than mask pain. It causes us to lose faith in ourselves and in our relationships with others."[1] While much of the silence of the church may come from fear, there are more subtle temptations at work. The very structure of an over-busy life can lead to a growing incapacity to care, a growing incapacity to step into the shoes of another and feel their pain. Acedia is particularly dangerous for a people who are called to be a compassionate people, a people who suffer (*passion*) with (*com*) others.

While discipleship in the practices of lament and compassion is expressed most fully in the life and teachings of Jesus Christ, we can find signs of God's prophetic movement in many places. In his paper titled "Rumours of Glory," Karl Martin explores how God can speak prophetically in the midst of popular culture: "With very few structures to support formal lamentation in contemporary Western societies, and with the nearly total absence of lament in most forms of Christian worship in those societies, popular culture texts, perhaps primarily by default, can serve as aids and encouragement for lament." Martin explores the prophetic nature of the music of Bruce Cockburn. For example, in examining Cockburn's song, "Stolen Land," Martin concludes that "by linking the past violence against Native Americans to current practices, Cockburn brings the past into the present and requires his listeners to consider the ongoing violence practiced against indigenous people." The prophetic nature of this art particularly comes alive in the "images of the incarnation sprinkled throughout Cockburn's canon."

The final chapter in this section is a public confession and lament from Rev. Jin S. Kim, pastor of the Church of All Nations (PCUSA) congregation in Minneapolis, St. Paul. Rev. Kim first delivered this message publically at the 218th General Assembly of the PCUSA Worship Service on June 24, 2008. Jin gives a brief history of the relationship between Korean-Americans and African-Americans, and in particular the way this relationship played itself out in the church. He comments on the role that race and ethnicity have played in misshaping the church in the United States, and the complicity of the church in fomenting racism at all levels. He is particularly concerned with the role that Korean-American Christians have played in the oppression of their African-American brothers and sisters: "No, we're not as white as Europeans, but at least we're not black. As Asian people who have been offered the crumbs of white

---

1. Quote from an interview with Kathleen Norris published online at: http://us.penguingroup.com/static/pages/specialinterests/religion/2008/acediaime-norris.html.

privilege in exchange for silence and invisibility, we've traded in our birthright of dignity for a bowl of pottage." Jin moves beyond theological reflection to real confession and lament as he witnesses and models publically the confession, contrition and lament to which we are all called.

10

A Voice is Heard at Ramah: Lament as the Form and Shape of the Prophetic Imagination
Emmanuel Katongole

(In memory of Archbishop Oscar Romero: On the 30th Anniversary of his Martyrdom)

I feel both honored and humbled to be asked to give the opening address at the start of this four-day conference on the Nurturing of the Prophetic Imagination.

I am not only humbled and honored by the invitation, but I also feel intimidated by the task ahead of me. First, because the theme of "the prophetic imagination" is one we are all very well familiar with, thanks in great part to the work of Walter Brueggemann. Therefore, since most of us have read, studied and even taught Brueggemann's work, there will be very little that I will say that will be unfamiliar. I hope my remarks this evening will be viewed as nothing but a commentary on and an extension to Brueggemann's fine work, whose key influence is both a source of inspiration and an invitation to further exploration.

Secondly, I am inspired, but also intimidated by your presence at this conference. In your life and work, whether in the academy, in churches, in inner-city communities, in Washington and other state capitols throughout the U.S, and beyond, you represent and embody what the life of the prophetic imagination is all about.

However, there is another presence in the room and with us these next four days whose memory is at once a source of intimidation and inspiration. I mean of course, the El Salvadorian priest, bishop and activist, Oscar Romero, who was assassinated on this day thirty years ago (March 24, 1980). I do not know whether the organizers of this conference knew when they first planned this event that its opening would coincide with the anniversary of Oscar Romero's martyrdom, but the timing could not be more perfect. For who better embodies the shape of the prophetic imagination than Archbishop Romero in his journey from a quiet, cautious cleric, who sought to maintain the status quo, to a prophet of justice and peace, a champion of the poor and oppressed? Oscar Romero's personal journey, his ministry and leadership and indeed his martyrdom provide a good outline of the nature and shape of the prophetic imagination.

There is still another presence which I would like to invoke to be with us in this room and throughout this conference. (This is what happens when you invite an African to speak: all she or he does is to call upon the spirit of different ancestors! But as many Africans know, this is a serious and dangerous exercise.

For ancestors do not simply become part of an audience. When ancestors show up, they take over. This is what the world of spirit possession is all about!) The other voice—the ancestress—I would like to invoke is much removed from us in time, but her voice offers the clearest example of what the life of the prophetic imagination is all about. Her presence comes in the shape of a voice of an anguished mother, who cries bitterly and refuses to be consoled. I am of course referring to Rachel of Matthew 2:18.

If the task of prophetic ministry is, as Brueggemann notes, "to hold together criticism and energizing" so as to allow the new social reality of God's promise to emerge,[1] that task is only made possible by lament. In this case, Rachel's lament is at once a gift and discipline that makes the prophetic imagination possible. To nurture the prophetic imagination is to nurture and keep alive the discipline of lament. What I would like to do is offer a sketch of how and why this is the case. Reflecting on Rachel's cry allows me to do so. However, before I begin, there are a number of key observations about the text of Matthew 2:18 that I wish to point out, all of which bear witness to the significance of lament as both a gift and discipline.

Matthew 2:18: A Voice in Ramah

Near the beginning of his Gospel, Matthew invokes the memory of Rachel's lament in 2:18:

Then were fulfilled the words spoken through the prophet Jeremiah:
A voice was heard in Ramah,
weeping and loud lamentation,
Rachel weeping for her children;
she refused to be comforted, because they are no more. (ESV)

Five key elements stand out in this verse, elements I would like briefly to reflect on in order to make explicit why and how the gift and discipline of lament is integral to the task of the prophetic imagination. These elements are: (1) memory: "this is how Jesus came to be born ... "; "when Jesus was born"; (2) A voice is heard from *Ramah*; (3) it is the voice of Rachel; (4) crying for her children and refusing to be comforted; and (5) thus fulfilling the words of the prophet Jeremiah.

Memory: "This is how Jesus came to be born . . ."; "when Jesus is born"

The evangelist Matthew locates the cry of Rachel at the beginning of his Gospel, and we learn that the immediate context of Rachel's cry is the story

---

1. Walter Brueggemann, *The Prophetic Imagination* (2d ed.; Minneapolis: Fortress, 2001; first ed. 1978), 4.

of the slaughter of the innocents in Matthew 2. But this story itself is framed within the story of the birth of Jesus. Before Matthew tells the story of how Mary, who had been engaged to Joseph, was found to be with child from the Holy Spirit, he announces in Chapter 1, "This is how Jesus came to be born," and then in the next chapter, he tells the story of a series of events that happened "after Jesus had been born at the time of King Herod."

Highlighting this context is important, for if the birth of Jesus is, as Brueggemann says, a decisive energizing event initiating a new social reality, what Matthew now provides in his version of the birth narratives are the conditions of possibility for the new social reality. Three elements stand out clearly. First, that newness does not come without a struggle between the old and the new, between the world of Herod and the world of the newborn king. Thus the rage of Herod that results in the slaughter of the innocent children is the last gasp of the old order and the desperate attempt to hold on to the old way.[2]

Secondly, Matthew's account of how Jesus came to be born is an opportunity to reveal the characters of those who respond to it, and whether they recognize and receive the birth as the gift it is. Herod and the chief priests and scribes are frightened by the news of the birth and cannot accept its significance. But the birth is welcomed as a gift by those at the margins of Herod's empire—an innocent young virgin (Mary), a simple and obedient carpenter (Joseph), and the foreign outsiders who come searching for the child (the magi).[3]

Thirdly, if the birth of Jesus represents the birth of a new social reality—the Kingdom of God—this new social reality does not come without a price: in this case the slaughter of the innocents (Matt 2:1–17).

A Voice from Ramah

The voice of Rachel comes from a particular location—Ramah—which has significant historical meaning. Lying about ten miles north of Jerusalem, Ramah is considered the traditional burial place of Rachel. In 599 BCE, when Jerusalem was destroyed by the Babylonians, those taken captive were assembled in Ramah before being moved to Babylon (Jer 40:1). The Ramah in the Gospel of St. Matthew is possibly the Ramathaim-Zophimthe—the birthplace of the prophet Samuel and the seat of his authority (1 Sam 2:11; 7:17)—and it has also been variously identified with Arimathea and with the modern Ramallah. At any rate, the significance of "Ramah" is its location outside Jerusalem (the center of power).

---

2. Ibid., 82.
3. Ibid., 103.

It is the Voice of Rachel

It is the voice of an anguished *woman*, a mother. Rachel, Jacob's wife, desperately wanted to have children, but for many years could not, until finally she conceived and gave birth to Joseph. According to Genesis 35:16–21, Rachel died giving birth to her second child (Benjamin) and was buried on the way to Ephrath (Bethlehem). A long-standing tradition places her burial site northeast of Jerusalem, at Ramah.[4]

Crying for her Children and Refusing To Be Comforted

Rachel cries bitterly and refuses to be comforted, which is another way of saying she refuses consolation. Consolation can take many forms, but one constant form is forgetfulness, which is often the effect of wanting to move on quickly. Consolation might also take the form of distance as one tries to separate oneself from a painful experience. Additionally, it might take the form of silence. For Rachel, to "refuse to be consoled" is to refuse to forget; it is to refuse to remain silent; it is to refuse to be distant.

As Kathleen Billman and Daniel Migliore point out, there are two aspects to Rachel's crying: first she cries for herself, for her own loss—she can no longer have, hold, love or embrace her children. But she also cries on *their* behalf, because they are no more: "Although the children's cries have been silenced by death, Rachel continues to cry out on their behalf, to remember their suffering."[5]

Then were Fulfilled the Words Spoken through Jeremiah

Matthew invokes the memory of Rachel's crying by noting that "in this way the words spoken through the prophet Jeremiah were fulfilled." It is, however, not immediately clear or evident what this "fulfillment" refers to. In order to get a sense of what is "fulfilled," one needs to read the entire section of Jeremiah 31, which begins with Rachel's lament (v. 15) and ends with the prophet's declaration of the new thing which "God has done in the land" (v. 22). In fact, it is by working through this section of Jeremiah's prophecy that one comes to see clearly the gift that Rachel's lament is as it points and leads to a "new thing" in the land.

Jeremiah 31:15–21: The Gift of Lament

In a wonderful article, "The Gift of a Poem: A Rhetorical Study of Jeremiah 31:15–22," Phyllis Trible provides a helpful overview of the movements within this section of Jeremiah. The overall effect of Trible's analysis is to point to verse

---

4. Fred Strickert, *Rachel Weeping: Jews, Christians and Muslims at the Fortress Tomb* (Collegeville, MN: Liturgical Press, 2007), 69.

5. Kathleen Billman and Daniel Migliore, *Rachel's Cry: Prayer of Lament and Rebirth of Hope* (United Church Press, 1999), 2.

22: "The LORD has created a new thing on earth—a woman encircles a man," as the climatic conclusion of Jeremiah's proclamation. I find this observation highly insightful for it shows that this is what Matthew might have had in mind when he reminded his audience of Rachel's lament, thus making the connection that in the lament accompanying the slaughter of the innocent children, God had created a new thing, thereby fulfilling the words spoken through the prophet Jeremiah. However, in order to get a full sense of this "fulfillment," it might be helpful to follow Trible's analyses of the movements within the text of Jeremiah 31:15–22 and so make explicit the gift of lament, which is inexplicably connected to the "new thing"—the new creation—that God is bringing about in the land. Trible identifies five movements in the text: Rachel weeps (v. 15); Yahweh consoles her (vv. 16–17); Ephraim confesses (vv. 18–19); Yawheh contemplates (v. 20); and Jeremiah commands (v.21) and announces (v. 22). What these movements clearly show is that Rachel's wailing (and her refusing to be consoled moves Yahweh (who consoles Rachel), but also moves Ephraim (in exile) who confesses and repents (vv. 18–19). Then, in turn, Ephraim's confession and repentance moves Yahweh, who consoles Ephraim and promises a return:

> So there is hope for your future,
>   declares the LORD.
> Your children will return to their own land (31:17).

In other words, Rachel's wailing sets in motion a series of movements of anguish. If Rachel's anguish is her refusal to be consoled by anything else other than God, God's consolation of Rachel is nothing other than God's own anguish, not so much for Rachel, but for Ephraim (Joseph's second son). This anguish then prompts Ephraim's own anguish and repentance (vv. 18–19), which is addressed to God.

Having heard Ephraim's locking in grief, Yahweh considers him (v. 20) with a question which combines both intimacy and distance. What the hesitation shows, Trible notes, is how Rachel's weeping is really Yahweh's weeping.[6] Are the children for whom Rachel weeps not also the children of God?

> Is not Ephraim my dear son,
>   the child in whom I delight?
> Though I often speak against him,
>   I still remember him (31:20).

---

6. Phyllis Trible, "The Gift of a Poem: A Rhetorical Study of Jeremiah 31:15–22," *Andover Newton Quarterly 17* (1977), 274.

In the end, the cry of Rachel for her children is really Yahweh's cry. Yahweh is the woman crying for her children:

> Therefore my heart yearns for him;
>   I have great compassion for him,"
> declares the LORD (31:20b).[7]

There is therefore a clear parallel between Rachel and Yahweh. The voice of Rachel is the voice of God the mother, and as Rachel mourns the loss of the fruit of her womb, so Yahweh from the divine womb mourns the same child. It is within the context of this parallel that one begins to appreciate the reversals that Rachel's anguish triggers: first, the human mother, Rachel, refuses to be consoled, but then the divine mother consoles her. As a result, the text moves from the desolate lamentation of Rachel to the redemptive compassion of God, and the "divine mother changes grief into grace."[8] This reversal is confirmed by the verbal link between "bitterness" and "guideposts." It is the same word, *tamrurim*, that Trible notes is used in both both verse 15 and verse 22: "The nouns *tamrurim* appear in the end of the first line of both strophes. In the former instance the word means bitterness, in the latter, guideposts. A poem that begins with the mother bitterly crying for her lost children concludes with the prophet commanding them to make guideposts for their return home. Despair becomes hope."[9] Another significant reversal occurs in the text, this time pertaining to gender: "along the way a new thing has happened to the children. They change sex. At first male; at last female. Ephraim the son becomes Israel the daughter. Jeremiah speaks to the daughter. This change of imagery converges upon the center of the poem to surround male with female."[10]

The overall effect of these reversals is to point not only to the "new thing God is creating in the land," but also to the urgency of this new creation. Thus, Jeremiah speaks imperatively and impatiently. After all, since restoration has been granted by God, the nation ought to return immediately:

> Set up road signs;
> put up guideposts.
> Take note of the highway,
> the road that you take.
> Return, O Virgin Israel,
> return to your towns (31:21).

---

7. Trible's translation brings out the sense of divine motherhood even more clearly: "therefore my womb trembles for him; I will surely show motherly compassion for him" (Ibid, 276).
8. Ibid.
9. Ibid.
10. Ibid.

A third significant reversal, connected with the promise of return, is that the promised return to the land is in fact a return to the Lord:

How long will you wander,
O unfaithful daughter? (31:22)

Moreover, it is this question that leads to the final climatic line, according to which the "the new thing" is not simply a promise, but a reality that God has already actualized:

The LORD has created a new thing on earth—
a woman encircles a man (31:22).

This, in the end, is what the prophet Jeremiah announces—what God has done, God's new creation—and as Trible notes, "this new thing requires a new verb *bara*—a verb used throughout the Old Testament only for the creative work of God."[11]

Next, there is a fourth significant reversal in the text that has to do with the fact that the new creation is "in the land!" Yahweh, who promised that "they will return from the land of the enemy" (v. 16), now creates a new thing in that very land.[12]

That "a woman encircles a man" is another reversal, and it points to the rather unexpected, un-derived nature of the new reality God has created in the land as Rachel's lament turns into hope. Trible puts it thus:

> Accordingly, female surrounding the male is Rachel the mother embracing her sons with tears and with speech; it is Yahweh consoling Rachel about Ephraim; it is Yahweh declaring motherly compassion for Ephraim; and it is the daughter Israel superseding son Ephraim. And it is more than these images. Female surrounding man has power to dry up the tears of Rachel; to fulfill the compassion of Yahweh; and to overturn the apostasy of Israel. And it is other than all these images, for it is Yahweh's creation of a new thing in the land.[13]

I have found it helpful to draw extensively from Trible's essay as it makes evident that the new future, "a new thing in the land" that God promises, comes

---

11. Ibid., 277.

12. This seems to be quite consistent with Jeremiah 29:5–7: "Build houses and settle down; plant gardens and eat what they produce. Marry and have sons and daughters; find wives for your sons and give your daughters in marriage, so that they too may have sons and daughters. Increase in number there; do not decrease. Also, seek the peace and prosperity of the city to which I have carried you into exile."

13. Trible, "The Gift of a Poem," 279.

into visibility only through the anguished lament of Rachel. To be sure, it is not Rachel's lament itself that creates the new future—that future is God's gift (thus the use of the verb *bara* in verse 22). It is the same creative gift that God promises through the prophet Isaiah: "Remember not the former things, nor consider things of old. Behold I am doing new things; now it springs forth, do you perceive it?" (Isa 43:18–19). What lament opens up is a possibility for us to "perceive" and accordingly "dwell" within this fresh dispensation of "a new thing in the land." Lament places us into, and sustains that movement of, creative restlessness through which a new future comes to be at once revealed and received. It is in this sense that lament is a gift, as it makes possible the much larger and unexpected gift of a future on the other side of anguish.

Learning Lament or The Discipline of Lament

If lament is a gift, it is not one that is automatically accepted. In fact, given that we usually try to run away from any situation that would cause us anguish, we need to learn lament. Here again, Matthew 2:18 has a lot to teach us about the practice of lament. Rachel's lament is a very particular type of anguish: it is a voice from a particular place, *Ramah*, and the voice of a particular woman, *Rachel*, who refuses to be *consoled*. In this last section, let me examine the implications of these particularities in order to see what learning lament might entail.

Relocation (Unlearning Distance)

As noted earlier, Rachel's voice comes from Ramah, a place of burial and bondage into exile that is located "outside" of Jerusalem. But Ramah is also a metaphor for those places at the margins of power—places we tend to regard as poor, violent, unsafe or backward. If lament and therefore newness come from Ramah, then part of the prophetic task is to call the community into journeys—pilgrimages[14]—and other forms of relocation that bring individuals and the community to these marginal and abandoned places: the slums, the desert, the Mexican border, the inner city.[15] These journeys provide an opportunity to see what we must see and will not; to experience what we must experience but most fear to experience (and which we cannot experience when we stand *in* Jerusalem). Standing at Ramah is about learning to see, name, hear and feel the

---

14. On pilgrimage as a practice of relocation that brings us into friendship at the margins, see Christopher Heuertz and Christine Pohl, *Friendship at the Margins: Discovering Mutuality in Service and Mission* (Grand Rapids: InterVarsity Press, 2010); and also Phileena Heuertz, *Pilgrimage of a Soul: Contemplative Spirituality for the Active Life* (Grand Rapids: InterVarsity Press, 2010).

15. See Abraham Joshua Heschel, "What Manner of a Man is a Prophet?" in *The Prophets* (Harper Perennial Modern Classics, 2001); see also Miguel A. De La Torre, *Reading the Bible from the Margins* (Orbis Books, 2002).

anguish of those on the other side of power. It is only when we are able to stand in the Ramahs of our time that we are able to see the captives who sit in the dust or those condemned to a life of exile by those in power. It is at Ramah that we are able to see Rachel's grave—which might be another way to say the unmarked graves of young mothers and their innocent children. Standing at Ramah we can hear their cries in a way that is not possible from inside Jerusalem. At Ramah, we learn not only to hear but feel their bitter anguish in a way that triggers, as in the case of Ephraim in the text of Jeremiah, our own anguish and repentance. Through the gift of standing at Ramah we are able to hear the bitter wailing of the many young mothers and their innocents, who even beyond their graves threaten us with resurrection, that is, with the gift of "a new thing" and a new world that God is calling into existence.

Here one is reminded of the poem by the Guatemalan poet and theologian, Julia Esquivel, "Threatened with Resurrection":

> It is something within us that doesn't let us sleep,
> that doesn't let us rest,
> that won't stop pounding
> deep inside,
> it is the silent, warm weeping
> of Indian women without their husbands,
> it is the sad gaze of children
> fixed somewhere beyond memory,
> precious in our eyes
> which during sleep,
> though closed, keep watch,
> systole,
> diastole,
> awake...
>
> What keeps us from sleeping
> is that they have threatened us with Resurrection![16]

Weeping and Refusing to Be Comforted: Unlearning Numbness

To stand at Ramah is not only to hear Rachel's cry, it is to have our own world shattered, to learn to mourn and, like Rachel, to refuse easy consolation. The significance of this observation is to confirm Brueggemann's observation that the task of the prophetic imagination is to cut through the numbness that is

---

16. Julia Esquivel, "They Have Threatened Us with Resurrectiton," *Threatened with Resurrection: Prayers and Poems from an Exiled Guatemalan,* (Elgin, IL: Brethren Press,1994), 59–64.

so characteristic of modern society.[17] Much of Brueggemann's understanding of this challenge reflects and draws from the Canadian theologian Douglas John Hall, who in a highly instructive study, *Lighten our Darkness*, notes that the pathos of modern society (particularly in North America) is the inability to face failure and loss: "The pathos of our condition is not that we have failed. . . . The pathos of it is that we cannot bring ourselves as a people to contemplate our failure. Therefore our condition is all the more problematic, dangerous, and infinitely sad."[18] Hall traces this failure to the typically modern view of the human being as the center of the universe, of man's inherent goodness and freedom (the shapers of our destiny), as well as man's limitless abilities: "We belong to society that was assured it could hope. Hope would not disappoint us, for we were participants in a process and the end of the process was good. We belong to a people that was taught to think positively."[19]

Hall's observation suggests that this positive outlook or optimism is a form of consolation that hides the realities of failure and grief from us.[20] Christianity itself has tended to be, within this positive outlook, a source of consolation: "The Christianity that has become as the dominant religious institution of this continent is totally, perhaps inextricably, identified with the positive outlook . . . This Christianity is nothing more nor less than the official religion of the officially optimistic society."[21]

What Hall's analysis also helps to confirm is that the world of Jerusalem (our Washington D.C.) and the penchant for policy, law, order, success, civilization and economy can often serve as a form of consolation, whose effect is to prevent us from seeing the nature, depth and extent of the suffering perpetuated with these forms of power. But even coming to realize this fact itself requires us to step out of the rarefied world of beauracratic politics and of the status quo into the Ramah of slums and villages.[22]

Here we are reminded of the journey that transformed Fr. Romero from a quiet, careful, pious cleric who sided with the establishment and sought to maintain the status quo to the fiery advocate on behalf of the poor and voiceless.

---

17. See Brueggemann, op cit, see especially xx, 41–46.
18. David Monroe and Douglas Hall, *Lighten Our Darkness* (CSS Publishing, 2001), 16.
19. Ibid, 60.
20. Coming from a different angle, the Irish-born British poet, philosopher and novelist, Iris Murdoch, notes the difficulty of the modern self in facing truth and failure, instead constantly searching for fantasy and consolation, even in art and suffering. Cheryl K. Bove expresses these points thus: "The enemy of the moral excellence is fantasy which is untruthful and a form of consolation . . . Suffering can be a consolation because 'it can masquerade as purification.' . . . True suffering is almost unbearable, so the human tendency is to make it into something else, a form of consolation, a protection from the truth" (Cheryl K. Bove, *Understanding Iris Murdoch*, University of South Carolina Press, 1993), 25.
21. Hall, op cit, 74.
22. See Heschel, "What Manner of a Man is a Prophet?"

The turning point was March 12, 1977, when Oscar's priest and friend, Rutillio Grande, who had been organizing the poor in a rural parish, was gunned down on his way to evening mass. Upon learning of the murder, the archbishop drove through the night to the little village parish of Aguilares, where his friend lay dead (with the two other people who were killed with him), and celebrated mass. Afterwards, he spent hours listening to stories of suffering local peasant farmers—and hours in prayer.

It was this pilgrimage from San Salvador to the village of Aguilares and the vigil for his priest friend that shattered Romero's San Salvador-centered view of the world and his role as a priest within that world, and that offered Romero a new vision of the world and a new way of being in the world. Returning to San Salvador in the morning after the vigil, Romero had a meeting with his priests and advisers, and announced that he would not attend any state occasions nor meet with the president—both customary activities for his longtime predecessor— until the death was investigated. As no investigation ever was conducted, this decision meant that Romero attended no state occasions whatsoever in his three years as Archbishop, and he also constantly spoke out against government repression and demanded social reforms on behalf of the poor.

If pilgrimage offers relocation to Ramah, practices like vigils[23] teach us how to mourn in a way that not only offers a way to name and lament loss, but also create fresh possibilities of living into a world in which our consolations have been shattered.

Urgency (Unlearning Complacency)

If lament—that is, standing at Ramah—is able to pierce through the numbness of consolation, it can offer a glimpse of a different world—as a form of groaning (as if in childbirth [Rom 8:22]) and of eager expectancy. To learn lament is to live in the world with an edge of restlessness and urgency. Thus, in Jeremiah 31:22 the prophet speaks hurriedly to Ephraim:

> Set up road markers for yourself;
> make yourself guideposts;
> consider well the highway,
> the road by which you went.

But if as Paul reminds us in Romans 8:22, "For we know that all creation has been groaning as in the pains of childbirth right up to the present," the sense of urgency that lament cultivates is the expectancy of a new birth ("This is how Jesus came to be born"), then that is why to learn to live at Ramah is to learn to

---

23. On vigil as a practice and discipline of re-location, see Emmanuel Katongole, and Chris Rice, *Reconciling All Things* (Grand Rapids: IVP, 2008), 90–92.

be a patient midwife! The world of the midwife is the world of expectancy, but also the world of mundane, simple, patient but busy forms of preparations as one waits to receive the gift of a new birth. That is why nurturing the prophetic imagination requires and involves intense forms of advocacy and mobilization, and this might involve organizing, marching, lobbying, etc. However, important as these actions are, they are not the end, but the necessary preparations, so to say, for the new day about to be born. Again, the words of Julia Esquivel in the poem, "At Daybreak,"[24] capture very well what the politics of both waiting for and hastening the new day calls for:

> We must get up early to hasten the sunrise,
> To see the day break sooner ...
>
> We will hear the birds singing again,
> Greeting the *new day*
> Near the waterfall ...
>
> However, if daybreak is to come,
> We must tenderly nurture this pregnancy,
> We must hurry along,
> We must move in on the clumsy dreams,
> The absurd plans of the uniformed gorillas ...
>
> At *daybreak*,
> Widows will be surrounded by family,
> But for now we must rise early
> In order to hasten *the new day*.

Anointing for Resurrection (Beyond Wastage)

But just as Matthew's proclamation of the good news—of the new reality that the birth of Jesus ushers in—commences with the story of the slaughter of the innocents and the lament of Rachel's voice that is heard in Ramah, the same gospel ends with the story of Jesus' own murder and the anointing and burial of Jesus' body performed by Joseph from Arimathea (Ramah), who "went to Pilate and asked for the body of Jesus" (Matt 27:57–61). He took the body, anointed it, wrapped it in a clean linen shroud and placed it in a new tomb. The significance of this story is to point to Ramah as the bookend, indeed the very essence, of the gospel. To the extent the gospel is an invitation into the story of

---

24. Julia Esquivel, "They Have Threatened Us with Resurrectiton," *Threatened with Resurrection: Prayers and Poems from an Exiled Guatemalan,* (Elgin, IL: Brethren Press,1994), 51–57.

Jesus, it is an invitation to Ramah. It is an invitation not only to hear Rachel's cry of lament but also to hold tenderly (like Joseph). It is to love and anoint those who have been abused, killed and discarded by the powers. Thus if Ramah is about mourning the innocent that are easily sacrificed by the schemes of power and the preservation of the status quo of the old order, it is also about learning the art of care and binding (anointing) the wounds of the poor, the weak and those who are easily sacrificed by the economic and political calculations of the world.

From another angle, the story of Joseph's anointing is the refusal to give up on what has been wasted or discarded by the politics of the day and to stubbornly believe in the resurrection. That is why Joseph's anointing of the body of Jesus is but a way of preparing and anticipating Jesus' resurrection. That is why what the story of Joseph from Arimathea points to is a new form of politics, a new form of sacrifice (*sacra facere*: making sacred) which anoints the poor, thus preparing them for resurrection—for "the difficult rising," as Tania Runyan calls it in her poem, "Buried With Him in His Death":

We fought for one more sputter
of the old life. Even though a breeze passing
over your sieve of skin could send you
screaming, you muscled up your diaphragm
to whisk more air into the fire.

I held my own terrors to my chest:
failures and brush-offs, cancers and crashes,
all the anxieties I had grown to love
heaving and cracking like your ribcage
until we both gave out.

Then there was the mess of prying us loose:
wailing women and splintered lumber,
flesh stubbornly sticking to the nails.
But what swift hands, that Joseph of Arimathea,
what purposeful footsteps crunching the ground!

He wrapped us in linen and spices.
Only the hapless world could think of packing
fifty pounds of aloe around a dead man's wounds.
But we drank it in like deserts
until finally even the lizards scurried home.

I lay in the cave and wanted to touch you,
but my hands were no longer mine.
They closed in on themselves like daylilies.
The stone rumbled over the window of light,
and then our difficult rising began. [25]

A Community of Lament and Doxology

To live at Ramah is not only to learn lament, it is also to learn praise. That lament and doxology are bound together may be the reason why the evangelist Matthew weaves together the stories of Rachel and Mary. While their son is still an infant, Mary and Joseph flee with him to Egypt to escape the slaughter of the innocents by Herod. As the evangelist tells the story of their flight, he reminds us of Rachel's cry, weeping bitterly and refusing consolation (Matt 2:16–18).

That is why, from this point of view, the text of Rachel's lament accomplishes the same proclamation and declaration of reversal that the evangelist Luke achieves with the story of Mary's *Magnificat*. For if Rachel's lament and her refusal of consolation make room for authentic doxology for the new thing that God creates in the land, Mary's praise and exultation show full awareness of the reality of pain and loss. For Mary, like Rachel, will lose her child, and the sword of grief will pierce her heart, too. The implications, as Kathleen Billman states, are obvious:

> Rachel and Mary are thus bound together as sisters of faith in the biblical tradition. Even though the church has often remembered Mary but forgotten Rachel, the two belong together in the prayer and practice of Christian faith. Together they remind us that the danger of praise without lament is triumphalism, and the danger of lament without praise is hopelessness."[26]

That Rachel and Mary are bound together points to the life of the prophetic imagination as a life that is able to sustain social engagement at the intersection between lament and doxology; repentance and promise; memory and renewal; grief and hope; anguish and praise; critique and energizing; resistance and innovation; a life of No and a life of Yes. Maintaining this dialectic is an invitation to learn to be at once prophetic and imaginative, for as Brueggemann notes, "prophetic faith in a flat, confrontation mode, without imagination, is a non-starter ... *Prophetic* must be *imaginative* because it is urgently out beyond the ordinary and the reasonable.[27]

---

25. Tania Runyon, "Buried With Him In His Death," *The Christian Century* (March 23, 2010). Also at http://taniarunyan.wordpress.com/2010/03/

26. Billman and Migliore, op cit, 3–4.

27. Brueggemann, *Prophetic Imagination*, xiv–xv.

That is why worship is not only a good place to start when thinking about nurturing the prophetic imagination, it is also the school *par excellence* of what it means to live at Ramah and to hear Rachel's bitter cry. In worship, Christians learn to hear and become this voice, as a way to see and celebrate the new future that God creates in our midst. To make this claim is not only to see lament as both a gift and a way of living, but also to redefine worship as the form of Christian praxis that brings together the church and the street!

11

When Beauty Speaks, Truth Answers
Kathleen Norris

I am certain that beauty is prophetic, that it does what God—through the prophets—is asking us to do: to see anew, to open our closed, hardened hearts; to truly listen to God and not the world's distracting noises about power and wealth, or our own internal absorbed chatter. Beauty can break through our defenses, and take us where we neither expect nor want to go: thus, beauty both partakes of and expresses the prophetic imagination—it can change us, attune us to what is really going on around us—and that makes it God's instrument.

Also, I suspect that in biblical terms, beauty operates a lot like wisdom. In the Bible, wisdom is with God, at the beginning of creation, and St. Paul calls Jesus "the wisdom of God." But one thing the Bible makes clear about wisdom is that when we abandon her—when we seek information rather than knowledge, value false certitude and comfort over the pain and mystery of experience; when we go our own foolish ways, seeking possessions and power, even when we know better, or would know better if we were listening to the prophets—wisdom retreats; she leaves us to our own devices, and waits for a time when we grow vulnerable again, and she might pierce our hearts, and make us see anew. I think that's how beauty works on us as well. Beauty bides her time until she sees a chance to break through our defenses.

Beyond that fragile little thesis, I am uncertain as to how to proceed, except with poetry and story. I am heartened by Walter Brueggemann's image of Israel in his potent little book, *The Prophetic Imagination*. He reminds us that throughout history, the people of God are "equipped only with narrative, story, and poem." And yet, he insists, these seemingly paltry things—well-remembered ancient stories, and a poetic language with which to speak them—are what enable God's people "to persist long past empire."[1] Brueggemann, like any prophet, is right, and one way we know is that we are still remembering and telling the stories of Israel and its prophets some 15 centuries after the Roman Empire, and many empires that followed it have collapsed. And now, in what many believe to be the waning days of the American empire, it is good to hear Brueggemann remind us that the people of God always have to maintain their faith while living within the arrogant, unjust schemes of empire; that is their job. And "narrative, story, and poem," along with the tools of "irony, whimsy, and

---

1. Walter Brueggeman, "Alien Witness: How God's People Challenge Empire," *The Christian Century* (March 6, 2007), 30.

shrewdness," are the means by which Brueggemann says they survive empire, and always will.

I need to warn you, in case you haven't already guessed, that I am not a linear thinker, and this is not a linear essay. I hope you will bear with me, as I relate a few stories about beauty and truth. My father often told me that what turned him into a musician—what called him to his vocation—was hearing a pipe organ for the first time. He was a Methodist preacher's son and grandson—my great-grandfather was a circuit rider in West Virginia and a chaplain in the Confederate Army—and my father had grown up singing in choirs accompanied by worn and badly tuned pianos in little country churches in West Virginia and South Dakota. But one year his family lived in the town of Mitchell, home of South Dakota Wesleyan, and the church there had a pipe organ. Now, maybe you never thought of Mitchell, SD—or any place in South Dakota—as a cultural center. Like Galilee or Nazareth in ancient Israel, it is definitely a backwater on the world's map; those in power doubt that much good can come from such a place. But in God's hand, beauty and surprise can work wonders.

Hearing that pipe organ changed my father's life. It made him a musician, and his music became his ministry, as a church choir director, Navy bandmaster, classical cellist and finally as a Dixieland band leader whose band's motto was "Playing the truth in Hawaii." My dad was serious about that; he truly ministered through his music. And I think Walter Brueggemann himself could attest to that; he once came to my parents' church in Honolulu as a "theologian in residence," and he and my dad really hit it off. I figured out why the first time I heard Brueggemann speak: He and my dad shared not only a deep desire for truth and justice, but a wild, free-ranging and irrepressible sense of humor.

I read somewhere that the poet James Wright had a similar experience of beauty despite an impoverished childhood in an industrial region of eastern Ohio. When one of his teachers discovered that a symphony was presenting concerts in a nearby city, she took a group of students to hear it. Nothing in Wright's experience had prepared him for this. He later said that the music made him weep, because he had not known that such beauty existed in the world. And it changed him; he reached beyond his small, constricted world and became a scholar, and a poet, someone who could see a town in northern Italy as a swallow near sunset, "folding / its face in one wing," and then look again to see "Bardolino risen from the dead," the city that had been in darkness suddenly revealed in a blaze of sunlight. It's important that James Wright reminds us that "every fool in the world can see this thing" and ignore it, just pass it by, "make no more / Of it than of Christ, frightened and dying / In the air, one wing broken, all alone."[2]

---

2. James Wright, "A Rainbow on Garda," *The Journey* (New York: Random House, 1982).

And Mary Oliver—that poem, "Singapore," in which she pokes gentle fun at her reputation as a "nature writer," whose poems are usually populated with more deer and seashells than people. I love her humble admission of feeling for the airplane ticket in her pocket, that reassurance that she has a way out of this uncomfortable place. But then she looks again, and becomes something more than a tourist; she becomes a pilgrim, and sees this stranger as she really is, as beautiful, and she wonders, amazed, at "the light that can shine out of a life," any life. And then she asks what is perhaps the ultimate prophetic question: "If the world were only pain and logic, who would want it?"[3]

My next story about the power of beauty is my own. There is a poem I wrote about an experience I had at the annual Medieval Institute in Kalamazoo, which I believe is the largest gathering of medieval scholars in the world. I had no business being there with my lousy B.A. in literature from Bennington College. My invitation had come through the radical hospitality of the Benedictines. They had asked me as a poet to talk about another poet, the 13th century Mechthild of Magdeburg.

The key to the poem is in that line about Cistercian men and women singing "the Salve Regina to a perfect, oceanic stillness." I had gone to a far side of the campus to what I'd been told was a monastic prayer service, and expected to observe, from the sidelines. Instead, I was commanded to join in—"This is *not* a spectator sport" is a direct quote from the monk who led us in singing. At the time, I was shocked way out of my comfort zone, but now I am grateful for that sudden baptism, that full-body immersion in Gregorian chant.

The "Salve" is a hymn in praise of the Virgin Mary that ends every day in a Cistercian/Trappist monastery. I had never heard it before, and didn't know how to sing it, but that is how you learn Gregorian chant—by doing it with people who know what they're doing. I have good pitch, and a decent singing voice; still, learning Gregorian is a bit like trying to roller skate on ice. But you don't fall, because the other voices carry you along—and that's the point. It is a communal activity: many human voices sounding as one. There is no melody, or beat; the music simply flows like a force of nature. The beauty of it shook me to the core; I knew that something momentous had occurred, that my life had changed.

My experience had some elements of what Walter Brueggemann calls prophetic—recognizing that the old frames no longer fit, that you need a new way of seeing and hearing, without knowing how it will come, or where it will lead. That was in 1990; I was already writing essays that would appear four years later as my book *Dakota*; and more to the point of my topic today—beauty and the prophetic—I was already collecting material for what would eventually be published as *Acedia & Me* nearly 20 years later. It's a book about the spiritual

---

3. Mary Oliver, "Singapore," *House of Light* (Boston, MO: Beacon Press, 1990), 72–73.

morphine we survive on in present-day America. We know the pain is there, but we'll do anything to distract ourselves so we don't have to pay attention to it. Our obsession with celebrities, for example, and so-called "reality TV" blinds us to the ugly realities of everyday life for so many in the world. You didn't know the U.S. Army has ground troops fighting in the Philippine jungle? Or that the food needs of the unemployed are stretching food banks to their limits? It's okay; just go back to "Access Hollywood" or the Shopping Channel.

My point in telling these stories is to remind us that beauty is foundational and formative; we *need* beauty, to shake us up, to break open our hard hearts. And isn't it good for us that God's creativity is inexhaustible; God finds limitless ways to reach us through beauty. We can be moved by something in nature, as James Wright discovered in the play of sunlight and shadow in northern Italy. We find it in each other, in ordinary encounters with loved ones, or with strangers. Worship can be another avenue to beauty: We may hear the words of a familiar scripture story in a new way, and its words penetrate our thick skulls and numbed hearts. But I suspect that the disturbing wonder of beauty reaches us in church most often through music, because it touches another part of our brain, the pre-verbal; it moves us on a physical level and reminds us that the Christian faith is incarnational, a whole-body religion and not just a head trip.

The beauty and mystery of Gregorian chant, and poetry for that matter, is something that can only be experienced and savored; it can't be fully explained, or explained away. That is part of what makes it prophetic, and also deeply unpopular. In *The Prophetic Imagination*, Brueggemann describes the mindset of the royal, dominant system as "a management mentality which believes there are no mysteries to be honored, only problems to be solved."[4]

Surely we recognize ourselves in that description. In our attempts to control and domesticate everything under the sun, including legitimate grief and despair, and even God, it's as if we believe that if we just sound professional enough, fully credentialed and authorized, then all that disturbs our bogus sense of serenity will simply disappear. George Orwell, a true prophet of our language—who gave us the word "doublespeak"—has a passage in his essay "Politics and the English Language" that reveals our predicament nicely. Here is a passage from Ecclesiastes 9:11 in the King James: "I saw under the sun, that the race is not to the swift, nor the battle to the strong, nor yet bread to the wise, nor yet riches to those of understanding, nor yet favor to those of skill; but time and chance happeneth to them all."

And here is Orwell's modern translation: "Objective considerations of contemporary phenomena compel the conclusion that success or failure in competitive activities exhibits no tendency to be commensurate with innate

---

4. Walter Brueggemann, *The Prophetic Imagination* (2d ed.; Minneapolis: Fortress, 2001; first ed. 1978), 43.

capacity, but that a considerable element of the unpredictable must invariably be taken into account."[5]

Now remember what Walter Brueggemann says about the language of those who seek to perpetuate unjust systems of power and control—their language depends on the abstract and general, and avoids the concrete and specific; whereas the language of the poet and the prophet is just the opposite. It gives us images we can see, taste, touch, smell and hear, even when those images are ugly and are painful to see.

Orwell gave us one uncomfortable example of how our own mindset and language have been corrupted. Here's another that reveals that this process has been going on steadily for the last 150 years. Just look at the change in how we describe the damage caused to soldiers by their experience of the violence of warfare: In the Civil War, it was referred to as "soldier's heart"; in World War I, it was "shellshock"; the veterans of World War II were described as having "battle fatigue"; and now we call it "Post-Traumatic Stress Disorder." We've moved from "soldier's heart," a sadly evocative term that anyone might comprehend, to a clinical, medical term. I see this as an evasion of both beauty and truth, an attempt to describe the condition away and hand it over to the professionals, so that we no longer have to face it.

One important thing about the prophets in their quest to reveal truth and beauty, is that they do not run from ugliness, pain or grief. Sometimes they even embrace the darkness, not to frighten us, but to make us see, to make us sense, as they do—these are Walter Brueggemann's words—that "something is 'on the move' in the darkness that even the lord of darkness cannot discern."[6] It is God's primordial, creative darkness. I once was left pondering that darkness after hearing Psalm 88 in a monastery choir—one of the very few psalms that does not end with a doxology, but a lament; and it was followed by a reading from Esther, in which she fasts and prepares to risk her life to save her people.

Esther *is* alone in that moment, and feeling powerless in her lament; yet she signals a total shift in power that puts an end to genocide. As I worked her words into my poem, I was reminded of Jesus in the Garden of Gethsemane, and put him into the poem as well. Both Esther and Jesus might be seen as fulfilling Walter Brueggemann's idea of a prophetic undermining and dismantling of an arrogant, imperial power. Jesus, of course, does this in the most radical way, by accepting even death in order to reveal to us the way to new life.

So where are we with truth and beauty? I do think that when truth speaks, beauty responds. Walter Brueggemann reminds us that prophetic language, like poetic language, must be lyrical: "Speech about hope cannot be explanatory and

---

5. George Orwell, "Politics and the English Language," *Collected Essays* (London: Secker & Warburg, 1961), 360.
6. Brueggemann, 15.

scientifically argumentative; rather, it must be lyrical in the sense that it touches the hopeless person at many different points."[7] Lyrical language is not abstract: If we keep repeating words like "oppression," "brokenness" and "injustice," people will start tuning us out. The task of the prophet, or the poet, is to put live words out there, and then trust the listener to do the rest. Some will hear and be moved; others will turn away.

But when lyrical, living words do connect with us, miracles happen; lives change. We recognize (in Brueggemann's terms) "a newness [we] cannot generate."[8] But we have to struggle to find those fresh words. Way back in the 1960s, Thomas Merton, another prophet of our language, warned us that the overpowering consumerism of American society had corrupted our language so that "to say God is love is like saying 'Eat Wheaties.'"[9] Today, in a world even more permeated by advertising, phrases such as, "Our God is an awesome God" have lost their power. The word "awesome" has largely been stripped of its original meaning as dread and righteous fear, becoming an empty word. (It doesn't help that the language of religion itself has become co-opted by advertising: I once saw an ad for a swimsuit that asked, "Why pray for a miracle when you can wear one?")

Even given that, the language of the prophetic imagination is a large part of its power. It also draws power from envisioning. The prophets try to make us see what God considers beautiful. This is a major theme of not only the prophets, but the Psalms and Gospels, especially the Beatitudes. Isaiah 58 is a good example of this: We are asked to take a good look at a society in which human needs are met—the hungry are fed, the sick are cared for and no one is left out in the cold, on the margins. People are freed from the unjust power and control systems we've created (and treated as if they are eternal, just the "way things are"). We may have created a desert for ourselves (and called it good, especially if the status quo benefits us), but God insists on making and watering a new garden, where all are welcomed and cared for as God's beloved.

The prophets offer us an image of a society we are asked to hope for and work for, knowing that while we may never see it come to pass, it is always worth envisioning. "Questions of implementation," Brueggemann reminds us, "are of no consequence until the vision can be imagined. The imagination must come before the implementation. Our culture is competent to implement almost anything and to imagine almost nothing."[10]

---

7. Ibid., 65.

8. Ibid., 77.

9. Thomas Merton, *The Springs of Contemplation: A Retreat at the Abbey of Gethsemani* (New York: Farrar, Straus & Giroux, 1992), 9.

10. Brueggemann, 40.

It is important to remember that the prophets are all about hope, and do not traffic at all in optimism. Biblical hope requires envisioning a common good for God's people; optimism merely settles for a slightly better version of the status quo as it benefits me. I just encountered a new slang term that says it all: "shoptimism." Just buy more stuff and you'll feel better.

In conclusion, I'd recommend turning to Walter Brueggemann to better understand the prophets, and give them better press. He makes clear that these people called by God are not angry ranters. Brueggemann reminds us that the prophets do not simply harangue, "scold or reprimand" us; they are much more anguished than they are angry. Especially Jeremiah. And it is in their anguish over the way that human beings treat each other that the prophets mirror God's compassion. They see what is wrong with us, the out-of-balance and distorted fantasies of power and well-being that we call normal. And they want us to see it, too.

Walter Brueggemann calls our attention to the compassion of Jesus Christ within the prophetic tradition. He considers the crucifixion as the "decisive event" in that tradition, and in our life of faith. It is a full flowering of both the criticism of social injustice and the energizing, even beautiful vision of the new that all prophecy contains. It is what Brueggemann calls "the full expression of dismantling that has been practiced and insisted upon in the prophetic tradition since Moses confronted Pharaoh."[11] That's a long thread to pull in the Bible, from the stories of Genesis, through the prophets, and into the Gospels. But it is there for us to see, and to grab hold of.

That's a good image to take with us: the dying Jesus as a potent sign of the destruction of worldly power. But it will be hard to keep this truth alive as we face down the baskets full of trinkets, plush bunnies and sugar eggs in the malls. In a culture devoted to denying death, it is difficult to assert that any death has meaning, and that from this death, in particular, we find a sure sign of God's compassion for us. In this death is truth: In it we find the hope, faith and love that make life beautiful.

---

11. Ibid., 99.

12

Rumours of Glory: The Prophetic Music of Bruce Cockburn
Karl Martin

> It is only a poem and we might say rightly that singing a song does not change reality. However, we must not say that with too much conviction. The evocation of an alternative reality consists at least in part in the battle for language and the legitimization of a new rhetoric. The language of the empire is surely the language of managed reality, of production and schedule and market. But that language will never permit or cause freedom because there is no newness in it. (26)
> –Walter Brueggemann, *The Prophetic Imagination*

There is a deep paradox associated with popular culture. Millions go to popular culture to keep from thinking, to numb themselves from confronting the reality of their lives and the lives of others, to simply be entertained and distracted. And yet popular culture has the potential to house amazingly prophetic texts, texts that reveal the truth about the human experience and challenge their audiences to view the world differently. George Lipsitz and other scholars of popular culture have argued that in our industrialized and over-individualized culture where people can often be cut off from more traditional communities, popular culture can serve as a repository of collective memory. Experiences that once might have been shared by families, close-knit communities and church congregations are now shared by popular culture audiences through the mediation of a popular culture text. As repositories of shared memory, popular culture texts have the potential to unite people in experiences of joy, but they also have the potential to unite people in lament, to open wounds that do not heal, to encourage their audiences to refuse to be consoled. With very few structures to support formal lamentation in contemporary Western societies, and with the nearly total absence of lament in most forms of Christian worship in those societies, popular culture texts, perhaps primarily by default, can serve as aids and encouragement for lament. These texts can teach us about the pain and sufferings of others whom we might otherwise never meet or know anything about.

Popular culture texts can also insure that the sufferings of others are never fully in the past. As commodities, commercially recorded music discs and other popular culture texts, once they exist in the culture, are more or less permanent artifacts. We can return to them merely as aids for nostalgic remembering; however, we can also turn to them as aids in the discipline of lamentation. By continually holding the cause for lament before us, recordings and films can help us return to the original source of our sorrow and grief. As long as we can view "Schindler's List" the Holocaust cannot remain fully in the past. If we truly listen to "Ohio" by Crosby, Stills, Nash, and Young, the tragedy of the shootings at Kent State University come back to us again. We can again suffer through an unjust death every time we select Bob Dylan's "The Lonesome Death of Hattie Carroll" on our iPods. If, as Emmanuel Katongole has suggested, lament is not only a spiritual discipline but a gift that opens space for God to do a new thing in the lives of those who lament, then popular culture texts (as well as other works of art), as sites of collective memory, can have a vital, if somewhat unexpected, role to play in nurturing a form of the prophetic imagination.

Popular culture texts, as works of art, can also either protect or destroy a sense of the mystery of human existence. Some narratives seem to explain all of human life in naturalistic terms while others protect a space for mystery, even for the unexpected and mysterious movement of God's spirit in God's creation. Over the decades, the immensity of outer space, for example, has come to millions primarily through the visual images of science fiction films and television programs rather than from reading scientific journals. If coupled together, the articulation of events over which we should lament and the protection of a space for God's movement in the world can give voice to what theologian Walter Brueggemann calls "the prophetic imagination." The music of Bruce Cockburn, I will argue, does just this. Throughout his long career, Cockburn has both given his listeners ample reason for lament while also announcing the possibility of God acting in creative and redemptive ways in God's creation.

In the spring of 1980, when I was a junior at Point Loma College (now Point Loma Nazarene University), I heard a song called "Wondering Where the Lions Are." I can't recall whether I first heard the song on the radio (it received significant air time that spring on San Diego radio and peaked at number twenty-one on the national Billboard chart that June) or on Cockburn's performance on *Saturday Night Live* on May 10th. What I do recall is that the song had an immediate emotional impact on me. To a lilting guitar rhythm, Cockburn sings:

> Sun's up, uh huh, looks okay
> The world survives into another day
> And I'm thinking about eternity
> Some kind of ecstasy got a hold on me
>
> I had another dream about lions at the door
> They weren't half as frightening as they were before
> But I'm thinking about eternity
> Some kind of ecstasy got a hold on me

Walls windows trees, waves coming through
You be in me and I'll be in you
Together in eternity
Some kind of ecstasy got a hold on me

Up among the firs where it smells so sweet
Or down in the valley where the river used to be
I got my mind on eternity
Some kind of ecstasy got a hold on me
And I'm wondering where the lions are...
I'm wondering where the lions are...
Huge orange flying boat rises off a lake
Thousand-year-old petroglyphs doing a double take
Pointing a finger at eternity
I'm sitting in the middle of this ecstasy

Young men marching, helmets shining in the sun,
Polished as precise like the brain behind the gun
(Should be!) they got me thinking about eternity
Some kind of ecstasy got a hold on me
And I'm wondering where the lions are...
I'm wondering where the lions are...
Freighters on the nod on the surface of the bay
One of these days we're going to sail away,
going to sail into eternity
some kind of ecstasy got a hold on me
And I'm wondering where the lions are ...
I'm wondering where the lions are ...[1]

Cockburn has said that the song was influenced by the novel, *The Place of the Lion* by Charles Williams, but he has also said that he wrote it after having dinner with a friend who worked in the defense industry in Canada. During a time of great tension between China and the Soviets, Cockburn's friend told him they could wake up the next day facing nuclear war. That night, Cockburn had another in a recurring sequence of dreams about lions, but this time the lions were less threatening than they had been in earlier dreams. Cockburn has said that he woke up from that dream to find that it was actually quite a beautiful day. The song, then, was born of the juxtaposition of potential doom and the experience of beauty; thus, the song expresses the mystery of this juxtaposition.

---

1. All lyrics and comments by Bruce Cockburn regarding his work are taken from www.cockburnproject.net, a website dedicated to the career of Bruce Cockburn.

Although I knew nothing about the song's genesis, this sense of wonder and surprise in the face of potential doom immediately struck an emotional chord with me.

Like many college students, I was seriously wrestling for the first time with the reality that the world was not as it should be. I could relate to you the specifics of those days for me—they were both societal and personal as I recall. But suffice it to say that even the imminent demise of Western civilization did not strike me as an impossible thing. And yet these realizations struck me in my Point Loma dorm room with a breathtaking view of the Pacific Ocean, so a song about the threat of doom in the midst of an experience of beauty made perfect sense to me. Little did I know at the time that the song was introducing me to the work of an artist whom I would find remarkably sustaining from that point in my life until now. It has always been a mixture of the sense of danger and the sense of awe I associated with that first song that I have found so compelling in Cockburn's music. In a later song, Cockburn succinctly states this juxtaposition: "One day you're waiting for the sky to fall/ The next you're amazed by the beauty of it all."

In his 1982 song "Maybe the Poet," Cockburn sings of the poet, "male female slave or free/ peaceful or disorderly/maybe you and he will not agree/but you need him to show you new ways to see." What Cockburn claims for the poet, I would claim for Cockburn, a Canadian folk-rock artist who began recording in 1970 and has released more than twenty-five albums in the more than forty years since. With songs both profoundly political and deeply personal, Cockburn is responsible for a remarkable body of work. He has become for me a wonderfully prophetic voice—especially in the way the prophetic voice is defined by Walter Brueggemann.

Brueggemann reads the Jewish scriptures as containing a confrontation between what he calls the royal consciousness and the prophetic imagination. The royal consciousness, associated by Brueggemann with the achievements of the kingdom of Solomon, is built upon an economics of affluence under which ample consumer goods are available to the people thus easing their anxiety about survival and ushering them into a world of perceived prosperity and stability. This affluence, unfortunately, is built upon a politics of oppression. The prosperity of the Solomonic kingdom is made possible only through oppressive social policy. Finally, criticism of the oppressive social policy is muted by the contention that God stands with the king rather than in judgment over the king. Brueggemann identifies this as a religion of immanence that implicitly challenges the freedom of God to act in history to counter the status quo because, leaders assert, God stands with the status quo rather than in judgment over it. Thus the leaders, claiming the blessings of God, take credit for the blessings of God. Criticism of the king, because it is equated with criticism of God himself, is essentially silenced.

To counter the royal consciousness, those articulating the prophetic imagination must complete two tasks: the task of prophetic criticizing and the task of prophetic energizing. To begin the task of prophetic criticizing, what Emmanuel Katongole associates with lament, the prophet must "*bring people to engage their experiences of suffering to death*."[2] To do this, the prophetic voice must "*offer symbols* that are adequate to the horror and massiveness of the experience which evokes numbness and requires denial."[3] The prophet must also "*bring to public expression those very fears and terrors* that have been denied so long and suppressed so deeply that we do not know they are there."[4] Finally, to criticize the royal consciousness, the prophet must "*speak metaphorically but concretely about the real deathliness that hovers over us and gnaws within us*," and to do so "with the candor born of anguish and passion."[5] Criticizing the royal consciousness certainly has an essential role to play, but, in Brueggemann's understanding, the prophetic task is not complete if it ends with prophetic criticizing because the fundamental goal of the prophetic artist is not social reform but rather a protection of a space where God is free to work.

The prophet must also energize the people with a message born of hope. The first step, according to Brueggemann, is "*the offering of symbols* that are adequate to contradict a situation of hopelessness in which newness is unthinkable."[6] The second task of the artist who would energize his listeners "*is to bring to public expression those very hopes and yearnings* that have been denied so long and suppressed so deeply that we no longer know they are there."[7] Finally, "The prophet must *speak metaphorically about hope but concretely about the real newness that comes to us and redefines our situation*."[8] Being neither a biblical scholar nor a trained theologian, I cannot comment with any authority on the contributions Brueggemann has made to these fields of knowledge. I can say, however, that his development of the paradigm of the prophetic imagination provides a very helpful tool for the analysis of the work of Christian artists, artists who attempt to both offer a cultural critique and maintain and promote a vision of a God who is actively engaged in sustaining the entire creation and promoting human flourishing.

---

2. Walter Brueggemann, *The Prophetic Imagination* (2d ed.; Minneapolis: Fortress, 2001; first ed. 1978), 46.
3. Ibid., 49.
4. Ibid., 50.
5. Ibid.
6. Ibid., 66.
7. Ibid., 67.
8. Ibid., 69.

I listen to a great deal of popular music, and I know of no artist who does a better job of bringing together a voice of lament and a voice of hope than Bruce Cockburn. I do not want to claim that Cockburn's work fits absolutely into Brueggemann's paradigm as much as I want to suggest that in any number of songs through the years Cockburn has identified the interlocking economics of affluence, politics of oppression and religion of immanence that Brueggemann cites as the core elements of the royal consciousness and also has given voice to the hopes and yearnings Brueggemann associates with prophetic energizing. Brueggemann's work, therefore, provides a fascinating lens through which to listen to Cockburn's work and recognize the gifts it offers to the listener.

A critique of the royal consciousness is everywhere evident in Cockburn's music, and it is clearly presented as a situation calling for lament. Time and time again in Cockburn's work we are confronted with suffering and grief and encouraged to refuse to be consoled. In line with Brueggemann's paradigm, Cockburn's music argues that far too often one nation's prosperity is based on the economic oppression of others, either within their borders or outside of the nation. In the title song from his 1983 album *The Trouble With Normal*, Cockburn sings, "Callous men in business costume speak computerese/Play pinball with the third world trying to keep it on its knees/Their single crop starvation plans put sugar in your tea/And the local third world's kept on reservations you don't see." Resisting this reality, the "Person in the street" shrugs and proclaims, "It'll all go back to normal if we put our nation first." As a result of the politics of oppression and the numbness of the average person:

> Fashionable fascism dominates the scene
> When the ends don't meet it's easier to justify the means
> Tenants get the dregs and the landlords get the cream
> As the grinding devolution of the democratic dream
> Brings us men in gas masks dancing while the shells burst

Numbed to the point where we are willing to call this tragedy "normal," we feel helpless to make any changes. In the confrontive chorus, Cockburn proclaims, "The trouble with normal is it always gets worse."

One of the most consistent reasons for lament in Cockburn's music is the relationship between industrialized societies and the two-thirds of the world from which those industrialized societies have often drained resources and upon which we have relied for cheap labor. In one of his early songs, "Burn," Cockburn specifically associates this "royal consciousness" with American state power. He sings, "Look away across the bay/Yankee gunboat come this way/Uncle Sam gonna save the day/Come tomorrow we all gonna pay." In a subsequent verse, Cockburn sings, "Something dead under the bed/Local diplomats turn their heads/never mind what the government said/They're either lying or they've been misled." Cockburn goes on to historically locate expressions of United States dominance when he sings, "Philippines was yesterday/Santiago and Greece today/How would they ever make the late news pay/If they didn't have the CIA?" In "This is Baghdad" from *Life Short Call Now* (2006), Cockburn again points out the gap between what the United States may intend to do in its relationships with other nations and what it actually does. In the song's final verse, Cockburn sings, "Carbombed and carjacked and kidnapped and shot/How do you like it, this freedom we brought/We packed all the ordnance but the thing we forgot/Was a plan in case it didn't turn out quite like we thought."

Cockburn's critique is not limited to the actions of the United States. In "Tibetan Side of Town," Cockburn turns his analysis to the relationship between China and Tibet. He sings, "Beggar with withered legs sits sideways on his skateboard, grinning/There's a joke going on somewhere but we'll never know/Those laughing kids with hungry eyes must be in on it too/with their clinging memories of a culture crushed by Chinese greed." In "The Mines of Mozambique," Cockburn considers the landmines left behind as products of war and sings, "Some men rob the passerby/For a bit of cash to spend/Some men rob whole countries dry/And still get called their friend." Such issues of global politics are immensely complicated. Cockburn's songs cannot offer comprehensive solutions, but by keeping the issues before his listeners, he can help focus our attention on the problems and encourage us to refuse to be consoled.

In a number of songs, Cockburn turns his attention to the relationship between the state power of the United States in relationship to indigenous people. "Kit Carson" tells the story of a man some might consider a western hero. Cockburn offers a different perspective. After recounting a conversation between Kit Carson and the president, Cockburn sings, "Kit Carson knew he had a job to do/Like other jobs he had before/He'd made the grade/He learned to trade in famine, pestilence, and war." He concludes the song with, "Kit Carson was a hero to some/With his poison and his flame/But somewhere there's a restless ghost/That used to bear his name/That used to bear his name." Carson's "restless ghost" is restless because of Carson's participation in the slaughter of the food supply of indigenous plains tribes. On "Indian Wars," a song for which Jackson Browne contributes harmony vocals and plays the dobro and Mark O'Connor plays a haunting violin, Cockburn sings, "Out in the desert where the wind never stops/A few simple people try to grow a few crops/Trying to maintain a life and a home/On land that was theirs before the Romans thought of Rome." In the chorus, Cockburn sings, "You thought it was over/but it's just like before/Will there never be an end to the Indian wars?/It's not breech-loading rifles and wholesale slaughter/It's kickbacks and thugs and diverted water/Treaties get signed and the papers change hands/But they might as well draft these agreements in sand." By linking the past violence against Native Americans to current practices, Cockburn brings the past into the present and requires his listeners to consider the ongoing violence practiced against indigenous people. The situation, Cockburn concludes, leads "the so-called white so-called race" to dig "for itself a pit of disgrace." Perhaps Cockburn's most penetrating song regarding the treatment of indigenous people—and the clearest expression of the need for lamentation—comes with the song "Stolen Land" from *Waiting for a Miracle* (1987):

> From Tierra del Fuego to Ungava Bay
> The history of betrayal continues to today
> The spirit of Almighty Voice, the ghost of Anna Mae
> Calls like thunder from the mountains—you can hear them say
> It's a stolen land
>
> Apartheid in Arizona, slaughter in Brazil
> If bullets don't get good PR there's other ways to kill
> Kidnap all the children, put 'em in a foreign system
> Bring them up in no-man's land where no one really wants them
> It's a stolen land

Cockburn follows these two verses with the chorus: "It's a stolen land—but it's all we've got/Stolen land—and there's no going back/Stolen land—and we'll never forget/Stolen land—and we're not through yet." In the song's final verse, Cockburn makes it clear that the lament of the chorus is not an end in itself. Rather, it is designed to lead the listeners to action—or perhaps allow the listeners to continually have their hearts broken by the truth the chorus affirms:

> If you're like me you'd like to think we've learned from our mistakes
> Enough to know we can't play god with others' lives at stake
> So now we've all discovered the world wasn't only made for whites
> What step are you going to take to try and set things right
> In this stolen land

In addition to the oppression of indigenous people within the borders of the nation state, another consequence of the politics of oppression undergirding the economics of affluence is the environmental degradation of the creation. Both "Radium Rain" and "If a Tree Falls" from the album *Big Circumstance* (1988) address environmental concerns. "If a Tree Falls" specifically associates damage to the creation as a product of human greed. Calling the rain forest the "climate control centre for the world," Cockburn sings that this "ancient cord of coexistence" is being "hacked by parasitic greedhead scam." In the second verse, Cockburn sings, "Cut and move on/Cut and move on/Take out trees/Take out wildlife at a rate of a species every single day/Take out people who've lived with this for 100,000 years—/inject a billion burgers worth of beef—/Grain eaters—methane dispensers."

In "Gospel of Bondage" from *Big Circumstance*, Cockburn links economic oppression to what readers of Brueggemann would recognize as a religion of immanence. He sings, "We're so afraid of disorder we make it into a god/We can only placate with state security laws/Whose church consists of secret courts and wiretaps and shocks/Whose priests hold smoking guns and whose sign is the double cross." He follows this verse with an expression of the freedom of God. "But God must be on the side that's right/And not the right that justifies itself in terms of might/Least of all a bunch of neo-Nazis running hooded through the night." The linkage between a politics of oppression and a religion of immanence is also seen in "Red Brother Red Sister." Cockburn plaintively sings, "Went to a pow wow, red brother/Felt the people's love/joy flow around/It left me crying just thinking about it/How they used my saviour's name to keep you down." Clearly, Cockburn's music rather consistently gives voice to what Brueggemann identifies as "prophetic criticizing."

A deep distrust of political leadership, which he often sees as merely self-serving, informs many of Cockburn's songs. In "Let the Bad Air Out" from *Breakfast in New Orleans, Dinner in Timbuktu* (1999) Cockburn sings, "Traitors in high places take my money, tell me lies/Take a walk past Parliament, it smells like something died/They ask for trust, but somehow I've got serious doubts/Open up the window, let the bad air out." On "People See Through You," Cockburn specifically calls into question the legitimacy of the structures of what could be called the modern equivalent of the royal consciousness—the modern nation state so deeply committed to protection of its own borders and the policing of its citizens. To an up-tempo rhythm he uses quite effectively to accompany a pouring forth of a biting lyric, Cockburn sings:

> You've got covert action
> Prejudice to extremes
> You've got primitive cunning
> And high tech means
> You've got eyes everywhere
> But people see through you
>
> You've got good maniuplators
> Got your store of dupes

You've got the idiot clamour
Of your lobby groups
You like to play on fears
But people see through you

You've got instant communication
Instant data tabulation
You got the forces of occupation
But you don't get capitulation
'Cause people see through you

You've got the sounding brass
You've got the triumph of the will
You do what you want to
And we pay the bills
You hype the need for sacrifice
But people see through you

You've got anti-matter language
Contrived to conceal
You've been lying so long
You don't know what's real
You're a figment of your own imagination
And people see through you

You've got lip service tributaries
You've got death fetish mercenaries
You hold the tickets to the cemeteries
You're big and bad and scary
But people see through you

While not denying the power of the nation state, Cockburn's song attempts to rob it of its legitimacy and thus rob it of its power to control. In "Laughter," Cockburn reduces such pretensions for control to the object of laughter when he sings, "Let's hear a laugh for the man of the world/Who thinks he can make things work/Tried to build a New Jerusalem/And ended up with New York."

When Cockburn turns his attention to helping people engage their experience of suffering, even suffering unto death, his work becomes very powerful. "If I Had a Rocket Launcher," one of Cockburn's best known and angriest songs, certainly encourages its listeners to engage the experience of suffering as they are transported to a Guatemalan refugee camp in Mexico under attack by helicopter gunships: "Here comes the helicopter—second time today/Everybody scatters and hopes it goes away/How many kids they've murdered only God can say/If I had a rocket launcher/I'd make somebody pay." The first few verses of "Santiago Dawn" describe an early morning attack on a Chilean shanty town: "Something moves in the still dark hours/Sunday in a shanty town/Eyelids open two by two/But not a single light goes on/Tension builds as the only sound/Is the quiet clash of metal and boots/And now and then an order barked/At the bullies in the drab green suits/Military thugs with their dogs and clubs/Spreading through the poblacion/Hunting whoever still has a voice/Sure that everyone will run." "Postcards from Cambodia" contains some of Cockburn's most distressing images:

> Outside Phnom Penh there's a tower, glass paneled,
> Maybe ten meters high
> Filled with skulls from the killing fields
> Most of them lack the lower jaw
> So they don't exactly grin
> But they whisper, as if from a great distance,
> Of pain, and of pain left far behind
> Eighteen thousand empty eyeholes peering out at the four directions

These are just three songs where to listen to Cockburn's music means to be taken to scenes of suffering and death and to be confronted with the violence of the world so often hidden from our eyes.

One of Cockburn's most biting songs is "Call it Democracy" from the 1986 album *World of Wonder*. The song gives us Cockburn's gift of prophetic criticizing at its most powerful:

> Padded with power here they come
> International loan sharks backed by the guns
> Of market hungry military profiteers
> Whose word is a swamp and whose brow is smeared
> With the blood of the poor
>
> Who rob life of its quality
> Who render rage a necessity
> By turning countries into labor camps
> Modern slavers in drag as champions of freedom

In a subsequent verse, Cockburn sings, "IMF dirty MF/Takes away everything it can get/Always making certain that there's one thing left/Keep them on the run with insupportable debt/See the local paid-off bottom feeders/Passing themselves off as leaders/Kiss the ladies, shake hands with the fellows/[And then it's] open for business like a cheap bordello/And they call it democracy." Cockburn's songs can be seen as tools for lament, for they lead us into settings of suffering and death and, often, simply leave us there. The listener who wishes to truly engage these songs must learn to live with the knowledge Cockburn supplies. The chorus from "Postcards from Cambodia" expresses the movement toward lament quite well:

> This is too big for anger,
> It's too big for blame.
> We stumble through history
> So humanly lame
> So I bow down my head
> Say a prayer for us all
> That we don't fear the Spirit
> When it comes to call

Thankfully, Cockburn has also been wonderfully adept at providing his listeners metaphors to communicate what it means to live with the knowledge of such suffering and death. Knowing that the vast majority of his listeners will never experience the terror of having their door kicked in by military thugs, Cockburn must provide them with images conveying the emotional impact of knowing such suffering and feeling a certain amount of helplessness in the face of such evil. He has done so with a series of images over the years. What does it feel like? It feels "like Fay Wray face to face with King Kong." One of Cockburn's early songs is entitled "Outside a Broken Phone Booth with Money in My Hand." We know we have resources, but we don't know where they can be put to use. In "Hills of Morning," Cockburn describes the human condition in this way: "Underneath the mask of the sulphur sky/A bunch of us were busy, waiting/Watching the people looking ill at ease/Watching the fraying rope get closer to breaking." In "Slow Down Fast," Cockburn chants at a breathless pace, "One-eyed sun leering through the haze/Hordes of loveless marching while the little drummer plays/Nail in the coffin rats in the maze/Dancing arm in arm towards the looming end of days." In another song, the singer wonders if he "will end up like Bernie in his dream/A displaced person in some foreign border town/Waiting for a train part hope part myth while the station changes hands." In "Hoop Dancer," Cockburn describes a laugh he utters as "a true 20th Century sound/A little crazed and having no tonal center." We are, as Cockburn sings in "You Pay Your Money and You Take Your Chance," "The numb and confused/The battered and bruised/The counters of cost/And the star-crossed." One of his most evocative images is found in the first verse of "Pacing the Cage" from *The Charity of Night* (1996):

> Sunset is an angel weeping
> Holding out a bloody sword
> No matter how I squint I cannot
> Make out what it's pointing toward
> Sometimes you feel like you've lived too long
> Days drip slowly on the page
> You catch yourself
> Pacing the cage

Even in the midst of these observations about what the human condition feels like, Cockburn affirms the leadership of God. In a loose paraphrase of the 23rd Psalm, Cockburn attributes to God the journey that has taken him to sometimes dark places in the world and dark places in his own spirit. "Strange Waters" is from *The Charity of Night* (1996):

> I've seen a high cairn kissed by holy wind
> Seen a mirror pool cut by golden fins
> Seen alleys where they hide the truth of cities
> The mad whose blessing you must accept without pity
>
> I've stood in airports' guarded glass and chrome
> Walked rifled roads and landmined loam
> Seen a forest in flames right down to the road
> Burned in love till I've seen my heart explode
>
> You've been leading me
> Beside strange waters
>
> Across the concrete fields of man
> Sun ray like a camera pans
> Some will run and some will stand
> Everything is bullshit but the open hand
>
> You've been leading me
> Beside strange waters
> Streams of beautiful lights in the night
> But where is my pastureland in these dark valleys?
> If I loose my grip, will I take flight?

You've been leading me
Beside strange waters
Streams of beautiful lights in the night
But where is my pastureland in these dark valleys?
If I lose my grip, will I take flight?

In the third part of prophetic criticizing, Brueggemann claims the prophetic artist must speak of the death that haunts us, a fear of death that leaves us "questing for new satiations that can never satisfy," a quest that drives us "to the ultimate consumerism of consuming each other."[9] Cockburn expresses this sentiment in "Fascist Architecture" in which the singer, along with the listeners who sing along, confronts his own complicity in the destructive relationships so common under the royal consciousness. "Fascist architecture of my own design/ Too long been keeping my love confined/You tore me out of myself alive." For me, the most penetrating, even devastating, song came as "Broken Wheel" from *Inner City Front* (1981):

Way out on the rim of the galaxy
The gifts of the Lord lie torn
Into whose charge the gifts were given
Have made it a curse for so many to be born

This is my trouble—
These were my fathers
So how am I supposed to feel?
Way out on the rim of the broken wheel

After wailing the prayer, "Lord, spit on our eyes so we can see/How to wake up from this tragedy," Cockburn sings this last verse:

Way out on the rim of the broken heel
Bleeding wound that will not heal
Trial comes before truth's revealed
So how am I supposed to feel?

This is my trouble—
Can't be an innocent bystander
In a world of pain and fire and steel
Way out on the rim of the broken wheel

---

9. Ibid., 50.

If Cockburn had only produced songs of prophetic criticizing, he could take his place alongside artists such as Bob Dylan, John Mellencamp, Bruce Springsteen, Neil Young and Jackson Browne—heady company indeed. All of these songwriters have written deeply and profoundly about injustice and human misery. Cockburn's distinctive gift is that he is able to write and sing such material while also exploring the essential mystery and beauty of the world and affirming the freedom of God to act in history to bring about newness and hope. As we turn to what Brueggemann identifies as prophetic energizing in the songs of Bruce Cockburn, we see his full range as an artist. As Cockburn himself has written, "It's time for the singers of songs without hope to take a hard look and start from scratch again."

Cockburn has consistently embraced a sense of wonder in his songwriting, and, in so doing, counters any sense of the inevitability of suffering and injustice that might be drawn from his own biting social criticism. Cockburn early announced the embracing of possibility in his song "Laughter" quoted above. His statement of the pretensions of human accomplishments, the limits of what humans allow themselves to dream, opens up the possibility for the actions of God in the world. In "Hills of Morning," after Cockburn characterizes the human condition as one of "feeling ill at ease" while a "fraying rope gets closer to breaking," Cockburn sings:

> Women and men move back and forth
> In between effect and cause
> And just beyond the range of normal sight
> This glittering joker was dancing in the dragon's jaws

That this "glittering joker" is an image of Christ is made clear in the prayer of the chorus following this verse:

> Let me be a little of your breath
> Moving over the face of the deep
> I want to be a particle of your light
> Flowing over the hills of morning

From this prayer, Cockburn moves into the third and fourth verses before ending with the chorus:

> The only sign you gave of who you were
> When you first came walking down the road
> Was the way the dust motes danced around

Your feet in cloud of gold

But everything you see's not the way it seems—
Tears can sing and joy shed tears
You can take the wisdom of this world
And give it to the ones who think it all ends here

The image of Christ "dancing in the dragon's jaws" captures a sense of wonder, of possibility for hope in the midst of danger. It is a concrete image designed to embody hope. The imagery of tears singing and joy crying is further disruptive of what might be considered natural categories of human experience. All of this is rooted in a hope born of the belief in a higher order of wisdom, a wisdom not associated with the wisdom of the world. "Rumours of Glory" also attempts to capture a sense of another order. In the second verse, Cockburn sings:

Smiles mixed with curses
The crowd disperses
About whom no details are known
Each one alone yet not alone
Behind the pain/fear
Etched on the faces
Something is shining

Like gold but better
Rumours of glory
Rumours of glory

In "What About the Bond," Cockburn acknowledges the challenge of continuing to hope, of continuing to order one's life in a wisdom not born of this world. "It's all too easy/To let go of hope/To think there's nothing worth saving/And let it all go up in smoke." The title track of Cockburn's 1986 album, *World of Wonder*, opens with this verse: "Stand on a bridge before the cavern of night/Darkness alive with possibility/Nose to this wind full of twinkling lights/trying to catch the scent of what's coming to be in this/World of wonders." What quoting the lyrics cannot capture is the beauty of the songs themselves communicated through Cockburn's singing and his incredible guitar playing. All of these messages come to the listener in songs filled with the emotional power lyrics acquire when wedded to musical accompaniment.

His most direct affirmation of the significance of mystery comes in one of his most recent songs, a languid tune simply called "Mystery":

And don't tell me there is no mystery
Mystery, Mystery
And don't tell me there is no mystery
It overflows my cup

This feast of beauty can intoxicate
Intoxicate, intoxicate
This feast of beauty can intoxicate
Just like the finest wine

So all you stumblers who believe love rules
Believe love rules, believe love rules
Come all you stumblers who believe love rules
Stand up and let it shine
Stand up and let it shine

Taken out of the context of Cockburn's other songs, these songs of mystery and wonder could be mistaken for a cheap mysticism. But placed in the midst of Cockburn's critiques of the royal consciousness and his specific symbols of hope, they take on a deeper meaning. It is to these symbols of hope that I would now like to turn. Some of these symbols of hope can be found in the actions of particular people Cockburn has encountered in his travels through the years. In "Dust and Diesel" Cockburn sings of being taken in by people in Nicaragua. "Now we make music for the time to pass/Tired men and women raise their voice to the night—/Hope the fragile bloom they've grown will last." In "Santiago Dawn," Cockburn offers the image of "sisters and brothers" "coming home/To see the Santiago dawn." In a subsequent verse, Cockburn sings, "I got a dream and I'm not alone/Darkness dead and gone/All the people marching home/Kissing the rush of dawn."

Of course, as a Christian, Cockburn's most penetrating images of newness and hope can be found in images of the incarnation sprinkled throughout his canon. One is in the previously cited "Hills of Morning." In "Cry of a Tiny Babe" Cockburn recounts the birth narrative of Jesus. In the chorus he sings, "Like a stone on the surface of a still river/Driving the ripples on forever/Redemption rips through the surface of time/In the cry of a tiny babe." The final verse allows Cockburn the opportunity to suggest the newness offered to human beings in this gift:

There are others who know about this miracle birth
The humblest of people catch a glimpse of their worth

For it isn't to the palace that the Christ child comes
But to shepherds and street people, hookers and bums
And the message is clear if you've got ears to hear
That forgiveness is given for your guilt and your fear
It's a Christmas gift [that] you don't have to buy
There's a future shining in a baby's eyes

This brings us to the last and perhaps the greatest gift Cockburn's music provides—instruction and inspiration for how to live in this "world of wonder," even with the knowledge of so much that is wrong and unjust, and how to lament with the confidence in the activity of God in God's world. We live in a world called to the telos of the beloved community. In "Great Big Love," Cockburn acknowledges his surprise that human beings are capable of love and locates the source of the love in God's actions when he sings, "Never had a lot of faith in human beings/But sometimes we manage to shine/Like a light on a hill beaming out to space/From somewhere hard to find." How are we to live? Cockburn's music is not short on suggestions. In "Starwheel," he admonishes his listeners, "Don't go playing no shell game with God—/Only Satan's going to give you odds/We're given love and love must be returned—/That's all the bearings that you need to learn/See how the starwheel turns." This love can be transformative. In "After the Rain" Cockburn ponders its possibilities:

After the rain in the streets light flows like blood
I can just taste salt on the humid wind

Here comes that gasoline
Spreading hungry rainbow over shiny black tar

I'm blown like smoke and blind as wind
Except for when your love breaks in
Maybe to those who love is given sight
To pierce the wall of seeming night
And know it pure beyond all imagining
Engine throb street cruise light bullet car flash
Hollow beauty night gleam oily river tension glass

Ultraflame! Glittering dust falling in slow motion
Clouds tumbling one over another into apparent emptiness

It's like a big fist breaking down my door
I never felt such a love before

Maybe to those who love it's given to hear
Music too high for the human ear
And clear as hydrogen to go singing

To live in this knowledge that God is at work in God's creation, we have to silence the voices that would tell us we are living in a fantasy world. Cockburn confronts these voices in "More Not More" from *Humans* (1980) when he sings, "Don't I hear them talking?/Don't I know what they say?/I'm a fool for thinking/Things could be better than they are today." After singing these lines, he asserts with great pathos, "There must be more ... more." Perhaps speaking to himself as much as to his audience, in "Don't Forget About Delight" from *You've Never Seen Everything* (2003), Cockburn sings, "Amid the rumours and the expectations/and all the stories dreamt and lived/Amid the clangour and the dislocation/and things to fear and to forgive/Don't forget/about delight/Y know what I'm saying to you/Don't forget/about delight."

Cockburn's admonishment to work for a better world even in the midst of suffering and death, and his conviction that this kind of life must be fueled by hope in God's freedom to act in history, is perhaps best demonstrated in his song "Where the Death Squad Lives" from *Big Circumstance*:

> Goons in blackface creeping in the road—
> Farm family waiting for the night to explode—
> Working the land in an age of terror
> You come to see the moon as the bad news bearer
> Down where the death squad lives
>
> They cut down people like they cut down trees—
> Chop off its head so it will stay on its knees—
> The forest shrinks but the earth remains
> Slash and burn and it grows again
> Down where the death squad lives
>
> I've got friends trying to batter the system down
> Fighting the past till the future comes round
> It'll never be a perfect world till God declares it that way
> But that don't mean there's nothing we can do or say
> Down where the death squad lives
>
> Like some kind of never-ending Easter passion,
> From every agony a hero's fashioned
> Around every evil there gathers love—

> Bombs aren't the only things that fall from above
> Down where the dead squad lives
> Down where the dead squad lives
>
> Sometimes I feel like there's a padlock on my soul
> If you opened up my heart you'd find a big black hole
> But when the feeling comes through, it comes through strong—
> If you think there's no difference between right and wrong
> Just go down where the death squad lives
>
> This world can be better than it is today
> You can say I'm a dreamer but that's okay
> Without the could-be and the might-have-been
> All you've got left is your fragile skin
> And that ain't worth much down where the death squad lives

For years, Cockburn's music has served his audience well, has provided both prophetic criticizing and offered energizing, hope-filled messages. In one of his early songs, Cockburn sings about "Trying to keep the latent depression from crystallizing." Perhaps many in his audience find themselves doing just that on a fairly regular basis—I know I do. And as I do so, I reflect on the many wonderful songs Cockburn has given to us. He functions for me as a prophetic voice in my life. A world traveler who has seen more human misery than I will ever see, Cockburn has remained hopeful. And if he can do so, he gives me hope that I can as well. He gives hope for the future because he declares it to be God's future. He reminds me that "all this world is hallowed ground." That last line is from a song that has long struck me as a kind of benediction. As it should be, I'll let Cockburn have the last word:

> These shoes have walked some strange streets
> Stranger still to come—
> Sometimes the prayers of strangers
> Are all that keeps them from
> Trying to stay static
> Something even death can't do
> Everything is motion—
> To the motion be true
>
> In this cold commodity culture
> Where you lay your money down
> It's hard to even notice

That all this earth is hallowed ground—
Harder still to feel it
Basic as a breath—
Love is stronger than darkness
Love is stronger than death
The gift
Keeps moving—
Never know
Where it's going to land.
You must stand
Back and let it
Keep on changing hands
Hackles rise in anger
Heat waves rise in sex
The gift moves on regardless
Tying this world to the next
May you never tire of waiting
Never feel that life is cheap
May your life be filled with light
Except for when you're trying to sleep
The gift
Keeps moving—
Never know
Where it's going to land
You must stand
Back and let it
Keep on changing hands

13

Walking Humbly
Jin S. Kim

> God has told you, O mortal, what is good; and what does the Lord require of you but to do justice, and to love kindness, and to walk humbly with your God?
> —Micah 6:8

The Birth of a Multicultural Church

One of the reasons I was asked to preach is to share with you the amazing things that have been happening at Church of All Nations in Minneapolis, MN, the congregation I am so privileged to lead. In January of 2004 a group of mostly second generation Christians of a Korean immigrant church in the Twin Cities was blessed by our "mother church" to launch a multicultural community called Church of All Nations. We were chartered with great fanfare, but no one knew if a hundred mostly young Korean-Americans could actually become a Church of All Nations; many thought the name was a bit premature, if not presumptuous.

Today, we have an adult membership and worship attendance of about 250. We are currently 32% Asian, 37% white, 20% black and 10% Latino, with over 20 nations represented in our membership. Our pastoral and teaching staff includes people who hail from Korea, Kenya, Sudan, Brazil, Japan and the US (both Euro- and African American). Our session also reflects the major racial ethnic groups of our congregation.

We are one of a handful of congregations in the US with no ethnic majority and sizable groups of the four major racial categories of white, black, Asian and Latino. But we actually have even more denominational diversity than ethnic diversity, and draw as many Catholics, Episcopalians and Lutherans as we do Pentecostals, Baptists and Evangelical Free.

Our highly visible commitment to ecumenical unity may be one reason why most of our new members have no Presbyterian background. We seem to draw equal numbers of "evangelicals" and "progressives," Republicans and Democrats, traditionalists and dreamers, and a lot of what I call "posts"—those who see themselves as post-modern, post-ideological, post-denominational, post-foundationalist, post-missional and post-emergent—we're even post-trendy.

From the beginning, the crafting and nurturing of our congregational identity was seen as paramount. Our central mission is to do the ministry of reconciliation, and it is happening in all kinds of wonderful ways here. For instance, in January of 2006 we moved from our "mother church" to a declining white PCUSA congregation founded in 1884 called the Shiloh Bethany

Presbyterian Church in an urban suburb called Columbia Heights. Seven months later Shiloh Bethany had a congregational dissolution and all of their members became members of Church of All Nations, handing us the keys and the title to the building.

Incidentally, 1884 is the year that PCUSA missionaries first arrived on the shores of my home country, Korea. So we came full circle, historically speaking. Not one Shiloh Bethany member left after the merger—praise God! One of the key reasons for this union was the growing recognition of the need to be a new kind of church for an increasingly multicultural population in Columbia Heights and the entire Twin Cities area. Church of All Nations fits that need very well.

Exactly a year later, in August of 2007, an independent Pentecostal Brazilian congregation which also had a multicultural vision asked if they might merge with us. We became 10% Latino overnight! As the co-pastors of the Seara Brazilian Ministry have testified, it was love at first sight. And I can tell you, a full year into this journey, we are still on our honeymoon. We have wonderful friendship, collegiality and mutual respect among our six international pastors, and a culture of inclusion and investment with our many full-time interns. Our diverse staff tries to model for our congregation a way of walking humbly with each other and modeling for the church the ministry of reconciliation.

We witness many signs of growth in our midst, but the most important thing is that people are filled with joy, hope and genuine love for each other across all kinds of lines, crossing barriers erected by church and society, history and culture. For decades now, Shiloh Bethany members have prayed that their sanctuary would be full again, and that the building would be restored to its original condition. Who knew that God would answer the prayers of this typical, declining white church through a young, multicultural church? Who knew that a church chartered just two years before would own a sizable building overlooking a beautiful lake?

Many of us who began this journey assumed that we would be dealing with much more conflict as many cultures and worldviews add to the complexity of congregational dynamics. What we have discovered, to our delight, is the exact opposite. The very decision to join a church in which one chooses to be a minority seems to draw the kind of people who are willing to "lay down their sword" of power and privilege, and to walk humbly with God. The Korean American founders had to set the example first. Today, we all seem to be caught up in a virtuous cycle of lifting up and valuing other individuals and cultures, to "consider others better than oneself." The culture of public confession, corporate repentance, joyful celebration and vulnerable relationality that we have cultivated at Church of All Nations is key to understanding the dynamism and eschatological hope evident in our life together.

We live in the time between the "already" and "not yet." Our church also sees itself between Pentecost in Acts 2 and the coming kingdom in Revelation 7, when all nations, tribes and tongues will glorify God together in one voice. We feel called to be an ecumenical church that embodies the major spiritual roots of the early church—to be simultaneously Rational, Sacramental and Pentecostal. We are also convinced that only intentional movement away from rigid denominationalism toward visible unity will lead the global church to recover its identity as one, holy, catholic and apostolic. We are a high-risk, low-anxiety church where anything is possible, including the possibility of failure. The only poverty we contest for ourselves is the poverty of imagination. We feel so blessed with God's abundance and grace. With humans, this is impossible. Thanks be to God who makes all things possible!

A Brief History of Race in America

Now let me share a bit about the theological, historical and sociological reflecting that goes on at Church of All Nations on a daily basis, especially regarding race in America. From the not-so-long-ago ruckus over Barack Obama's former pastor Jeremiah Wright, it's clear to me that we still don't know how to engage this topic in either church or state. After all, racism remains the mega-idolatry in the meta-narrative of American history. Race is the third rail that will electrocute anyone who touches it. I was grieved over this episode, as I believe that Dr. Wright will be remembered as one of the great prophets of his generation. Do we need reminding that it was the African American church that kept the prophetic tradition alive in America? The Black Church has been the only consistent, alternative voice to the dominant narrative generated by empire.

As a Korean American, I speak as a historical newcomer to this debate. When I was growing up in 1970s South Carolina, we didn't even have a category for Asians or Hispanics—there were so few of us in the Deep South back then. I had no ethnic group to belong to, except when I went home to a mother, a father, a brother and sister that looked like me. Thanks be to God that I also had the Korean immigrant church on Sundays to look forward to—the Korean Community Presbyterian Church of Columbia, S.C. where my pastor was the Rev. Sun Bai Kim, my lifelong mentor. The immigrant church served as a spiritual and cultural oasis for people like my parents.

But one of the painful things that we have to grapple with is the larger social context in which the white church, black church and immigrant churches find themselves today. White Presbyterian missionaries from the US came to Korea in 1884 and made the outrageous claim that "the God who made us is the same God who made you." In other words, they taught us that a sovereign God made all of humanity and all of creation. A century later a lot of us growing up in America realized that that is not quite the case. Your doctrine might teach the sovereignty of God and a shared humanity but your churches sure don't embody it. You opened up your Bibles to us, but made it crystal clear that your churches are not open to blacks, Asians and Latinos.

It's painfully obvious that India is not the only country with a rigid caste system. From the birth of this republic our founding fathers enshrined into the constitution the notion that blacks would be counted as 3/5 of a person. Only since the passage of the Voting Rights Act in 1965 have African Americans as a whole been legally enfranchised and able to vote. Is this country not founded on the unstated principle that whites should be on top, middle-colored people in the middle, and blacks at the bottom? Have we not determined as a society that only whites are fully human, middle-colored people almost-human, and blacks and American Indians sub-human?

Now I want to ask, over 40 years after Dr. King's assassination: How did we get into this mess? Clearly, nations have tried to dominate other nations from the beginning—that's nothing new. What's new was that when "in 1492, Columbus sailed the ocean blue ..." to the so-called New World (new to the Europeans), he sailed as a Christian. Attila the Hun was not a Christian; Genghis Kahn was not a Christian; Alexander the Great was not a Christian; the Egyptian Pharaohs were not Christians. When the Egyptians warred against the Hebrews and prevailed, that meant that the Egyptian gods were stronger than the Hebrew god. So you're supposed to go to war, to prove that your tribal god is mightier than your enemy's tribal god.

So how then do Christian nations behave in the same brutal way that non-Christian nations have behaved since the beginning of time? How do we justify oppression, slavery, the theft of land, theft of labor, genocide, rape and exploitation of every kind done unto non-European peoples? How do these Christians break every one of the Ten Commandments, violate the Beatitudes and defy every teaching of Jesus in perpetrating a global holocaust on to non-white peoples around the world? How do Christian nations do that? It's really simple: Invent racism.

European nations had to invent the notion that darker skinned people are not fully human so that they could justify this unrelenting global war of terror. Well into the 19th century, American intellectuals, politicians and religious leaders debated whether black people had souls. White people needed to buy into the myth of the inferiority of others by saying to themselves: "We know that God made all of humanity, but if we can just convince ourselves that dark skinned people aren't really human, we can do whatever we want." Or, "Certainly, these African heathens cannot be as civilized as we are! Can they really be considered fully human like us?"

It's clear that racism is a philosophical construct, one invented by Christian nations to absolve themselves of the atrocities of empire, to do what every power-hungry nation has done to another, and still call themselves Christian. It's one of the biggest self-deceptions ever invented in human history. And that self-deception continues to undergird American life.

Do we realize that when an ethnic group tries to wipe out another ethnic group in Asia, it is called genocide, but when white settlers wipe out over 10 million Native Americans over a period of 250 years, so that only a couple of hundred thousand are left today, we call it Manifest Destiny? When whites brutally oppressed blacks in South Africa, that was called apartheid, but when whites in America did the same thing, we called it Jim Crow. When people from the Middle East set off bombs among civilians, we call it terrorism, but when white supremacists bombed black businesses, homes and churches all over this country during the Civil Rights era, we called it "unfortunate." Is not 400 years of unrelenting oppression against Native and Black Americans a form of "state-sponsored terrorism"? We Americans don't alter our history; we simply euphemize it and euthanize it. This penchant for the whitewashing of history is one reason why all Christians should reflect seriously on South Africa's Belhar Confession,[1] a foundational document in our self-understanding at Church of All Nations.

There is a powerful myth at work in America—the myth of the white man as the good guy, the righteous sheriff who comes to clean up the town, the cowboy protecting the pioneers from the "naked savages," the homesteader who pulls himself up by his bootstraps—forget about the fact that he pulled himself up on top of land that was stripped from someone else and labor that was stolen from someone else. There is no affirmative action program more grandiose than the one invented for white people in America. How often have we heard about the bootstraps? Give me all that stolen land and stolen labor and see if I don't have stretch marks from all that pulling.

It's not that there is a deliberate attempt to distort history. It's that there is such a powerful need in America to maintain a parallel myth of the white man as the hero that it overwhelms actual history and prevents white people from speaking honestly about the past, and therefore taking responsibility for the present. Most damning of all is that white *Christians* are just as prone to drinking this imperial Kool-Aid as anyone else, and so become incapable of offering genuine confession and repentance. Another obstacle is that the grip that radical individualism has on the Western mind prevents white people from confessing corporately about structural sin and injustice. How many times have we ethnic minorities heard, "My great-grandparents immigrated after the Civil War." Or, "I'm not a racist—I have a black friend." Or, "We've always lived

---

1. http://images.rca.org/docs/aboutus/BelharConfession.pdf

in Minnesota and so never owned slaves." To which my response is, "So we Minnesotans never wore cotton or smoked tobacco?"[2]

How do we boldly and explicitly confess our past so that our memories can be healed? How do we penitently confess that we are still complicit in the structures of injustice that still fund our so-called commonwealth? What does it mean for us to walk humbly with our God and with one another in this time and place, and model a constructive way forward as a beloved community?

From Martin Luther King to Rodney King

Remember the Rodney King incident and the riots that ensued in Los Angeles in 1992? We had 400 years of white racism against blacks, and when black people exploded in anger at the white police brutality finally caught on videotape for all the world to see, it ended up being blacks and Koreans fighting it out in South Central L.A. How did this happen? Koreans started coming to this country in the late 1960s, after the passage of the Civil Rights Act. How did Korean immigrants get caught up in the middle of the racial fear and hatred between blacks and whites that goes back to the time when Europeans first stepped foot on this continent in the early 1600s?

I am not at all suggesting that we Korean people are not culpable in this great American tragedy. Like all immigrants before us, we used the same strategy to "get ahead." In the mid 1800s, millions of Irish were escaping the great potato famine ravaging their land. American nativists considered them European refuse dirtying up America. They were greeted by angry mobs who shouted, "Go back to Ireland!" and "They're here to steal our jobs!" Sound familiar? But the Irish immigrants' response was essentially: We know we're starving, diseased, uneducated "European scum," as you say, but at least we're not black. After the second generation lost their Irish brogue, they were accepted as "white" and became part of the great American melting pot. Of course, we are well aware that this melting pot only worked for European immigrants and had always intentionally excluded darker skinned Americans.

A few decades later after the Irish, the Italians started coming. They were a little darker, a little hairier, but they made the same case: "Hey, we know we're not as white as the Anglo-Saxons here. And we know we're from southern Europe and Catholic and not as 'American, baseball and apple pie' as you people who have been here before us. We're not even as 'white' as the Irish, but at least we're not black."

And so in America, Italians got to be white people. In America, even Jews got to be white people over time. Where else in the world could the Jewish

---

2. Incidentally, I support the continued use of the term "ethnic minority." Just when we are approaching an era when that term will be used for white people for the first time in American history, we want to change the rules?

people have gained that kind of social acceptance? What a country! This is no small feat considering the historic bias against new immigrants from the earliest days of our republic. Benjamin Franklin, one of our most illustrious founding fathers, said about the Germans, "Why should the Palatine boors be suffered to swarm into our settlements and, by herding together, establish their language and manners to the exclusion of ours? Why should Pennsylvania, founded by the English, become a colony of aliens, who will shortly be so numerous as to Germanize us, instead of our Anglifying them?" He claimed that the non-English immigrants were not "purely white," and that the Germans, Russians and Swedes were of a "swarthy complexion."[3]

However many generations it took, Germans, Swedes, Norwegians, Irish, Italians and Jews all got to be part of melting pot whiteness in America because there was a common target of hatred called blackness. Now what do we do with the middle-colored people, like Latinos and Asians? With racist laws forbidding interracial marriage, third generation Asian Americans looked just as Asian as the first generation. We could lose the accent, but we couldn't lose our non-European looks. For instance, my Korean wife was born in Montgomery, Alabama, and our children are third generation Korean Americans, but they look just as Korean as their grandparents who came from Korea in 1975. Now here's the clincher. Even though we Koreans can't get rid of our Asian-ness enough to enter fully into whiteness in this country, "At least we're not black."

So here's the deal we middle-colored people made with the white power structure of this nation: "Let us enter into your elite educational institutions, let us work in your corporations, let us live in your neighborhoods. We know you flee when black people move into your neighborhoods, but hey, slow down. We're Asians; we're not black. No, we're not as white as the Europeans, but at least we're not black." And so we Asian immigrants used the same strategy as every immigrant group before us, stepping on the backs of black people to enter into white privilege.

As Asian people who have been offered the crumbs of white privilege in exchange for silence and invisibility, we've traded in our birthright of dignity for a bowl of pottage. We have failed to understand that in our day and time, that bowl of pottage is the petty crumbs of empire. We have chosen the path of least resistance rather than the straight and narrow path of solidarity with the poor, the marginalized and the rejected of society. O Lord, how now do we recover our humanity and our prophetic imagination?

I think it's tragic that the Rodney King incident incited such violence between the African American community and the Korean immigrant community. But I understand. The 1970s, '80s and early '90s was the time when

---

3. http://www.vernonjohns.org/vernjohns/sthfrnkl.html

many Korean immigrants got their start in low-cost, urban neighborhoods. Now if you go to South Central L.A., there are hardly any Korean-owned businesses there, as newer immigrants have taken over. You see what I'm saying? Korean immigrants have been here long enough now not to need to be in the poorest neighborhoods. "Well, we're movin' on up, to the east side, to a deluxe apartment in the sky." From a Korean perspective, it was tragic that the Rodney King incident exploded just in that brief moment of immigration history when Koreans owned businesses in South Central L.A. The dream of Martin Luther King seemed to turn into the nightmare of Rodney King.

On the other hand, it's not just a historical accident. It's a historical pattern that my people were a part of. That it happened to us might be tragic, but that this sort of ethnic conflict occurred at all in the 1990s is indicative of how hidden the structures of racism are on a day-to-day basis. Is this how a new immigrant group becomes "American"? And what does that say about whether we are Christian or not? Are we genuinely Christian when we ourselves participate in this historic pattern of injustice in this country?

So I want to conclude by walking humbly with God and with you, my Christian sisters and brothers. On behalf of all Korean immigrants in this country, I apologize to you, my African American sisters and brothers, and ask your forgiveness. On behalf of all Korean immigrants, I also apologize to our Native American sisters and brothers for benefitting from the land that was stolen from you. And on behalf of all Korean Americans, I apologize to my white American sisters and brothers, for when we as Asians gladly exploit the "model minority" myth for our own advantage, we are complicit in perpetuating racial divisions and the dehumanization of us all. I humbly ask all of you: Please forgive me and my people, by the grace of God. And may that same grace of our Lord Jesus Christ, the love of God, and the communion and fellowship of the Holy Spirit, be with you all, now and forever. Amen.

Part IV: A Eucharistic People

Mark H. Mann

It might seem a bit strange to end a book on the prophetic by talking about the Eucharist. We think not. In fact, it is our belief that participation in the Eucharist—often referred to as Holy Communion or the Lord's Supper—is very likely the most prophetic thing that we do as Christians.

The central rite of the Christian church is the Eucharist. It was instituted by Jesus himself during his last meal with his disciples the night of his betrayal and arrest, and from the earliest days of the church it has been practiced regularly by some Christians whenever they gather.

This is not to say that all Christians are in agreement about the Eucharist. Some affirm that the practice is an actual reenactment of the sacrifice of Christ that mediates the living presence of the risen Lord to the gathered community; others say it is a memorial service through which believers acknowledge and are transformed by piously recalling Jesus' sacrificial death. Some believe that Christians should practice the Eucharist as often as they meet together; others affirm that it is such a special event that it should only be practiced annually or quarterly, such as is done with key Christian holidays. Some believe that it can only be performed by priests who can trace their ministerial ordination back to the early apostles through a well-defined line of bishops; others that leading Eucharistic celebration is the prerogative of all believers in Christ. Some have complex and highly involved rites involving the entire congregation, while others recite brief and simple "words of institution" when passing out communion to the gathered.

Beyond these differences, most Christians nevertheless affirm the importance of Eucharistic practice and of course the absolute significance of the events and theological truths engaged whenever Christians "come to the table" for communion. Indeed, of the seven sacraments of the Catholic and Orthodox traditions, and the two that most Protestants acknowledge, only the Eucharist is both available to all Christians *and* practiced more than once and on an occasional basis. At the very least, in some sort of general, practical sense, we may speak of the Christian church as a *Eucharistic people*.

To call ourselves a Eucharistic people, however, says something far more about the church than simply that Christians happen to practice the Eucharist and agree that it is in one way or another important; Christians also mostly affirm that participation in the Eucharist is a pivotal moment in our interaction with God and an event through which we can be—indeed, ought to be—transformed after the image and likeness of Christ. This goes without saying for those Christians who affirm in some sense the *real* presence of Christ in

Eucharistic practice, but also for those, as is the case with the many of evangelical Christians, who affirm a memorialist view. According to this view, given its chief formulation by the Swiss Reformer Huldrych Zwingli, the Eucharist is essentially a service of remembrance wherein we recall the great sacrifice of Christ and celebrate the grace that has *already* been given to us in salvation by faith in Christ. But Zwingli himself actually affirmed the benefit of participation in the Eucharist as an act that assures of God's saving grace and thereby strengthens and empowers Christians for faithful service to God.

Ultimately, however, the prophetic nature of participation in the Eucharist is not reliant on the particular view one holds—whether memorialist, real presence or one of the various attempts to mark out a middle ground between these two. One way or another, the Eucharist is prophetic because of the prophetic nature of the event that it points us to—the sacrificial death and glorious resurrection of Jesus Christ.

Jesus Christ is the prophetic Word of God *par excellence*. Jesus is the Word of God made flesh, the voice of the Creator spoken into Creation, the pure light of God's character, will and way reflected into the world and into human history. And Jesus reveals the character, will and way of God most profoundly in his surrender to death on a cross (Phil 2).

The cross of Jesus can and should be understood as central to Christian faith in many ways, all of which are firmly grounded in the scriptural witness and Christian tradition. As a prophetic event, we come to see Jesus' death as a condemnation of all our worldly hopes and commitments, our institutions and systems, our *normal* ways of being, acting and living in this world. Jesus' life, words and teachings are the perfect, pure and blameless life, words and teachings of God—calling all persons and preparing the way for all of creation to be reconciled with God. But rather than embrace the Word made flesh, the world utterly rejects Him in the greatest act of violence imaginable, revealing powerfully Jesus' claim that the Kingdom of God and the kingdoms of this world stand in stark contrast to one another. In Jesus' Kingdom, the first will be last, a leader will serve, the master washes disciples' feet, and no distinction is to be made between the free and the slave, the insider and the outsider.

In this sense, the cross of Jesus is a call to have our eyes opened to the countless ways that the world's ways of seeing, believing and acting have become our ways of seeing, believing and acting as the church. In this sense, the cross—and therefore the celebration of the cross in the Eucharist—is both a call to and act of repentance from the many ways that we have become defined by and addicted to the ways of the world. Similarly, the cross of Jesus is a call to lamentation, for on the cross the very author of life is being executed by the people to whom he has come to bring life abundantly; on the cross the absolute weight and darkness of sin and evil is crushing down upon the One alone who is innocent of sin and evil and is the only hope of overcoming sin and evil. The cross, then, is a Ramah from which the divine Rachel weeps for the death of her son, a place of powerlessness and ultimate resignation where we, the so-called faithful, must come to terms with the humiliating truth of the depth of our sin, and therefore even our own participation in the execution of our Lord. At the foot of the cross, a place to which we come every time we participate in the Eucharist, we mourn our own sinfulness and embrace anew the extent to which the death of the One on the cross is the death that we deserve.

But of course the cross is not merely a call to have our eyes opened or a call to lament, for the cross is not *only* the great tragedy of the execution of the God-man, Jesus. The cross can only be understood fully in light of its fulfillment in the resurrection, in which sin, evil and death are overcome by the power and love of God. In this way, the cross is also a call to participation in the resurrected life of Christ, a new way of living and being in the world in which God's will is accomplished and God's way lived out in the world in and through the church. This is what we mean when we speak of the people of God as *a Eucharistic people*. It is the gathering of the faithful to remember and experience anew the death *and* resurrection of Jesus, to be transformed into Christ's image and likeness as the living Body of Christ in the world.

Yes, that is right! The Eucharist is a celebration of what God in Christ has done for us and a transformative event for the people of God that unites us with Christ, draws us anew into his death and resurrection, and sends us out into the world to be the living, breathing, loving, serving, dying, rising life of Christ. This is true in both a personal sense as well as a communal and political sense.

In the Eucharist we find our sins forgiven and our fellowship with God and with our sisters and brothers in Christ renewed. For this reason, many Christian churches preface the breaking of the bread and the sharing of the cup with a confession of sin, an absolution of sin and a time for exchanging words of peace and love for one another. In this three-step process, we are reconciled anew with Christ and given the opportunity to be reconciled to others against whom we have sinned or who have sinned against us. Personal renewal then bleeds appropriately into renewal of relations and of the community, for we are not reconciled to God simply as individuals, but as a body whose life both irreducibly includes and yet all at once transcends the sum total of all of its parts. In *remembering* what Christ has done, we once again become the members of the Body of Christ—we are "re-membered."

This calling to be the broken Body of Christ, both individually and corporately, creates some natural tensions and challenges. As both individuals and a community, we are called to be holy, to be literally and completely *drawn together* and *set apart* for God. This means that the church is to be essentially defined by its relation to Christ, to function and live in the way that Jesus lived and called his disciples to live. In this community, this "kingdom of God" called "the church," the first will be last, the master will wash the feet of the servant, the lamb will lie down with the lion and not be devoured, the naked clothed, the hungry fed, the stranger made at home, the widow and the orphan cared for, the Year of the Lord's favor proclaimed. And the Body of Christ is not to be all of these things just for itself, but for the whole of the world and all of creation.

This establishes what is the core tension and vital question of the prophetic imagination: what does it mean for the church to be *in* but not *of* the world? How does the Body of Christ transmit the love, the grace and the holiness of God into the world without becoming sullied and corrupted by the world? This is a hard and complex, perhaps impossible to answer with complete clarity considering the complexity and interconnectedness of our world. Sin is not merely a matter of individual moral choices, but also becomes embedded in and perpetrated through personal, relational, communal and social habits, systems and institutions. Caring for the "least of these," then, can never simply be a matter of individual Christians or churches welcoming and providing for individual widows and orphans, as important as such acts of Christian charity might be. So also must the Body of Christ acknowledge and be concerned with the various systems of evil that perpetrate sin, violence and unrighteousness.

But here is where the prophetic calling of the church becomes complicated, where the church struggles to be in but not of the world. Even as we seek to participate in God's reconciling work in the world, so also do we face the temptation to take on the ways of the world to accomplish what we understand to be the justice of God. We have seen this again and again throughout the history of the church—Christians seeking to gain and wield power for the sake of the good, only to find themselves the new perpetrators of evil through the misuse of power. But this is not the *way* that the Body of Christ is called to act in the world. Instead, the Body is called to act as Jesus himself acted—by giving up all pretentions for power, by being broken and spilled out into the world, by embracing solidarity with the poor, the brokenhearted, the widow and the orphan, the imprisoned, naked and hungry. This is what it means to be the Body of Christ; this is what it means to be a Eucharistic people.[1]

Two of the authors in this section explore these themes pretty explicitly. In the first, Brent Peterson seeks to come to make sense of the dichotomies between Jesus' avid stance on nonviolence and popular evangelical Christian support for violence, including governmental practices of torture. His conclusion is that many Christians have confused their allegiance to Christ with allegiance to the nation state, failing to distinguish carefully between the kingdom of God and

---

1. The influence of both John Howard Yoder and William T. Cavanaugh should be apparent here. See especially Yoder's *The Politics of Jesus* (Grand Rapids: Eerdmans, 1972) and Cavanaugh's *Torture and Eucharist* (Oxford: Blackwell, 1998).

the kingdoms of the earth. Peterson then argues that if the church were to take more seriously its identity as the embodied life of Christ as forged in union with Christ in the celebration of the Eucharist, it would find itself called to a different form of political allegiances in the world—not one tied to any particular nation, party or platform, but instead sacramentally poured out into the world in ways that embrace a commitment to nonviolence and refuse to see others as enemies.

Nathan Kerr's chapter echoes many of the themes and convictions that we find conveyed by Peterson, but framed differently. Kerr's central concern is the inversion of the relationship between the church and world in the work of theologians (or, as Kerr calls them, "missiological fundamentalists") like Robert Jenson and Stanley Hauerwas. Jenson in particular, claims Kerr, understands the mission of the church to be a culture into which the world is to be drawn. Rather, argues Kerr, drawing upon both the Apostle Paul and Karl Barth, the message of the cross is one that calls for the church to exist *for the sake of the world*, to be poured out into the world in solidarity with the poor and the broken. This is the essential witness, mission and holiness of the church—which is most sharply defined in the sacrament of the Eucharist—by living, working and praying in solidarity with the world.

While never mentioning the Eucharist explicitly, what we find in the next two chapters provide powerful expressions of what Peterson speaks of in terms of the Kingdom of God, and Kerr as the Body of Christ living in solidarity with the world. The first, in what might be the single most inspiring chapter in this volume, Stephen J. Bauman and Wendy Wellman Sinnema, both of whom worked for the Christian NGO World Relief, discuss recent successes of economic development programs among the poorest and most marginalized people on earth—women in countries like Kenya, Rwanda and Burundi. What Bauman and Sinnema find is that programs such as theirs have empowered countless women to rise above their circumstances, take a greater measure of control over their lives and finances, and find a sense of hope and dignity previously unimaginable. Most significant among their findings, especially as we consider the church as a Eucharistic people, is the extent to which these women have been empowered by their participation in Christian community (the church!), and in turn have become instruments of empowerment for others in similar conditions.

The penultimate chapter in this section is an interview with Bill McKibben, activist and popular writer on environmentalism, global warming, sustainable economic practices and a host of other issues facing our world today. McKibben is perhaps best known for his 1980 *The End of Nature*, the first popular book to begin to put together scientific research on global warming and provide a comprehensive picture of the human contribution to climate change. For decades McKibben was a prophetic voice "crying in the wilderness," calling people to understand, take responsibility for and seek to undo the terrible cost of our addiction to fossil fuels. People are finally listening, but McKibben describes how much work still needs to be done, the cost of our not doing it and the countless obstacles that still remain in our making any real progress before it is too late. The interview, conducted by Dr. Dean Nelson of PLNU, is pure McKibben: funny, poignant, inspiring and, in the end, brutally honest. It is hard to make the case that the interview fits well into this section, and yet it is a piece that we simply could not leave out and it so beautifully embodies all that this book seeks to say, even if not with the clear theological categories that we wish it might. McKibben is a modern day prophet whose work in many ways embodies all that we wish to hold up with this book.

As powerfully as any other writer today, McKibben embodies what it means to open one's eyes and take a long, hard look at reality as we have made it, and to call us to account for just how "screwed up" we have become. Moreover, in McKibben's writing one also finds a deep sense of lamentation. He offers no quick fixes, no easy answers. Indeed, he often wonders aloud for us all to hear whether we are really up to the task of making the kinds of changes that we need to make to save civilization as we know it in face of the tremendous obstacles we face.

Nevertheless, McKibben is also not without hope. His work exhibits great sorrow at the way things have become as a result of human sin, but he is also a true believer, a Sunday school teacher in a small town Methodist church in Vermont who is still that voice in the wilderness, calling for change and providing hopeful ideas for making change. And his hope has been expressed even more profoundly in his activism. Through his tireless efforts with a group of college students in that same small Vermont town and the wonder of the World Wide Web, McKibben founded what in a few short years has become the most influential environmental network in the world (350.org), and which in 2010 organized the single largest one-day demonstration in the history of humanity. Hope indeed! Prophetic hope, grounded in God's love for the world, which Christians celebrate each time they gather to celebrate the Eucharist.

In the final chapter of this section, and this book, we return more explicitly to ecclesiological and sacramental themes. In this chapter, Jamie Gates, Robert Gailey and Larry Bollinger confront a current debate within evangelical theology between so-called "managerial" mission (emphasizes strategic planning and measurable outcomes) and "holistic" mission (emphasizes care for the whole person). In the end, the authors argue that both sides have missed the point in certain respects by failing to ground their emphases in an understanding of the church as the Body of Christ and centered in Eucharistic practice. As such, the authors argue, the church does not have a mission[2] so much as it is a mission[3] in all that it does—a foretaste of God's kingdom to come on earth. In the end, we find that the church as mission is a community called to embody the prophetic imagination: a Eucharistic people called to having its eyes and ears opened, called to live in lamentation and true solidarity with both God and the world.

---

2. A specific task.
3. A group of believers that seeks to be the Body of Christ in the world.

14

The Eucharistic Imagination of Hope and Martyrdom: The Kingdom of God

Brent D. Peterson

Will the Kingdom of God ever be fully consummated? Will Christ return again in the fullness and glory of the kingdom? If one were to ask Christians these questions, it seems likely that many would affirm positively. A primary hope of the church's explicit celebration at Easter is that Christ's resurrection is a first-fruits (a beginning) and a promise of the general resurrection of the dead. Despite hope in the full coming of the Kingdom of God, it appears many Christians live as if this life on earth is the source of their "real" hope and joy. The primacy of this life is often embodied through a voluntary captivity to a host of fears. More than simply a sadness that many live in fear rather than joy, such fears among Christians encourage many to support violence against any "others" viewed as threats. Most specifically I will consider and contrast the liturgy of torture versus a eucharistic imagination of hope and martyrdom.

Torture: A Liturgy of Fear

On April 30, 2009 *US News and World Report* cited the results of a Pew Forum on Religion and Public Life. This survey reported that sixty-two percent of white evangelicals and fifty-one percent of white non-Hispanic Romans Catholics believe it is necessary to "sometimes" or "often" use torture on suspected terrorists. It was most intriguing that only forty percent of persons who are not affiliated with Christianity felt torture was justified.[1] The results seemed to indicate that one was more likely to support the use of torture if one claimed to be a Christian. Is there not a disconnect in believing the Kingdom of God will fully come and torturing other humans? What is at the roots of torture? It seems one primary motivation is fear. Fear of what? Perhaps many things, but ironically the primary fear is likely physical death.

Torture As Dismembering Anti-Liturgy

Why the use of torture? William Cavanaugh suggests that many Christians look to the nation-state (empire) as their means of security rather than God and the gift of the present and coming kingdom. William Cavanaugh suggests the rise of the empire (modern statecraft) is predicated on the transfer of authority

---

1. www.usnews.com/blogs/god-and-country/2009/04/30/poll-most-evangelicals-and-catholics-condone-torture-in-some-instances.html.

from familial and local associations to the state, and the establishment of a direct relationship between the state and the individual.[2] In many ways the empire's use of torture is a type of anti-liturgy, a de-politicization of the *polis*. This direct relationship seeks to dismember bodies from one another and often then limb from limb. Cavanaugh is convinced that "torture is a kind of perverted liturgy, a ritual act which organizes bodies in the society into a collective performance, not of community, but of an atomized aggregate of mutually 'suspicious individuals'."[3] Not only do persons look to their nation-state for security, they often become skeptical of fellow humans who are *different* from themselves.

Torture As Exploitation of the Poor

The perversion goes deeper. The empire (nation-state) is not a nameless faceless other, some dark lord. All empires consist of human rulers with bodies they seek to protect. The empire is often in the hands of the powerful, wealthy and elite. It is more than a sad irony that often those who are tortured and those who do the torturing are from the lower socio-economic classes of the empire. In the United States, many who come from economically disadvantaged families see enlisting in the Armed Forces as a means toward a "brighter future." Promises of *seeing the world* and *adventure* are joined next to words such as honor, duty and bravery. If this imagination is not strong enough, money is also given to help one pay for an education during and after making war. Mark Allman notes that Martin Luther King decried racism, poverty and war as three major evils that are deeply interrelated. King "declared war as an act of theft on the poor, he lamented the fact that war disproportionately kills the poor and persons of color."[4] King saw that those with power use the poor and weak to put their lives on the line for the benefit of the rich, elite and powerful.

Torture Denying Personhood for Victim and Perpetrator

Not only does torture segment the population and exploit the poor, many are denied the responsibility of violence they receive and propagate. Not only are those who are tortured faceless bodies that are discarded, those who commit the torture are also nameless and faceless hiding under the authority of the empire. Allman suggests that, for Augustine, when the empire commands persons (re-named as soldiers) to kill or torture for the empire, "they are not acting as private citizens, thus the action of killing [torture] is not their own."[5] Augustine states, "In fact one who owes a duty of obedience to the giver of

---

2. William Cavanaugh, *Torture and Eucharist*, (UK: Blackwell Publishing, 2003), 9.

3. Ibid., 12.

4. Mark J. Allman, *Who Would Jesus Kill: War, Peace, and the Christian Tradition*, (Winona: MN, Anselm Academic, 2008), 91.

5. Ibid., 167.

the command does not himself 'kill'—he is an instrument, a sword in its user's hand."[6] Allman offers further analysis of Augustine:

> When an individual sheds blood with vengeance (motive) or without permission (authority), that persons commits a sin; but as a tool or delegate of the state, the soldier can kill without sinning, so long as the soldier does so dispassionately (without taking delight) and in service to the common good.[7]

Augustine names sin not in the acts of killing (and torture) but in whether they are acting under the authority of the state in the service of "good." While soldiers are absolved, according to the empire's laws, they are denied the dignity of the guilt, pain and despair of taking and torturing fellow human bodies.

Golgotha: God's Blessing of Violence

What is to be the church's response to the violence and breaking of bodies in the world? As noted above, in the name of Christ, the church has tortured, burned, dismembered and brutalized human beings. Part of the challenge emerges when a center of the Christian story seems to indicate that not all violence and torture is evil. In fact, many Christians affirm the benefits of Christ's flesh being torn and body brutalized as central to salvation. "He was wounded for our transgressions, bruised for our iniquities, by his stripes we are healed ... Yet it pleased the Lord to bruise Him" (Is 53). The tension remains. There is much confusion about what is so good about that Friday at Golgotha. Is this day good because humans killed Christ? In response to this question many Christians would employ several generic and collapsed "pop" atonement theories and offer an unequivocal, "Yes." Christ's death procures, purchases, or pays off what I owe. If Christ's bloody death was "good" then clearly God needs and celebrates the use of violence and torture. If this is true the church should continue to discern the times and places when God wills and empowers violence and torture to achieve holy ends.

However, this is misconstrued, if not idolatrous. What is worthy of celebration is not that Christ was killed, but that Christ refused to resist, refused to defend himself, refused his need to be, and allowed himself to be killed. Christ demonstrated that the only way to truly receive the life God offers is to offer one's life back to God, come what may. That is what is doxologically good about that Friday. As Christ laid down his life, he offered the church a picture of who it is invited to become, the broken body and shed blood. The emphasis is not that Christ's body and blood were tortured, but that Christ *offered himself*

---

6. Augustine, *City of God,* trans. Henry Bettenson (Harmondsworth, Eng.: Penguin, 1976), Book 1, Ch. 21.
7. Allman, 169.

in love as gift to the Father by the Spirit for the world. Christ's sacrificial offering is central to the Church's sacrificial participation in the Lord's Supper.

Along with God's supposed blessing of violence, could it be the case that Christians' fear really fosters a posture that supports war and torture and an allegiance to a government above God? Are Christians really afraid to die? The New Testament states powerfully that Jesus' entire life and ministry offers the greatest gift of all—life (John 10:10). The gift of life that God offers not only heals the disease of sin, but releases persons from the fear of death (Hebrews 2:15). Furthermore, this life God offers in Christ finds completion by casting out fear (I John 4:18). The invitation to be released from fear is one of the greatest gifts that our seasons of Advent and Lent offer. The gift of Christ's birth, life, death, resurrection and ascension is the healing to no longer be held captive to any fears, including the fear of death. Along with a refusal of fear, what does a Christian prophetic imagination looks like? What is the proper imagination for people who affirm not only Christ's resurrection of the dead, but of his return and consummation of the Kingdom of God? The problem for Christians is not simply fear; the problem is a loss of a Christian eschatological prophetic imagination.

Eucharistic Imagination

An alternative to a liturgy of torture is a eucharistic imagination. This eucharistic imagination considers the church as a sacrament of the kingdom, an imagination not of fear but hope. In this exploration I will, *first*, suggest that the eucharistic imagination undoes the posture of enemy. *Second*, as the church is renewed as the body of Christ it is invited into the gift of martyrdom. *Third*, the martyr-church is a sacrament of the kingdom, a visible testimony to what God is doing in the world. *Finally*, such a prophetic imagination celebrates the hope that the Kingdom of God will be consummated. In light of the present and coming kingdom, such a prophetic imagination invites Christians to live presently in love for fellow creatures without the presence of fear.

Eucharistic Imagination: Undoing of the Posture of Enemy

This contrast of imagination of empire and Eucharist leads to a very distinct ethical stance toward those viewed as one's enemies. In the civil state, and too often in the church, peace comes through the conquest of enemies. Conversely, the eucharistic imagination moves the church into three powerful liturgies. First, the Spirit invites the church to healing and life by refusing to consider any other person or creature as enemy. Cavanaugh argues that a Christian politic is based not on the defeat of one's enemies, but on identification with the "victims through participation in Christ's reconciling sacrifice."[8] The Eucharist

---

8. Cavanaugh, 11.

is a divine-human encounter re-*membering* the church as a social body that is defined not by defeating enemies but by self-giving, serving and loving the other. Loving one's enemies often comes first by being present and facing them by the Spirit. Such ethics constitutes the church's politics in the Kingdom of God. This eucharistic imagination moves the church to confession and repentance for posturing any other human as evil, other and enemy. From a profane other, to a person with a beautiful face and particular name, the church seeks healing, transformation and reconciliation.

Second, this eucharistic imagination of brokenness seeks not the defeat but the conversion of one's enemies. Being present and facing those who consider Christians as enemies is a posture seeking reconciliation. However, it is noteworthy that this desire to seek peace and reconciliation with enemies may put one at odds with one's native empire (nation-state). Cavanaugh asserts that the Eucharist produces a "communion stronger than that of any nation-state, than my identity as a member of the body of Christ is ultimately more important than my country of birth."[9] Questions arise: where does my ultimate allegiance and loyalty lie?[10]

Martin Luther King, Jr. offered an embodied expression of this eucharistic brokenness for the world. Following the work of Mohandas Gandhi, King was committed to active nonviolent resistance. The goal of King's active nonviolent resistance wasn't simply to challenge authority or change unjust laws; it was to convert the oppressor: "the objective is not to defeat the enemy, since that will only cause them to be humiliated and desire revenge. No, the goal is to end injustice as well as the attitudes that cause it. In short, the aim is conversion: to change not only actions but hearts as well to turn enemies into friends."[11]

This is the imagination of the Kingdom of God that began in Christ and continues through the church as the body of Christ empowered by the Spirit. Opposed to torture as an anti-liturgy and a social imagination of fear, control and oppression, the social imagination of the Kingdom of God is one of relentless love that leads one to lay down one's life, not simply for one's friends, but for those who may regard Christians as enemy. "The Eucharist aims at the building of the true body of Christ in time, his *corpus venum*, which the church both is and is meant to be."[12] A eucharistic imagination of brokenness

---

9. Ibid., 18.

10. I was recently struck by the multiple reports of Libyan pilots who were ordered to fly planes loaded with full armaments to bomb the "rats." These pilots did not see them as rats but their fellow brothers and sisters and thus disobeyed. Of course their willingness to refuse to kill their own brothers and sisters is admirable. Yet I wonder if I or they would have been as reluctant to carry out orders if their targets were brothers and sisters who live under a different flag.

11. Allman, 92.

12. See Jean Luc Marion, *God Without Being;* trans. Thomas A. Carlson (Chicago: University

is a participation in the present and coming Kingdom of God, a kingdom of peaceableness in God's glory.

Third, Jesus' command to love one's enemies and pray for those who persecute you offers an imagination of a world without enemies. When the church follows Christ's commands to love and pray for enemies, what does the church no longer have, but enemies? The church refuses to treat any other human being or creature as a nameless faceless other that it can either ignore at best, or torture or kill at worst. While the church can refuse to consider any other as enemy that does not mean that persons cannot still view Christians as enemies. The hope of the Eucharist imagines the full redemption of creation where the category of enemy will be undone.

The Gift of Martyrdom

Refusing to consider any other human as enemy will put one at odds with one's nation-state. Furthermore, Christians refusing to claim any other as enemy will face "enemies" not with hands raised with weapons, but with hands lowered with arms open to love. Such a *defenseless* posture may result in physical destruction by those who still consider Christians as enemy. A eucharistic imagination neither seeks nor is afraid of being killed. The church's encounter with God in Christ by the Spirit at the table renews the church as the body of Christ. This renewal as the body of Christ empowers and sends the church to be broken and spilled out in doxological joy for the world. On some occasions the church's refusal to posture any person as enemy, instead opting to love boldly, will result in the gift of martyrdom. Martyrdom is largely misunderstood in the North American context. Apophatically speaking martyrdom is not seeking death, a strategy, suicide, or avoiding violence. It is a willingness to fully receive the gift of life offered by God, refusing to fear physical death for me or others I love.

Martyrdom is not a strategy or some "good" that is desired or sought after. Martyrdom is thoroughly eschatological, a testimony of the *already* and *not yet* of the Kingdom of God. The not yet of martyrdom is often the result of protagonists who are still blinded to the notion that life is not about protection from other humans postured as enemies. Just as the killing of Christ was not a strategy for any good purpose, so too when persons are martyred, sadness and laments should follow. Yet within the midst of sadness, hope irrupts into the present pain. Like the overpowering illumination on the Third Day, the church remembers those who have offered their lives to God as a gift and God received them as such. The saints and martyrs are the cloud of witnesses inviting and encouraging the church to also release their need to be, to truly find life by offering it back to God in Christ, come what may.

---

of Chicago Press, 1995), 176–82.

Martyrdom is not suicide, a careless throwing off or refusal of one's life. One cannot martyr oneself, or take hold of martyrdom. Similarly, the cross is not sought or seen as any good "means" to any other end. In fact, as Craig Hovey notes, we must refuse to give crosses a purpose: "The church bears its cross when it does not ask what purpose the cross serves."[13] Just as martyrdom is neither a "good" nor does it have a purpose, the church offers its life to God as its means of truly receiving the life God offers. Rather, as one is doxologically broken and spilled out as the body of Christ, the martyr's life is taken, bearing witness to the gift of resurrection life offered by God that refuses paralyzing fear, most powerfully for many the fear of physical death. Hovey notes that, too often, "Users of violence have abandoned their crosses for more effective means of achieving results."[14] When Christians abandon crosses in an attempt to preserve their present physical existence, they are rejecting the gift of resurrected life that God offers most powerfully at the Table.

Martyrdom is also not a means of avoiding violence, but refusing it. "Christian peace is in the shape of the cross because it cannot be a way of avoiding violence but only a way of refusing it: refusing it by suffering it and suffering it for refusing it."[15] Martin Luther King, Jr. ardently affirmed what Allman labels as absolute pacifism. Like martyrdom, pacifism is not about avoiding injustice, conflict or oppression, but seeks to undo the very structures of violence. This leads Hovey to conclude that it is martyrs and not soldiers who are moving the world, by the Spirit, toward peace.[16] Such a refusal of violence seeks to undo the vicious cycle of violence, enmity, revenge and retribution. By refusing violence, justice and peace come. One can look to the civil rights movement lead by King and James Lawson in which segregation was undone precisely because they sought to be very active and present, but with a presence that refused to be violent. "The way of Jesus requires the unseating of those modes of behavior, ways of life, desires and thoughts that are conditioned on scales of self-preservation, and security for one's life."[17] Martyrdom is a gift to life. It is an eschatological imagination that seeks to offer life, peace and justice to the world. Unfortunately, many followers of Christ are willing to be broken and spilled out as long as the physical, emotional and material cost is not too great. Persons are fine offering portions of their life, but not all of it. Consequently as Christians refuse martyrdom they embrace the torturing and breaking of their "enemies'" bodies.

An evaded cross is simply not God's way. The Son obeyed the Father to the point of death because he loves the Father as Son and therefore resembles

---

13. Craig Hovey, *To Share in the Body* (Grand Rapids, MI: Brazos, 2008), 47.
14. Ibid., 47.
15. Ibid., 48.
16. Ibid., 53.
17. Ibid., 60–61.

the Father in faithfulness, not because he was bound to execute a separate and sufficient arrangement for a preset course of events.[18] God does not will, but allows some to receive the gift of martyrdom. However, the invitation is for all Christians to offer their lives fully to God. This is the prayer of consecration and worship of Romans 12:1–2. To live into the eucharistic imagination is a refusal of violence, a refusal of torture, a refusal to fear, a refusal to have enemies, a refusal to grasp onto one's life as "mine." This eucharistic imagination is a refusal to break bodies and a willingness to be broken. This is the eucharistic vocation of the church to be Christ's broken body and shed blood in the world, sanctification. The church's willingness to embrace the life God offers is not finally centered on Christians. The church's invitation to faithfulness serves as a continual and further coming of the Kingdom of God.

The Church: The Sacrament of the Kingdom

By the Spirit and through the church, God is and will continue to bring the kingdom. In this way the church is a sacrament of the kingdom. As a sacrament, the church is an outward and visible embodiment of God's redemptive activity in the world. While the church is not the kingdom, it is empowered by the Spirit to embody and participate in the kingdom's continual coming. The church's refusal of enemies, torture and a willingness to be broken open and poured out before the world is a means by which God uses the church to bring the Kingdom of God further. As the continual embodiment of the broken body and shed blood, the church has no fears and thus is not afraid of death. Since physical survival no longer is the end that justifies all means, the martyr-church refuses to bless the use of physical violence. In fact, the Gospels themselves proclaim condemnation on any who seek to use violence for any "good." Jesus' rebuke of Peter in the garden alone offers a prophetic chastisement of any "just war."

The Kingdom of God Will Be Fully Consummated

The testimony of the New Testament offers a bold proclamation of hope that the Kingdom of God, which Christ inaugurated, will be fully consummated (Rev. 11:15; Eph 1:10). As the apostle Paul states in 1 Corinthians 15, when death is defeated and all things put in subjection, God will be all in all. A eucharistic prophetic imagination affirms an eschatology of both an *already*, alongside faith and confident hope that the *not-yet* will one day be. This is the very premise of the Lord's Supper. It is at the table that the church liminally encounters the Kingdom of God in its fullness. This sends (masses) the church out to allow God to continue to further bring the kingdom through them by the Spirit. It is with this hope and assurance that the church lives in continual hope, joy and peace. Without such hope, martyrdom becomes a perverted and

---

18. Ibid., 86.

twisted joke. Without this hope and confidence the church may be tempted to use violence and oppression to bring the kingdom by violent force. Jesus' life and ministry testify that the Kingdom of God will come through the power and love of laying down one's life for all others, especially enemies. Those who hold such a hope are released from fear, violence and the idolatrous need to grasp onto this physical existence, no matter the cost.

Conclusion

Christians must be captured again by the gaze of the eucharistic imagination of the present and coming Kingdom of God. The Kingdom of God will not come through the earthly empires of nation states often built upon the use and threat of violence as the embodiment of a liturgy of torture and fear and the exploitation of the poor. Conversely, it is through the martyr-church that God is and will continue to bring the kingdom as a sacrament of the kingdom. In light of this political allegiance, the church's most prominent political activity is the celebration and encounter with Jesus Christ in the Service of the Word and Table. This celebration not only empowers the church to live as Christ's body and blood in the world, it also celebrates the audacity of hope that one day the church will feast in the fullness of the heavenly banquet in the Kingdom of God. In light of the present and coming kingdom, such a prophetic imagination invites Christians to live presently in love for fellow creatures without the presence of fear. The Church's political allegiance is to the Kingdom of God as the body of Christ. This eucharistic imagination refuses to be held captive to fear, but rather in perfect love casts out all fear. This is the life God is offering to the world.

Archbishop Oscar Romero serves as a powerful iconic testimony of the promise of the kingdom, whose doxological sacrifice ended in his own life being taken:

> As a shepherd, I am obliged by divine mandate to give my life for those I love—for all Salvadorans, even for those who may be going to kill me. If the threats are carried out, from this moment I offer my blood to God for the redemption and for the resurrection of El Salvador ... Martyrdom is a grace of God that I do not believe I deserve. But if God accepts the sacrifice of my life, let my blood be a seed of freedom and the sign that hope will soon be a reality. Let my death, if it is accepted by God, be for my people's liberation and as a witness of hope in the future.[19]

---

19. Quoted in Bryan Stone, *Faith and Film* (St. Louis: Chalice Books, 2000), 86–76.

15

In Solidarity With the World: The Holiness of the Missionary Community

Nathan R. Kerr

> Our church has been fighting during these years only for its self-preservation, as if that were an end in itself. It has become incapable of bringing the word of reconciliation and redemption to humankind and to the world. So the words we used before must lose their power, be silenced, and we can be Christians today only in two ways, through prayer and in doing justice among human beings. All Christian thinking, talking, and organizing must be born anew, out of that prayer and action. ... It is not for us to predict the day—but the day will come—when people will once more be called to speak the word of God in such a way that the world is changed and renewed. It will be in a new language, perhaps quite nonreligious language, but liberating and redeeming like Jesus's language, so that people will be alarmed and yet overcome by its power—the language of a new righteousness and truth, a language proclaiming that God makes peace with humankind and that God's kingdom is drawing near.
>
> – Dietrich Bonhoeffer

I

It is commonly assumed that the "holiness" of "the church," whatever else it entails, *must* consist of some kind of ontological, moral, or cultural (cultic) otherness from "the world." It can hardly be disputed, right? "We" are (the) "church"; "they" are (the) "world." If "we" are to be "holy," then there most certainly must exist those socio-historically identifiable markers—the Sacraments, Ecclesiastical Offices, the Bible, the Tradition—by which "the Church" ensures its own inner constitution vis-à-vis whatever worldly forces threaten from the outside. So we must affirm, we are told, if we are genuinely to believe as we do in the one, holy, catholic and apostolic Church.

But what if this is not how it is to be at all? What if such an account of the church's holiness neglects "the world" by fundamentally misrepresenting it? What would it mean to consider the world as *transfigured* in Christ, and thereby to eschew the safety and security of Christianity's own religious "identity" and the church's own ecclesiological "integrity" for the sake of the church's *solidarity with* this world? Can we think "church" not simply in terms of its *antithesis from* but rather its *openness to* this world? Can we think "holiness" as a matter of solidarity especially with those who are poor, marginalized, oppressed and crushed to the point of death under the strong arm of the earthly powers that be (even, and especially, where those powers take "ecclesiastical" shape)? Can we think the liberation of these poor and oppressed ones as the very event of holiness itself? Do we even have a way of speaking ecclesially that can entertain these questions?

II

In what follows, my aim will be to reconsider what we mean when we say that the church is "holy" by rethinking the nature of her "apostolicity." I want to do this by offering an "apocalyptic" reconsideration of the church as an "event," by suggesting we think the church as an *event of mission*. At the same time, I offer this reading as a means of critically assessing a certain consensus emerging within Christian life and thought today, which assumes that the church is most properly "missionary" only when the church *is* its own "holy culture." Such a conception of the church as its own holy culture leads inevitably to a certain kind of missiological fundamentalism. By "missiological fundamentalism" I mean the kind of careless thinking about the church that, by defining the church's *being* in terms of its cultic (that is, "religious") otherness from the world, treats of its various liturgical practices, institutions, doctrines and morals as self-justifying, such that the missionary task is reduced to that of Christianity's survival as its own discrete culture. Against this line of thinking, I shall contend that once we are set free from the illusion of supposing that the church's holiness is bound up with the preservation of such a "Christian culture," an apocalyptic reconstrual of the church-world relation opens for us a conception of ecclesial holiness that is positively missionary, without reserve.

III

Let me begin by providing an example of the kind of "missiological fundamentalism" that I am talking about. The theological trend of considering Christianity as its own distinct culture is one that is far-ranging and crosses a number of confessional lines. But here I want to focus upon the ecclesiology of Robert Jenson, for it is Jenson (along with his contemporary Stanley Hauerwas) who has most impressively and thoroughly articulated what he takes to be the missionary imperative of constructing a thick "Christian culture." Jenson defines a "culture" as "a group of deliberately human practices and artifacts" that can be taken in themselves to form a mutually determining, internally coherent "system of signs."[1] Put simply, for the purposes of this essay, we might say that a "culture" is that particular code of behavior that a given people constructs out of its group-specific institutions, behaviors and patterns of language. For Jenson,

---

1. See Robert W. Jenson, "Christian Civilization," in *God, Truth, and Witness: Engaging Stanley Hauerwas*, ed. L. Gregory Jones, Reinhard Hütter and C. Rosalee Velloso Ewell (Grand Rapids: Brazos, 2005), 155. Cf. also idem, "Election and Culture: from Babylon to Jerusalem," in *Public Theology in Cultural Engagement: God's Key to the Redemption of the World*, ed. Stephen R. Holmes (Carlisle, UK: Paternoster, 2008), 48–49.

the church's missionary witness is a function of the particular code of behavior that is embodied in the church's tradition of liturgically cultic practices, and such witness is visible to the world as the discretely "Christian culture" that is constructed from out of these practices. I shall return to this relation between liturgical practices and cultural construction momentarily, when considering the role the eucharist plays within such an ecclesiology. But for now let us consider the connection between "Christian culture" and "mission" within Jenson's ecclesiology.

Jenson's aligning of mission with the construction of a Christian culture is a direct consequence of his taking up the generally Catholic conviction (a conviction so apparently consistent with "the Great Tradition" as to now be considered beyond doubt) that the church is the mediator of salvation (*mediatrix salutis*), or the place of salvation (*locus salutis*) for this world. As the one cultural community uniquely "inspired" by the Holy Spirit, the church itself is to be considered "the active *mediatrix* of faith."[2] This is a fundamental tenet of Christian evangelism and mission, for Jenson. The risen Christ is now present and available to us only in the earthly reality of the Church as the Body of Christ. It is as "the Church" alone that Christ is now shown to be an object for the world; "Christian culture" *is* "the availability of Christ in and for the world."[3] Thus the existence of a distinctively Christian culture comes to be "the *condition of the possibility* of faith."[4] Note here that Jenson is establishing a direct *causal* link between the existence of the church as its own lived culture and the outworking of the event of the world's reconciliation to God in Christ. The church is the mediator of salvation because the church *is* the place where the world undergoes its process of reconciliation to God in Christ; as the active *mediatrix* of salvation the church's existence as a culture is on some real level causally determinative of the reconciliation of the world to God in Christ.

In order to understand just what is meant by this, we need to be clear about the relation between the church and the world presumed in this account of Christian culture. Contemporary defenders of Christian culture assume that there is a fundamental *ontological* gap between the church and the world. That is, the church is something that the world is not. Furthermore, the world is in a way that requires the mediation of the church for its reconciliation to God, its salvation. Jenson argues for this point on the basis of the conviction that Christian culture exists as the "inner" ground of the world's "outer" existence. Insofar as the world *exists* at all, it is just *there* as the "raw material" out of which God will create the Christian culture that is the church and bring it to perfection

---

2. Robert W. Jenson, "You Wonder Where the Spirit Went," *Pro Ecclesia* 2.3 (1993): 303.
3. Robert W. Jenson, "Christ as Culture 1: Christ as Polity," *International Journal of Systematic Theology* 5.3 (2003): 325.
4. Jenson, "You Wonder Where the Spirit Went," 303.

in Christ.[5] It is important not to miss what is being said here: the world only exists for the sake of the building up of the holy culture that is the Christian church. The very idea, which Jenson espouses, that the church is as antecedently "prior" in God's intention for creation from all eternity requires that we think of the world as an ontological abstraction—its "being" is just that it is the required "other" over-against which the church exists, for the sake of becoming its own holy culture in and of itself. Indeed, we might say that the very idea of "the world" subsists (is sustained in its mode of "being") in the church, inasmuch as the goal of creation, from beginning to end, is to become the church. Simply put (and this is the basic slogan not only of Jenson's theology but of all missiological fundamentalisms as such): "The world (exists) for the church."

We are now in a position to see how this construal of the church as its own holy culture and its corresponding account of the church-world relation is determinative of the mission's *content* and its attendant missionary forms. Quite simply, the mission's content is that of the church's own interior culture, and the *form* of the missionary task is that of induction into the particular modes of ritual practice, moral vision and cultic formation that make up that interior culture. And so Jenson writes: "If ... we are aware of the mission, and of the mission's situation in our particular time, we will not try to adapt the church's culture to seekers, but seekers to the church's culture."[6] Whatever else we might take this statement to mean, the key point is this: it is the given existence of the church as its own distinct and inviolable "holy culture" that determines "the mission's situation" at every turn. The goal of the mission thus turns out to be induction into the church's cultic life for the very purpose of the cultivation and survival of "Christian culture." As such, the church's primary mission is just to be itself, as its own distinct culture. Or, to cite the one oft-repeated mantra of the so-many defenders of this very missiological fundamentalism: "The Church *is* the mission." Thus, as Jenson emphasizes, the church can be said to be holy only by way of its "being as much its own specific culture as it can manage."[7] And because the world "subsists" in the church, the church's mission is to be involved in the induction of the world—the other—into its own specific mode of culture-making, for the sake of the world's transformation into the holy culture that the church just *is*. Thus, all genuinely missionary activity is itself reduced to the churchly function of Christian culture-making.

Such a reduction is evidenced by the way in which the defenders of this cultural Christianity tend to render the sacramental practices of the church

---

5. Robert W. Jenson, "The Church's Responsibility for the World," in *The Two Cities of God: The Church's Responsibility for the Earthly City*, ed. Carl E. Braaten and Robert W. Jenson (Grand Rapids: Eerdmans, 1997), 4.

6. Robert W. Jenson, "Catechesis for Our Time," in *Marks of the Body of Christ*, ed. Carl E. Braaten and Robert W. Jenson (Grand Rapids: Eerdmans, 1999).

7. Robert W. Jenson, "Christian Civilization," 159–60.

themselves as mere practices of Christian culture-making. This can be seen especially in accounts of the Eucharist which view it primarily as that one practice wherein the ordering of the Christian culture is fundamentally "actualized." What I have in mind here is the perspective of those who see the sacraments, particularly those of Baptism and Eucharist, as the fundamental means of induction into a given culture. As one contemporary missiological fundamentalist puts it (in terms consonant with the definition of culture laid out above), "The Eucharist is a complex ritual involving the juxtaposition of signs *and* words. It contains within itself a whole web of meaning that, for anyone who participates in it regularly, is hard to miss."[8] On this view, the Eucharistic liturgy is rendered as a cultic ritual which supplies the indispensable "grammar" by which one is assimilated into and participates in the church's own Christian culture. The primary function of the Eucharist is thus to serve as an identity-defining marker for what transforms Christians into a living communal culture that is "not of this world."[9]

The critical point I want to make here is to show how Eucharistic and liturgical practice is instrumentalized as a means of ontologically securing what the church is in-itself vis-à-vis the world. To be sure, there is a sending dimension to the liturgy that corresponds to the communal-cultural dimension of holy gathering, which is the primary referent of Eucharistic practice. And this sending dimension is functionally missiological. Thus, one can say on this view that "the Eucharist is mission" and thus is done "for the life of the world."[10] But the missiological direction is here self-reflexively determined; because the world subsists in the church, the sending into the world that occurs is only for the sake of the world's induction back into the gathered holy culture that is the Christian community. Eucharistic practice here functions in perfect accordance with the posited ontological gap between the church and the world upon which the idea of a self-sustained Christian culture depends. Liturgical practice ecclesiologically construes the world as an other that can only recognize itself in recognizing its need for its own *conversion into* the church.

And herein lies the crucial point: When the church is conceived primarily as a culture, holiness always takes precedence over and determines mission, both ontologically and practically. And insofar as the church's holiness is bound up with and requires the maintenance of its own interior culture, any

---

8. Simon Chan, *Liturgical Theology: The Church as Worshipping Community* (Downers Grove, IL: IVP Academic, 2006), 89. For a similar perspective on the Eucharist as the normative affective practice of Christian culture-making, see James K.A. Smith, *Desiring the Kingdom: Worship, Worldview, and Cultural Formation* (Grand Rapids, MI: Baker Academic, 2009), 197–203.

9. Chan, *Liturgical Theology*, 27.

10. Ibid., 40, 84. Chan is here referencing the work of Alexander Schmemann, whose position, in my opinion, Chan severely misrepresents.

eccentric missionary movement will be circumscribed as inherently self-reflexive. In other words, the only way to think of mission at all will be to think of the world as an outside that is to be related to on the basis of the building up of the church's own interior life. As such, Christian mission will never come to entail genuine encounter with the world, in such a way as itself to be challenged and transformed by this encounter; much less will it involve *solidarity* with that world, in such a way as to identify with a world suffering and dying under the sway of hostile powers and principalities. Christian mission will simply exist to propagate the holy culture that it must assume it always-already is, as if that were the very end and goal of the church itself. And so the church on this view is most missionary, as Stanley Hauerwas states clearly, when it is most intentionally "self-regarding."[11]

IV

By now it should be clear that this kind of missiological fundamentalism takes us into a kind of ecclesiocentric cul-de-sac. And yet the irony of the church existing in this mode of intentional "self-regard" in order to set itself over-against the world should not escape us. For to seek to exist in and for itself in this way is what makes the world what it is, in the negative Johannine sense of the term. But the message of the Johannine and New Testament literature as a whole is precisely that for anything to be said to exist "in itself" as such is a delusionary abstraction. This is the good news of the gospel: the world in itself no longer exists, but is now *the world reconciled to God in Christ*. So what if the kind of thinking that seeks to live from the given reality of the church as its own holy culture vis-à-vis the world has precisely mis-represented both the church and the world, because it has mis-represented what it means for the world to be reconciled to God in Christ? What if the church-world relation were to be reconsidered precisely at the point where this reconciliation happens? What if the world were to exist in such a way as to witness to the fact that this delusionary abstraction of the world in-itself has been overcome in Christ? As Karl Barth states, "The world exists in self-orientation; the Church in visible contrast cannot do so."[12] Such "visible contrast" happens, we might say, as the Christian community finds itself to be given *in solidarity with the world*, for the sake of that world's reconciliation to God in Christ, and thereby refuses all concern for the integrity of its own ethic or culture *over-against* the world. In fact, such an attempt to maintain a distinctive identity in-itself would rather be the surest sign of the church's *conformity* to the world it seeks to set itself

---

11. Stanley Hauerwas, *Vision and Virtue: Essays in Christian Ethical Reflection* (Notre Dame: University of Notre Dame Press, 1981), 216.

12. Karl Barth, *Church Dogmatics* [*CD*], ed. G.W. Bromiley and T.F. Torrance, vol. 4, *The Doctrine of Reconciliation*, pt. 3.2, trans. G.W. Bromiley (Edinburgh: T. & T. Clark, 1962), 780.

against. For that is just what the world, as held in bondage to the powers of sin seeks falsely to be—namely, a self-securing reality or totality or an "integral whole."[13] But *that* world is precisely what we proclaim has been overcome in Christ. And so it remains for us to consider just what it means for the church to live in solidarity with the world "in Christ."

V

The heart of the problem with the missiological fundamentalism that I have been analyzing is essentially that of what we might call an *ontologizing* of the church as its own self-sustained holy culture. It assumes that the holiness of the church is a given reality of its being, and that whatever it does through its institutions, life and practices is a performance of that which it always already is. Because the church is a culture in its own right, it presumes to possess the resources to go on being the holy culture by which it has set itself over-against the world. As a systematic and self-enclosed domicile of holiness, no encounter with what comes from the outside will change or challenge its own holy status. Such a church becomes what one critic has called an "*autopoietic* system"—that is, it builds itself up from out of its own resources and actions.[14] Certainly, such a church has work to do and a task to perform, but that task is basically to do the work of maintaining that which it already essentially is, and to assimilate that world (which it is not) into its own given being.

We have already seen how this account of the church's holiness fundamentally misconstrues the world. But what if this misconstrual of the world is the result of an even more fundamental misconstrual of the church? What if such an account of the church's being is more a reflection of a mere idea of what the church is rather than a confession of the life the church truly lives as it is constituted by the reality of Jesus Christ? What would it mean to say that the church's very life, its reality as that people called to live and to work in witness to the coming reign of God, is something that is neither a given, stable quality of its being, nor something that is to be acquired, constructed and built up through its own resources and actions?

These are the questions that I mean to keep in mind as I now begin to speak of the church as an apocalyptic and missionary *event*. To say that the church is an *event* is to say that the church is that people whose existence is always being made new, as it responds to the call of God that goes out to it in each new moment. To say that the church is an *apocalyptic* event, is to say that the church is constituted in its response to this call by the life-giving power of the Spirit, who is always at work in ever-new ways to transfigure this fallen world by

---

13. Ibid., 775–76.
14. Vítor Westhelle, *The Church Event: Call and Challenge of a Church Protestant* (Minneapolis: Fortress, 2010), 42–43.

liberating it for freedom in Christ. And to say that the church is a *missionary event* is to say that the church lives *by* and *from* the world's transfiguration, and that it is always being made new only as it is being sent to live in solidarity with the world that God loves, the world reconciled to God in Christ.

So it is to an alternative account of the church as an apocalyptically *missionary event*, and to an alternative account of the church's *holiness*, that I now turn.

VI

This account of the church as event is derived from the conviction that the church's properly missionary relation to the world is finally incomprehensible apart from its grounding in a biblical logic of apocalypticism. So what I should like to do briefly is to outline the basic logic of what New Testament scholar J. Louis Martyn calls the "apocalyptic gospel," and then to examine the way in which this logic orients our understanding of the church as an event of mission.

In Martyn's account, the apocalyptic gospel describes the singular action of God in Christ to bring the "old world" (that is, the world conceived falsely as a thing in itself) to an end and to bring about a whole new creation.[15] The main point here is that it is in Christ—and in Christ *alone*—that this transfiguration of the world into a new creation has been made a living reality.[16] Furthermore, just as the *whole world* has been transfigured in the cross of Christ, so also a "whole new humanity" (Eph 2) has been made a *reality* in the cross and resurrection of Jesus Christ. The task of the church is neither to set itself up as this new reality vis-à-vis the world, nor to *mediate* this reality to the world by way of a given set of virtues and habits that it calls "Christian culture," but rather to *enact* this reality in solidarity with the world. Hence, Martyn summarizes the primary message of Galatians thus: "'*God has done it*!', to which there are two echoes: 'You are to live it out!' and 'You are to live it out *because* God has done it *and* because God will do it!'"[17] To sum up, the logic of biblical apocalypticism is this: In the cross and resurrection of Jesus Christ, God has come to the world and has acted decisively to bring an end to the sinful world as a thing "in itself"

---

15. For the basic outline of the following paragraph, I am drawing heavily upon the excellent brief summary of "Pauline Apocalyptic" as provided by Philip G. Ziegler, "Dietrich Bonhoeffer— An Ethics of God's Apocalypse?," *Modern Theology* 23.4 (October 2007): 581–82. Cf. also J. Louis Martyn, "The Apocalyptic Gospel in Galatians," *Interpretation* 54.3 (2000): 246–66.

16. This point is made especially clear, especially as it relates to the first chapter of Bonhoeffer's *Ethics* on "Christ, Reality and God. Christ, Church, and World," by Ziegler, "Dietrich Bonhoeffer," 585–87.

17. J. Louis Martyn, *Galatians: A New Translation with Introduction and Commentary*, The Anchor Bible (New York: Doubleday, 1997), 103. Quoted in Ziegler, "Dietrich Bonhoeffer," 582.

by reconstituting the world as the new creation in which human beings are freed for a genuinely kenotic, self-giving relation of love to God and to one another.

So to proclaim an apocalyptic gospel is simply to say with the New Testament that Good Friday and Easter Sunday are together the singular act of God that ushers in the new creation, which is the world's transfiguration in Jesus Christ. And herein lies the important point: This act encompasses *all things*. There is no longer any world as such that is to be known and related to outside of the one world that we have been given to know in its reconciliation to God that is revealed in Jesus Christ. And it is this reality of the world as reconciled to God in Christ that becomes the basis and starting point for a new way of thinking about the church in the world, and which leads us to an entirely different understanding of the church as missionary and as holy. To put it another way, the church is missionary and holy insofar as the church is to be lived out as an event *within* the singular apocalyptic event of the world's transfiguration in Christ.

It is 20th century theologian Karl Barth who has been clearest in identifying church as just such a missionary event. For Barth, we think most properly about the church only as we think about the church positively in its relation to what he calls "world-occurrence," by which he means the whole history of the world as it is brought under the reign and rule of God in Christ Jesus.[18] That is, we must not think the church in abstraction from the world into which Christ came, and which has been reconciled to God in Christ's death and resurrection. All thinking about the church begins and ends here, with this confession: "God was in Christ reconciling *the world* to Godself." But the great insight that Barth gives us is not only that the whole world is made new in the event of Jesus Christ's cross and resurrection, but that the church itself (because of the cross and resurrection) is unable to subsist apart from the world. That is, the church lives solely by way of its embodied witness to the ongoing, ever-new event of God's Word in the world, which is the ongoing, ever-new event of Jesus Christ's transfiguration of that world into the reality of the new creation.

For Barth, this is what it means to say that the church happens as a missionary event. The church exists as witness to the fact that the world has been transfigured—made new—in Jesus Christ. In itself, the church does not exist; apart from Christ's ongoing work of transfiguring the world and making it new, the church has no life. To say this is to say that the church only exists as it continually moves out of itself and into the places where God is at work to transfigure the world in Christ; the church lives as it goes to those places and lives as a real witness to the transfiguration of the world that is happening there.

---

18. Karl Barth, *Church Dogmatics* [*CD*], ed. G.W. Bromiley and T.F. Torrance, vol. 4, *The Doctrine of Reconciliation*, pt. 1, trans. G.W. Bromiley (Edinburgh: T. & T. Clark, 1956), 681-762.

This is why Barth insists that it is in its apostolicity, or its "missionary sending," that the church bears its one proper *nota ecclesiae*. For the church exists only by way of witness to what the church "is not" in itself—that is, only by pointing away from itself to the transfiguration of the world in Christ. And herein lies the basis of the church's distinct visibility in the world, or what Barth calls its "very special visibility."[19] What is *seen* when the church happens is not some Christian culture that subsists and is built up in-itself as over-against the world, but rather *the world's* very apocalyptic transfiguration, which is itself an event of the church's ongoing *conversion* to the missionary movement of self-giving love that is the way of God in Christ. Thus, in the end, the church is not other to the world in any ontological, or cultural, or moral sense at all. Rather, the church *happens* as it stands in solidarity with the world in its confession of what Christ has done and is doing for the world.

But just what is this transfiguration of the world of which we speak? And what does it mean to live in solidarity with the world for the sake of such transfiguration? And how is that missionary solidarity with the world uniquely the mark of the church's holiness?

To begin with, transfiguration is a way of speaking of new creation. The transfiguration of the world of which biblical apocalypticism speaks is the transfiguration of a world that is presently laboring under the weight of the powers and principalities of sin that hold this world in bondage and thrive on the kind of power that breeds poverty, oppression, marginalization and death. Thus, the apocalyptic transfiguration of this world occurs by way of a double-movement of liberation and freedom. This liberation occurs as Jesus Christ himself is sent into solidarity with the poor, oppressed and dying of this world, so that there he might live and die (in the way of the cross) with these poor and dying ones in such a way as to liberate them (through the power of the resurrection) for a new life over which the powers and principalities of sin prove powerless. This new life is the freedom of the Spirit for living and loving in the way of Jesus Christ himself. This is the very freedom which drove Jesus into solidarity with those being crushed by the powers for the sake of their liberation and freedom. And it is only because *the world* itself is being transformed and made new through Christ's cross and resurrection that this liberation and freedom are made possible. In other words, it is as Jesus Christ is sent to live and to die in solidarity with those dying under the weight of the powers of sin (and there to be raised to new life with them) that the transfiguration of the world occurs. And this transfiguration is an opening into a new way of living and loving and working that reveals the powers' claims (and that includes the claim of every so-called "culture," and especially that culture that would call itself the church) to the world to be illusory and passing away.

---

19. Ibid., 654.

It is in Christ's solidarity with the poor and suffering, and God's act to liberate the poor and suffering of the world, that the event of the world's apocalyptic transfiguration happens. But it is also the transfiguration of the world that manifests God's *doxa*, God's glory. It is here, at the point of the transfiguration of the world by which the poor and oppressed are liberated for the freedom to love, that God's holiness is made manifest. It is here, in the transfiguration of the world, that God shows Godself to be holy—not in some kind of quality of God's "being" in-itself, but precisely in a love that goes out for the sake of liberating the other to love freely. God's holiness just *is* God's missionary act of sending God's Son to live in solidarity with and to love a poor, outcast and broken world, for the sake of liberating that world to love in the very way that God's own Son loves.

This is what it means for the church to be holy *in solidarity with* the world. If the church's mission is to live as an embodied witness to the transfiguration of the world in Christ, then the church is holy as that people of the world that is set free to love in the way of Christ himself. And so it is precisely as a movement into solidarity with those persons who are poor, oppressed, marginalized and dying, in such a way as to live with these persons for the sake of that liberation by which these ones are given to live and to love freely in the way of Jesus Christ that church happens. In short, the solidarity with the world of which the missionary church is about is a solidarity with the poorest, most oppressed and marginalized, the dying and soon to be dead of this world. It is a conversion *into* a shared suffering of their reality (cross), for the sake of waiting and hoping for and receiving the unpredictably new way of life freed from the powers that God has promised to give these suffering ones here and now (resurrection). And it is *here*, in this mode of missionary solidarity with the suffering, poor and dying of this world, that the holiness of the church *happens*. To say this is to say that a church that lives in missionary solidarity with the world "is not" holy in itself; holiness is not a characteristic of its "being." Rather, the church is only ever holy in the most missionary of ways, as it is free to live for the world and in solidarity with the world, such that in doing so it not only points away from itself in witness to the transfiguration of that world in Christ. But it must do so in such a way that the world sees in that witness the *doxa*, the glory, the holiness of God.

We come now to one final point, which is to articulate the way in which our conception of the church's various liturgical forms and practices is reconfigured by understanding the church's holiness as a kind of missionary event. Understanding of the church as event does not dispense with the liturgical practices of the church, but rather heightens their significance at precisely this point: solidarity with the world. Liturgy is now no longer reduced to the function of locating and sustaining the church's identity and integrity as its own interior culture. Rather, it is a sign precisely of God's liberation of the church *from* itself as an institution of power and security, and its freedom *for* abandoned solidarity with the world that God loves in Christ. Here again, Karl Barth is instructive. Speaking of various aspects of the church's liturgy such as preaching, prayer, baptism, the Lord's Supper and church teaching, Barth says:

> [The church] cannot forget that it cannot do these things simply for its own sake, but only in the course of its commission—only in an implicit and explicit outward movement to the world with which Jesus Christ and in His person God accepted solidarity, for which he died, and in which He rose again in indication of the great revelation of the inversion accomplished in Him. For this reason the Church can never be satisfied with what it can be and do as such. As His community it points beyond itself. At bottom it can never consider its own security, let alone its appearance. As His community it is always free from itself. In its deepest and most proper tendency it is not churchly, but worldly—the Church with open doors and great windows, behind which it does better not to close itself in upon itself again by putting in pious stained-glass windows. It is holy in its openness to the street and even the alley, in its turning to the profanity of all human life—the holiness which ... does not scorn to rejoice with them that do rejoice and to weep with them that weep. ... And when it does this it cannot fail to be recognizable and recognized as apostolic and therefore as the true Church.[20]

With these words, Barth decisively reverses the basic ontological and functional premise of missiological fundamentalism and its liturgical practice—"the world for the church"—and gives it the exact opposite expression: "The church for the world." We might put this even more sharply: the church is *only* for the world. The church is not "for the world" in a sloganeering way, for the sake of returning back to itself and building itself up. Rather, the church is for the world as entirely *free from itself*, and it is for the world in this way because the church only lives—only *happens*—as perpetually sent out to embody the very solidarity with the world that God's Godself accepted in Christ.

This alternative, missionary conception of the church's liturgical life is exemplified in the way in which it gives us to think the sacrament of Eucharist otherwise than as presented by the cultured defenders of a given "Christian Tradition." It is a commonly held Christian teaching that Eucharist is above all the sacrament of the presence of Christ. That is to say, it is a sacrament whose practice is determined by the way in which Christ is redemptively present to

---

20. Ibid., 724–25.

the world. It makes sense, then, that if the church as its own culture is taken to be the objective presence of Christ to the world, as it is by missiological fundamentalists like Jenson and Hauerwas, then the Eucharist will ultimately be practiced as a self-serving celebration and re-affirmation of what the church always-already is in-itself. The Eucharist is set forth as the sign that here, in this culture, Christ is present. As we have seen, within such a perspective the Eucharist serves to "fix" Christ at the center of the church, to orient the church to that center, and thus is only performed "for the world" for the sake of orienting the world to itself.

But the logic of biblical apocalypticism has taught us to think of Christ's presence to the world otherwise. The apocalypse of Jesus Christ is his presence to the world as the one who is everywhere being sent into solidarity with the poor, the oppressed, the suffering and dying of this world, for the sake of transfiguring that world in liberating these poor and dying ones for the freedom of new life. If *this* is the presence of Christ of which Eucharist is to be an embodied sign, then the Eucharist is itself an event in which Christ is present to us *in* the poor and oppressed of this world. And such poor and oppressed are present to us only in the mode of our missionary solidarity with them. What Eucharist signifies is precisely that there is no "church" that exists prior to and apart from missionary solidarity with the poor, as if the church were some categorical thing (call it a "culture," or a "*polis*," or an "essence," or an "ethic," it does not matter) already formally established vis-à-vis the poor of this world. The poor are not present to the church as an object of its mission, and "care for the poor" is not one subsidiary (even if centrally important) dimension of a broader, more encompassing Eucharistic liturgy, as so many missiological fundamentalists often risk portraying it. No, we do not move *from* the centrally gathered Eucharistic culture that we call Christianity to the poor, as if such a movement were a mere overflow or second step outside of what the Church is in-itself. Rather, we are given to do Eucharist with the poor because it is there, under the weight of the powers, where the poor and suffering are dying that Christ is revealed (in and by the Spirit) as God's life-giving presence. And it is as these poor ones are raised to new life that the event that is Christ's church visibly *happens*, as that holy people who have been sent by God in Christ to gather with these poor and suffering ones for the sake of witnessing to and working for the new life that is to be received as Christ acts in ever-new ways to transfigure their world.

VII

We began with the question of what it means for the church to be a missionary community. And we have been led to suggest that it is in the sacrament of Eucharist that this question receives its sharpest definition.

Indeed, we have been led to affirm that Eucharist happens as the sign of the fact that the church is missionary only as it lives *from* and *by* the poor, in solidarity with the oppressed and suffering persons of this world. For the church itself *is* the ongoing, ever-new event of the transfiguration of the world that happens where these poor ones are raised with Christ to new life. But we have also come to see that the great sin of the Church itself lies in the forgetting of that fact. Involvement in such forgetfulness runs straight through the whole tradition of the Great Western Culture we call Christianity. And it has come down to us today in a form of ecclesiological thinking that can only finally be realized for what it is: a witness against the very word and truth of Jesus Christ himself. Perhaps we could say that today, more than ever, we need to turn Bonhoeffer's way by putting the matter on its head. We must confess that our only hope is that finally the Word of God is living and active and at work to transfigure the world, and that such transfiguration will be given to happen here and now in such a way that what we call the church will once again be given to hear the Word of God and be transformed and renewed by it. In the meantime, we are given to live, and to work, and to pray—in solidarity with world.

16

Prophets Turning Profits: The Transforming Impact of Women's Savings Groups in Sub-Saharan Africa
Stephan J. Bauman and Wendy Wellman Sinnema

Introduction

Tucked among verdant, rolling hills and banana groves in the Makamba province of southern Burundi, a group of Burundian women begin their weekly meeting with prayer, song, and dance. They call their group "Rukundo," meaning "love"— a hopeful word for a country still recovering from more than a decade of ethnic civil war. Singing gives way to business: each member contributes the equivalent of a dollar—some less, some more—to a common pot, or "fund." Some receive small loans to pay for a wedding, a funeral, this month's school fees, or unexpected medical expenses for a sick child. Emergency grants are also available to members in distress. Members reach out to their communities and use their savings to help others. When asked about their experience, the women of Imbereheza speak of new-found respect in their communities; they tell stories of renewed hope and dignity.

In much of the world today, to be a woman is to be poor. Women comprise 70 percent of the poor, 66 percent of those who cannot read, nearly 80 percent of the world's refugees, and 75 percent of the sick.[1] While women comprise just more than half the world's population, they do nearly two-thirds of the world's work and receive only ten percent of the world's income.[2] They are the majority of the world's farmers, but own a mere one percent of property. Women care for most of the world's sick, but are less likely to receive treatment when they are ill. Childbirth remains the leading cause of death and injury to women worldwide. Women caught in war zones face rape as a weapon of the enemy and as the prize of the victors.[3] More than one million girls are trafficked each year, many into sex slavery. And then there are women who are simply "not here": economist Amartya Sen estimates that more than 100 million girls are missing from the world today due to years of "gendercide" in countries like China and India.[4]

These are staggering statistics. But there is hope. Emerging from the periphery are powerful expressions of promise, movements that overcome

---

1. Beth Birmingham, "Half the Sky and then Some," *Prism Magazine* (Winter 2010): 6.
2. David Barrett and Todd Johnson, *World Christian Trends* (Pasadena, CA: William Cary Library Publishers, 2003).
3. Hillary Rodham Clinton, "Remarks at the UN Commission on the Status of Women," *54th Session of the Commission of the Status of Women* (conducted at the March 2010 meeting of the United Nations, New York, USA): www.state.gov/secretary/rm/2010/03/.
4. Cited in "Gendercide: The Worldwide War on Baby Girls," *The Economist* (March 4, 2010): 13.

poverty and empower women around the world. According to the Microcredit Summit Campaign, 88 million women received micro-loans in 2007, many receiving the equivalent of $50 to $75 to start or maintain small businesses. Millions of women, working together in community-based groups, are saving small sums—often just a dollar or less weekly or twice monthly across Asia, Latin America, and Africa. This includes women who are among the most poor and oppressed in the world. A revolution is underway, a prophetic movement for women by women.

The evidence of the impact of this movement is compelling: small increases in income among women benefit the household—better education and nutrition for children, more visits to the local clinic for family members, and increases in household assets.[5] As moms earn, kids learn and eat better, too. Moreover, in some countries, husbands respect their wives more and treat them better as they contribute to the family income.[6] Importantly, many women form deep friendships with other savings group members. They depend upon their groups as a source of encouragement and a place to express their faith together. Savings group members help one another in sacrificial ways, and they reach into their communities to improve the lives of their neighbors.

This paper presents the emerging economic development initiative of savings programs as a prophetic movement of poor African women serving as modern-day prophets. Through their savings groups, these women foster "alternative communities" of empowerment among the poorest people in the world. Part I presents *principles* of empowered communities of women by relying on Walter Brueggemann's framework for prophetic ministry. Part II presents the *practices* of these empowered communities in Africa through savings groups.

Part I. Poor No More: Prophetic Communities in Principle[7]

Imagine a world where women are safe from exploitation, rape, and abuse, where women even in the poorest parts of Africa experience peace, joy, and hope. Dream of a world where women earn an equitable wage to put their children through school, where childbirth is not a death sentence and where educated mothers help their daughters with their homework.

Is this too much to hope for? Our task is to "bring to public expression those very hopes and yearnings that have been denied so long and suppressed

---

5. Elizabeth Littlefield, Jonathan Murdoch, & Syed Hashemi, "Is Microfinance an Effective Strategy to Reach the Millennium Development Goal," *Focus Note 24* (Washington, DC: Consultative Group to Assist the Poor, 2003).

6. Nicholas Kristoff and Sheryl WuDunn, *Half the Sky: Turning Oppression into Opportunity for Women Worldwide* (New York, NY: Knopf Publishing, 2009).

7. Note that "Poor No More" refers to the title of Peter Grant's book, *Poor No More: Be Part of the Miracle* (Oxford: Monarch Books, 2008).

so deeply that we no longer know they are there."⁸ As followers of Christ, it is incumbent upon us to lay hold of such a task, to become "prophets," as it were, towards a new, hopeful reality for those who suffer under oppression.

In his seminal work *The Prophetic Imagination*, Walter Brueggemann outlines an agenda for prophetic ministry: " ... to nurture, nourish, and evoke a consciousness and perception alternative to the consciousness and perception of the dominant culture around us."⁹ The "prophet" fulfills this mandate by fostering an "alternative consciousness" and an "alternative community" through two modes. First, the prophet critiques the dominant consciousness, with the goal of "dismantling it;" second, the prophet "energiz[es] persons and communities" towards a new reality.¹⁰

The Dominant Consciousness of Affluence

The "dominant" or "royal" consciousness is the attitudes and actions of the prevailing culture that may unknowingly oppress or marginalize. A primary outcome of the dominant consciousness of our day is the disparity between the rich and the poor, along with its link to injustice against women. Brueggemann sees Western culture, "ourselves," as representing this consciousness for today:

- Ourselves in an economics of affluence in which we are so well off that pain is not noticed and we eat our way around it;
- Ourselves in a politics of oppression in which the cries of the marginal are not heard or are dismissed as noises;
- Ourselves in a religion of immanence and accessibility, in which God is so present to us that his abrasiveness, his absence, his banishment are not noticed, and the problem is reduced to psychology.¹¹

Economics of affluence, politics of oppression, and religion of immanence are inextricably connected: "no one of them would occur or endure without the other two."¹² They work together to create a vicious spiral that insulates the affluent and isolates the poor. To dismantle this consciousness, we need to first understand it; in particular, we must examine the aspects of the dominant consciousness that give rise to the divide between affluence and poverty. This paper will refer to the other two factors, "politics of oppression" and "religion of immanence," indirectly through the lens of affluence and poverty.

---

8. Walter Brueggemann, *The Prophetic Imagination* (Minneapolis, MN: Fortress Press, 2001), 65.
9. Ibid., 3.
10. Ibid.
11. Ibid., 36.
12. Ibid., 29.

We live in a global village increasingly divided between decadence and destitution. Of the approximately six-and-a-half billion people in our world, about four billion live on less than $4 per day. The bottom billion live on less than $1 a day.[13] Almost all of these people live in developing countries. Nearly three-fourths of these are women.[14] Poverty is at the heart of oppression and injustice against women. It is inextricably linked to issues of injustice, from trafficking to abuse to "gendercide." Poverty is far more than material lack.[15] In its fullness, poverty can strip humans of their dignity. In the words of a woman from Moldova, "Poverty is pain; it feels like a disease ... it eats away one's dignity and drives one into total despair."[16] Its nature is complex, and its range of causes is difficult to identify.

Leaning on the works of Robert Chambers, John Friedmann, and Jayakumar Christian, Bryant Myers defines the nature of poverty as fundamentally relational. "[It's] about relationships that don't work, that isolate, that abandon or devalue."[17] In essence, broken relationships with God, others, the community, the environment, and self lead to problems in the spiritual, political, social, economic, and physical realms of society. The fragmented relationships that result lead to the major manifestations of poverty in the world today: dependency, humiliation, injustice, oppression, and physical need. Inadequate worldviews generally lead to unjust ideologies, demonic principalities invite oppression, and a weak ethical base leads to corruption. Social problems result from broken relationships with one another—the ramifications of personal and systemic sin.[18]

The full effect of poverty over a sustained period can cause what Augustine Muspole calls a "poverty of being," or what Jayakumar Christian calls a "marred identity" among poor women. "A lifetime of suffering, deception, and exclusion is internalized in ways that result in the poor no longer knowing who they truly are or why they were created. This is the deepest and most profound expression of poverty."[19] The outcome is that many poor women truly believe they are forsaken by God and cut off from expressions of his love. The net result of

---

13. Paul Collier, *The Bottom Billionth: Why the Poorest Countries are Failing and What Can Be Done about It* (Oxford: Oxford University Press, 2007).

14. Ibid., 29.

15. Brian Fikkert and Steve Corbett, *When Helping Hurts: Alleviating Poverty Without Hurting the Poor ... And Yourself* (Chicago: Moody Press, 2009).

16. Deepa Narayan, *Voices of the Poor: Can Anyone Hear Us?* (New York: Oxford University Press, 2000), 2.

17. Bryant Myers, *Walking with the Poor: Principles and Practices of Transformational Development* (Maryknoll, NY: Orbis Books, 1999), 36.

18. Systemic sin, or structural sin, is the effect of sin in policies, institutions, and even governments. For further reading, see Ronald J. Sider, *Rich Christians in an Age of Hunger*, new ed. (Nashville, TN: Thomas Nelson, 2005).

19. Myers, 76.

"poverty of being" is destructive, not only regarding the relationships to God and self, but also in relationships to others, the community, and society.

Three issues regarding the dominant consciousness of affluence and poverty are worth noting. First, to the extent that we seek to solve the issues of poverty with superficial solutions—a trend today especially among newcomers to issues of poverty—we risk deepening it. Superficial solutions usually stem from defining poverty too simply—as material deprivation, lack of education, or misunderstanding of God. Other simplistic solutions fail to understand the local context, language, and culture. Hasty solutions can lead to "playing God" in the lives of the poor, reinforcing feelings of inferiority.[20] In short, we set out to help, but we entrench poverty rather than alleviate it. Worst of all, we may not even know we are causing harm.

Second, poverty among women is often a double curse—the mindset is "Not only am I poor, but I am a woman." While poverty and gender are closely related, they are also distinct. For example, research strongly suggests that young women and girls in Africa are more vulnerable to HIV infection. In many developing countries, families are less likely to educate their daughters than their sons. Unlike uneducated boys, uneducated girls are more likely to be married as children (under 18), more likely to have children at earlier ages, and their children are more likely to die in childhood or suffer poor nutrition.[21] Domestic violence is another facet of the double curse. Too often a poor woman in rural Africa spends the day in backbreaking cultivation of the fields, fetching water and firewood, and caring for her family.

Third, religion can foster a dominant consciousness. The affluent can blindly buy into a "religion of optimism," believing that "God has no business other than to maintain our standard of living."[22] Such an attitude, unconscious as it may be, can suggest wealth is a reward and poverty a punishment to God's people. Dismantling the dominant consciousness of affluence and poverty requires us to ask honest theological questions on wealth and poverty. The Hebraic concept of *shalom*, the redemption of *all* spheres of life towards God's "intended harmony,"[23] is the antithesis to poverty and injustice. Shalom envisions a world of just and peaceful relationships—with God, self, and others, including between men and women. The idea of shalom is based in the *Imago Dei*: all people are created in the image of God with equal and infinite value and, importantly, creative potential. The ideal of shalom requires a reckoning in

---

20. Fikkert & Corbett.

21. UNICEF, *State of the World's Children 2009: Maternal and Newborn Health* (New York, NY: United Children's Fund, 2008).

22. Brueggemann, 37.

23. Bruce Bradshaw, *Bridging the Gap: Evangelism, Development, and Shalom* (Monrovia, CA: Marc Publishing, 1994), 18.

the relationships between the affluent and the poor. It begins with compassion and ends in hope.

Compassion as Critique of the Dominant Consciousness

Dismantling the dominant consciousness of affluence and poverty begins with compassion. In essence, compassion is both empathetic to the person and defiant against the system and the injustice that results. Jesus is the ultimate example. He criticized the prevailing "dominant consciousness" of the first century not with weapon or pen but with compassion. Brueggemann says,

> Compassion constitutes a radical form of criticism, for it announces that the hurt is to be taken seriously, that the hurt is not to be accepted as normal and natural but is an abnormal and unacceptable condition for humanness ... [The] compassion of Jesus is to be understood not simply as a personal emotional reaction but as a public criticism in which he dares to act upon his concern against the entire numbness of his social context.[24]

Compassion is both an act of solidarity and protest. Jesus demonstrated compassion towards the marginalized—Gentiles, tax collectors, and especially the peasant poor.[25] He dined with them. He healed them. He asked them to join him. Profoundly, Jesus incarnated himself among them—he became poor and lived among them—and, in so doing, he validated their "cry." But he also "criticized" their suffering by healing "many," (Mark 3:10) ultimately healing *all* through his death and resurrection.

Jesus also defied the gender rules of his day. A small group of women—friends, no less!—traveled with him and supported him financially (Mark 15:40–41). He spoke with a Samaritan woman at a public well, and her resulting testimony turned the adjacent town upside down. As John 4:39 says, "Many of the Samaritans from that town believed in him because of the woman's testimony." Jesus allows a "sinful" woman to touch him, anointing him for death. He forgives her and praises her as one who "loved much" (Luke 7:47). And following his resurrection, he reveals himself first to a woman, Mary Magdalene (John 20:16).

Jesus' crucifixion was the ultimate protest against the suffering and oppression of the world.[26] In this final act, the culmination of his compassion,

---

24. Brueggemann, 88.

25. In the Hebrew culture of Jesus' day, "... one's status in a community was not so much a function of economic realities, but depended on ... education, gender, family heritage, religious purity, vocation, and economics." Joel Green, *The Gospel of Luke* (Grand Rapids: Eerdmans, 1997), 210.

26. For a full treatment of this concept, see Jurgen Moltmann, *The Crucified God: The Cross*

Jesus criticized the dominant consciousness of his day and for all history, energizing a movement of followers. This movement has continued into our era. Indeed, compassion for the poor has moved to the mainstream in many churches. Poverty, HIV and AIDS, human trafficking, and disasters are getting attention like never before. Local churches in the developed world—many encouraged by the global church, many out of their own initiative—are formulating programs to reach those who suffer. In the Western world, tens of thousands are traveling to once-forgotten places in Africa, Asia, and Latin America every year.

The affluent side of the dominant consciousness is slowly awakening to the cry of the oppressed. Issues of poverty are becoming known and we must continue to awaken to issues of gender as well. As the new consciousness emerges, compassion as criticism must continue if we are to overturn the divide between the affluent and the poor.

Imagining Communities of Hope

As we turn from dismantling the dominant consciousness to constructing an alternative one, we must focus on the special role of local churches and communities in energizing movements of change. The new consciousness must be birthed and sustained within a community—the community of God. The hope that is energized must be "concrete" and must "redefine" the situation of those who suffer.[27] While compassion can awaken the world from its numbness, only a movement of hope can create an alternative consciousness, a new community. It does this by offering a new way of life for poor women.

There are two primary characteristics of this movement of hope. First, alternative communities must be anchored in the gospel. Only the gospel in all its fullness, "by its witness—in word and deed and common life ... introduces the vision of a new world, a different world, a world for which it is legitimate to hope."[28] The gospel gathers a community towards worship, and in so doing it lays a foundational set of values to sustain the community beyond itself. That is, it orients the community towards others. The gospel calls forth concrete action *for the community* from *within the community*; it is an intrinsic call, one that is essential to sustain the alternative consciousness. The gospel is self-prophetic—it challenges the status quo to protect the new consciousness vis-à-vis the dominant consciousness.

Second, alternative communities must demonstrate a better future. As a result of the new community formed by the Christian gospel, women

---

of Christ as the Foundation and Criticism of Christian Theology (Minneapolis, MN: Augsburg Fortress, 1993).

27. Brueggemann, 67.

28. Lesslie Newbigin, *The Gospel in a Pluralistic Society* (Grand Rapids: Eerdmans, 1989), 129.

must experience empowerment in meaningful ways. Indeed, the proof of new communities is that women themselves contribute to change in their environments. Such change must translate into a better future for themselves and their children. Furthermore, poor women themselves must take the lead in these alternative communities. The future is not one that will be bestowed upon poor women by the affluent. Instead, alternative communities must clearly demonstrate the prophetic imagination through the poor themselves claiming their God-given dignity and realizing the promise of restoration in all its fullness.

Third, alternative communities must leverage the strengths of the community rather than depend on the outside. Too often well-meaning people in the Western world seek to help the poor by giving them things. Too often we assume the poor have nothing, no assets or strengths upon which we can build. However, such an approach only further solidifies the worthlessness and hopelessness that many materially poor people already experience. It does not have to be this way. Asset-based development—an approach that starts with the strengths and potential of poor people instead of their needs and deficits— turns this notion upside-down. Asset-based development begins by "asking the materially poor how they can be stewards of their own gifts and resources, seeking to restore individuals and communities to being what God has created them to be from the very start of the relationship."[29] It builds off the biblical premise that within every community around the world, God is and has been at work—that there is goodness in all of God's creation (Colossians 1:16–17). It builds off the biblical premise that even the smallest talent, if wisely invested, can be multiplied.

Part II. *Savings for Life*: **Prophetic Imagination in Practice**

Surrounded by the bleakness of broken relationships—with God, other persons, self and the environment—forming an alternative consciousness can seem like an impossible task. Yet alternative communities of hope are springing up in what some would call some of the most God-forsaken places. And the dominant consciousness of poverty is being dismantled by the very people it most effectively oppresses—women. Drawing on their strengths, their assets, and each other, poor women in sub-Saharan Africa and around the world are transforming their lives and their work. Through simple acts, poor women are creating Christ-filled communities in the here and now.

Saving groups help women and their families develop economically, socially, and even spiritually. Contrary to common assumptions, poor populations, even those living on less than $1 a day, save their money.[30] Research has found that

---

29. Fikkert & Corbett, 126.
30. Rani Deshpande, "Safe and Accessible: Bringing Poor Savers into the Formal Financial

poor people in the developing world, even the extreme poor, do in fact save. The poor save to meet social obligations, such as weddings, funerals, and festivals; to prepare for emergencies; to start or expand small businesses; and to respond to seasonal changes in cash flow. Generating savings reduces vulnerability, increases confidence, and raises standards of living—and the poor know this. Not only are they able to save from the money they currently earn, but by using disciplined savings practices the world's poor are breaking the cycles of poverty, reducing household vulnerability, and increasing economic advancement opportunities. Most importantly, as the poor save—especially poor women— they form new communities.

In the summer of 2008, World Relief's local HIV and AIDS partner organization in Burundi launched Shigikirana (meaning, "we support each other"), a *Savings for Life* program in rural communes of Bujumbura province. Working through the local partner's extensive church network, Shigikirana's aim is to change the lives of members of poor and rural communities through management of their financial resources by using a savings group methodology. In its first year and a half of operations, Shigikirana staff and local community agents have trained 4,248 people in the program's methodology and projects to reach 55,000 community members by the year 2015. As of the end of February 2010, Shigikirana's 3,749 active group members had together accumulated more than $29,000 in savings shares. Shigikirana is the first program launched within World Relief's *Savings for Life* network. The amount in savings accumulated thus far by the savers of Shigikirana *Savings for Life* is astounding, especially given that the 93 percent of Burundi's population live on less than $2 per day.[31] Since the time of the launch of *Savings for Life* programs, World Relief has established similar programs in Kenya and Rwanda.

Alone, a poor woman's financial resources are very meager. However, when poor women work together by pooling their assets, they multiply the little that they do have. The goal for women participating in community-level savings groups is to build and leverage what they already have and can earn through work and regular, disciplined saving practices. Rather than depending on relief funding from an outside donor or having external loan capital infused through a microfinance institution or bank, women exercise greater stewardship over the income they already earn. *Savings for Life* uses a grassroots methodology that reaches very poor and even illiterate women.

Savings for Life equips community trainers to mobilize and train groups of poor community members how to build and manage their own savings and lending fund. Meeting weekly or bi-monthly in their group of 15 to 25 people,

---

System," *Focus Note 36* (Washington, DC: Consultative Group to Assist the Poor, 2006).

31. "Burundi Fact Sheet," *Human Development Report: 2009* (New York: United Nations Development Programme, 2009).

poor people learn how to more effectively manage their household finances. As financial assets are mobilized, members take loans from the savings fund, and often use those loans to invest in individual enterprises or group business endeavors. The group members' financial assets are leveraged through the internal loan mechanism that creates profit, through an agreed-upon loan interest rate. Pooled funds are regularly distributed as small, individual loans to members. Members repay these loans with interest according to a group-determined schedule, not only replenishing the loan fund but also generating interest that can then be used to increase the total amount available for the members' investment and loan activities. The profit at the end of a group's savings and loan cycle (that lasts between nine months to one year) often exceeds 50 percent.[32] In addition to the business activities, savings group members are also involved in a participatory process for deciding how their group will operate, and they identify skills and qualities among their members that can be utilized in leadership roles. Savings groups are consistent with an important poverty alleviation principle—the materially poor become agents of change; that is, they are empowered to create and manage the poverty reduction efforts in their communities.

African Women as Modern Day Prophets

Hopelessness, shame, powerlessness, and a lack of self-worth among poor women constitute a "marred identity" or "poverty of being," which inhibits poor women from achieving their God-given potential. The goal of prophetic ministry is "to penetrate despair so that new futures can be believed in and embraced by us."[33] Penetrating despair begins a process of igniting hope and confidence in a woman suffering from poverty of being. In savings groups, women participate in a process that promotes dignity by showing them the capacity they have to become savers, lenders, managers, stewards, leaders, teammates, caregivers, and active social participants within the communities they live. In managing all of their own operations, they build financial management literacy and leadership skills. Many women, after participating in their own group, go on to mobilize other groups within the community. In Burundi, women in Shigikirana's savings groups are volunteering to act as "community sensitizers," traveling around their neighborhoods telling people about the groups that are forming and how God is working to transform their situation of poverty. The process of participation in a savings group kindles new energy as women lead dignified lives.

Essential to repairing their marred image is creating opportunities for the poor to engage productively in work, provide for their families, and utilize their

---

32. Shigikirana's *Savings for Life* program in Burundi, the first program to have had groups conduct end-of-cycle share outs, has groups seeing profits as high as 90 percent.

33. Brueggemann, 117.

gifts and talents. The woman saver exercises stewardship over the rewards of her work by managing her resources to care for herself and those around her. This represents a significant shift from a mindset of relief and dependency that often accompanies development work.

While *Savings for Life* does not exclude participation of men in these groups, the majority of group members globally in its programs are women. Women are encouraged to join and become active participants in groups to access financial services. Particularly in rural communities, women face some of the greatest blocks to accessing financial services, and their great need is one of the chief reasons why they are targeted by savings groups. In addition, it has been shown that economically empowering women is much more likely to benefit the situation of the entire family. When women are empowered with access to financial services, children have more food to eat and are more likely to attend school, family medical needs are financed, housing improvements made, and a cushion to prepare for life emergencies is created. Furthermore, participation in savings groups reignites a sense of dignity in the minds and spirit of women. Since groups set their own standards for membership (not World Relief or even community leaders), they enable some of the poorest in the community to join. Properly trained and supported, even an illiterate woman can successfully understand and apply the savings group methodology. Instead of applying criteria so often used by the dominant culture—wealth, prestige or social class—savings groups set standards that look beyond material assets and inward to the heart. Savings groups look to women's work ethic, integrity, creativity and faithfulness.

For impoverished families with chronically small cash flows, an unexpected crisis—such as illness, drought, or the death of a breadwinner—often has grim physical and emotional consequences. As Rutherford points out, "the awareness that such outlays are looming on the horizon is a source of great anxiety for many poor people."[34] Limited household income disables a poor woman from financing the costs of an unexpected period of illness or crisis. She may cope by selling off a nonproductive asset at a discounted value; worse, she may be forced to sell productive assets such as cows or the crops of a future harvest in order to pay for the emergency needs. The consequences of not enough cash to meet emergency needs may be far more severe. If a mother cannot afford medicine or a doctor's visit for a sick child, even basic illnesses such as diarrhea or pneumonia may quickly turn fatal. When there is no cash to buy food after a crop shortfall, children may chronically go hungry, and malnourishment may have lifelong consequences on their physical and intellectual development. And

---

34. Stuart Rutherford, *The Poor and their Money* (New York: Oxford University Press, 2001), 5.

the loss of family income due to death or illness can be disastrous to the fragile standard of living the family holds.

A lump sum of cash—even an amount that seems small in the West—can literally mean the difference between life and death for poor families facing financial crisis. Savings enables women to build up such a lump sum that creates a vital cushion and safety net they can use to respond to emergencies and meet their financial needs. They are able to purchase medicine to care for a sick child, pay for the burial costs of a deceased family member, finance minor home repairs after a natural disaster, and continue to feed their children when the harvest is lean. What would normally result in an increasing sense of despair and hopelessness that already plagues a poor woman becomes confidence rising—the woman with savings can ride out an economic storm and move towards greater household stability.

When a woman's vulnerability is reduced, she is "able to sing and dance, to heal and to forgive,"[35] instead of being consumed with worry about how her family will survive today and tomorrow. Women rejoice as they are able to use income for school fees and their children access the education so vital for a better life. They rejoice as their children receive food and medical care, growing into strong and vibrant adults. Indeed, these women, empowered to improve their lives and the lives around them, live out stories of hope in the midst of their communities. They are modern-day prophets.

Compassion as Critique in Action

The generosity of poor women is an astounding critique of the dominant consciousness. In sharp contrast to the individualism that pervades the Western world, women in savings groups work together sacrificially to help one another. They do not hoard their savings; instead, many groups demonstrate Christ-like compassion for others. These women engage in prophetic ministries of healing and compassion to others broken by poverty.

The social fund of a saving group is an emergency reserve used to support members in times of distress. Group members contribute equally to the fund at each meeting, in amounts usually one-fourth to one-half of the amount of share. The social fund acts similar to an insurance product. It is very unlike an impersonal insurance policy, however, because members decide when and how to use the social fund to show compassion to their peers facing crises. For example, one savings group in Kenya distributes $27 grants to members experiencing a death or severe illness in a family or for other major life events such as paying for the wedding of a family member.

The women in savings groups do not only serve one another; they serve their entire communities. Among the most marginalized within poor communities

---

35. Brueggemann, 112.

in sub-Saharan Africa are people living with HIV, as well as the orphaned and vulnerable children of deceased victims. Sub-Saharan Africa is the worst hit region in the world when it comes to HIV/AIDS. For example, in Rwanda, the prevalence rate for HIV among those aged 15–49 is 2.8 %; and 2 percent of the population aged 15–49 in neighboring Burundi is living with HIV.[36] In Kenya, 6.1 percent of people between the ages of 15 and 49 are living with HIV.[37] Besides the terrible physical effects, social stigma further isolates those suffering because of HIV and AIDS. However, just as Christ reached out to lepers and those considered "unclean" in his time, women in savings groups are serving the marginalized in their societies. They demonstrate enormous compassion that, as Brueggemann states, "expresses a new way that displaces old arrangements in which outcasts are simply out ... replacing ... numbness with compassion, that is, the end of cynical indifference and the beginning of noticed pain [which] signals a social revolution."[38]

In Gitega, Burundi, two savings groups are responding to the stigma and vulnerability experienced by people living with HIV and AIDS. The members in each of these groups were moved by the needs of two homeless, HIV-positive women living in their communities. In both circumstances, the groups supported the two women in building a house of their own. One of the groups used their social fund to purchase the materials, with one of the members participating in construction. In the second case, the group built the house but lacked the final funds for the construction of the roof. A town administrator passing by the house stopped and asked the group members what they were doing. When he heard how they were building a house not for one of their own but for a woman living with HIV, the administrator mobilized the remaining funds needed to complete the roof. Today, two women's lives have been radically changed as women in savings groups live out Christ-like compassion.

Another vulnerable population within a community is orphans and other children whose families have been affected by HIV/AIDS. Around 11.6 million children in sub-Saharan Africa have been orphaned by the AIDS epidemic alone.[39] Orphaned children suffer a range of effects, including emotional neglect, anxiety, depression, lack of educational opportunities, and lack of access to shelter, food, clothing, and health care. Many children, particularly those affected by HIV/AIDS, also face stigma and social isolation. Compassion towards this growing group is critical to creation of a new social reality within poor communities in Africa.

---

36. UNICEF, "Burundi," *Info by Country* (New York: UNICEF, 2010).
37. "Enabling the Rural Poor to Overcome Poverty in Kenya," International Fund for Agriculture Development, 2006.
38. Brueggemann, 90.
39. "Report on the Global AIDS Epidemic," UNAIDS, 2008.

Savings Groups as Communities of Hope

Leveraging and increasing one's financial assets in savings groups accomplishes far more than increasing income and physical assets. As Brueggemann points out, "the issues of God's freedom and his will for justice are not always and need not be expressed primarily in the big issues of the day. They can be discerned wherever people try to live together and show concern for their shared future and identity."[40] The woman who saves finds solidarity and encouragement in working together with her group. Group meetings provide a space for women to encourage each other, to discuss life concerns, to share on issues of faith and pray together. Anecdotal evidence from World Relief's *Savings for Life* programs suggest that the fellowship groups experience in working together is often the most important part of their participation.

As a woman's business grows and prospers, the entire savings group rejoices. If one member faces a financial setback, members help her problem-solve so that she can repay her loan to the group and continue saving. The savings group forms a web of relationships through mutual financial obligations, friendships, and shared tragedies and triumphs. Instead of individuals at the bottom of society buffeted by poverty and circumstance, they work together and become a close-knit team. The savings group becomes "a cord of three strands," that is not easily broken.

Women in Africa are also changing their churches. A pastor in the Ruziba district of Burundi says he was doubtful when he first heard of the savings methodology, and wasn't ready to promote it as a ministry of his church. But after visiting groups that had been operating in a nearby area, he decided to give it a try. The first group his church helped to mobilize saved more than $2,000 in the course of a year. He says now that his doubts are gone. He has seen the people in this group come together and achieve what he did not think would ever be possible. He says his church is now ready to go teach others in their community and in their region about what these savings groups can do. In promoting *Savings for Life*, the local Church responds to the biblical call of the prophets and Christ to respond to the economic needs of those in their communities.

Promoting the economic development requires a church that is empowered with appropriate tools for changing the situation of the poor in the church and community. Savings groups, because of their self-managed methodology, provide a way for the church to promote development, rather than relief, by increasing access to financial services for the poor. At the same time, because the groups run their own operations, own all their assets, and control all the lending to members, the church is able to maintain the "culture of grace" by focusing

---

40. Brueggemann, 117.

on discipleship, visiting the sick, counseling the distressed, and providing assistance to those in dire need.[41] The savings group and church complement one another's ministries and activities, as the church advances the cause of savings groups without becoming bogged down by running a "program." When church leaders fully grasp the importance of biblical principles behind poverty and stewardship, they encourage their members and those in the communities to join groups that use those same principles. Churches are able to assist in "changing the economic options for the materially poor so that they have an opportunity to support themselves."[42] Further, groups promoted by churches become vehicles for reaching out to non-believers in the community, who join groups and experience not only economic improvement but also the fruits of the Gospel by the believers among them. Churches, and the savings groups they promote, present an alternative consciousness that, as Brueggemann states "can energize the community to fresh forms of faithfulness and vitality."[43]

Conclusion

In being co-opted by the dominant royal consciousness, Brueggemann says that "we have been nurtured away from hope, for it is too scary."[44] Poor women often believe that the royal consciousness that creates the world in which they live is unending, unchangeable, and thus imagination and hope for a new reality do not exist. But the women saver experiences renew their hope for a new future.

---

41. Fikkert and Corbett, 209.
42. Ibid., 97.
43. Brueggemann, 59.
44. Ibid., 61.

Appendix A: Description of *Savings for Life* Methodology

The *Savings for Life* methodology begins by building upon an indigenous model of money management used by cultures across the globe for centuries, known as the Rotating Savings and Credit Associations (ROSCA) methodology. In a ROSCA, members of a community come together every week or every month to contribute a set amount of cash into a fund. At the end of each meeting, one person takes the entire "pot" of money to use for business investment or consumption needs. At the next meeting, every member of the group comes together and contributes the same amount of money again, with a different member of the group taking the pot. This continues until every member of a group has had a turn taking the lump sum of money, and then the cycle begins again. Even the most rural communities in the world have used this simple method of managing their finances and to create a way to save. While this method provides simplicity—no records need be kept, no fees or interests are charged on members—its greatest drawback is its inflexibility in the amounts individuals can choose to save as well as the time period in which they can "access" their savings (once per cycle through the group).

The specific approach used in World Relief's *Savings for Life* program enhances the ROSCA methodology. Known as the time-bound Accumulated Savings and Credit Associations (ASCA) methodology, it improves upon the ROSCA to create additional mechanisms that enable the poor to save in more flexible ways, accumulate a lump sum that remains with them at the end of the group's cycle, and let group members access various sizes of loans appropriate for their business and personal needs. To start the process, 15 to 25 community members come together and form a savings group. They commit to work together to save their money, borrow and repay small loans from each other with interest, and build an emergency "social fund" that will support each other in times of distress. The groups—meet regularly—weekly, bi-monthly, or monthly—and at each meeting contribute their savings in the form of "shares." A minimum value of a share (ranging from $0.25 to $1 in most groups) is set at the time of a group's initial formation, and members can purchase between one to five shares per meeting. As the savings fund accumulates, group members can access small loans from the fund. Loans have fixed terms and are repaid with interest (or what is called a "service fee"), which is determined by the group, not by World Relief. That fee is retained within the group in order to grow the group's savings fund. Since it is a time-bound process, a typical group savings cycle will last for about one year, at the end of which a "share out" is conducted. In the share out, all members get back the total savings they contributed plus a dividend of any interest on loans and fees paid into the group's fund over the year.

Savings for Life groups select all of their own group members. They consider qualities such as trust, honesty, and the ability to save regularly and repay loans on time. They select a five-member leadership committee, of which three are women. Groups undergo training in the methodology by a local trainer, who spends a period of one year providing training, mentoring, and support to the groups as they progress through their first savings cycle. Trainers help groups to set their own policies for operations and develop a constitution for how they will operate. All assets are owned by the groups, and all loans taken by members come from the group's savings fund. In addition, the training provided by the trainers includes a strong Christian foundation that emphasizes the biblical importance of saving and stewarding God's resources, as well as the importance of the church reaching out to the economic needs of the poor. While the trainers are sometimes staff of World Relief or World Relief's partner organizations, they are very often local community people who have been part of groups themselves and have committed to continue to mobilize and train new groups within their communities. The training of trainers approach in *Savings for Life* creates significant sustainability for the program—World Relief helps a group start, and eventually a member of that group becomes a local trainer who helps start and train more groups. Once the *Savings for Life* methodology is embedded in the communities through training of groups and local trainers, it can continue to be promoted through community members without World Relief's continued assistance.

17

Interview with Bill McKibben: An Environmental Prophet Crying in the Wilderness
Dean Nelson

Dean Nelson: I'm Dean Nelson, and it's our great honor to have Bill McKibben with us, a great environmental writer who has been a significant voice in understanding how the world works and where it's going. He's written twelve books; his next one is about to come out in just a matter of days. Bill McKibben, it's a wonderful pleasure to have you with us on our campus.

Bill McKibben: Very, very good to be here.

Dean: I'm so intrigued by your background. You went to Harvard; you were the editor, or at least a participant in the newspaper there, the Crimson, and you go right from your college newspaper to *The New Yorker*? Really? Who gets to do that?

Bill: It was a fluke, for reasons I'll explain. When I was a junior, I got a call at the Harvard Crimson one day, the voice on the other end of the phone saying, "This is William Shawn, the editor of *The New Yorker*"—the forty-years veteran editor of *The New Yorker*, probably the greatest magazine editor in American history—saying, "Would you like to come work for us when you get out of school?" And so of course I knew that it was people at the *Lampoon* calling to make fun of me. So I said a bad word beginning with an "F-you" and slammed down the phone. And six months later, the same voice appeared on the other end of the phone saying the same thing. So this time I thought, oh, maybe I was a little hasty. And the measure of what a gentleman Mr. Shawn was, and a gentleman of the old school indeed he was, was that we then worked together very closely for five or six years, his last five or six years at the magazine and my time there, without ever once, either of us, mentioning how our relationship had begun.

Dean: So you worked for *The New Yorker*, you wrote "The Talk of the Town"—

Bill: "Talk of the Town," yeah, which in those days was a very different animal. Not only was I writing anonymously, which I greatly enjoyed, but the one rule of thumb for "Talk of the Town" in those days was that it couldn't be about anybody famous, couldn't have anything to do with anybody in the news or famous or celebrity or anything. So it was great fun. I was all over New York doing all kinds of things.

Dean: So then you move into environmental writing, you're writing for *Harper's*, the *Atlantic*, *Outside*, *Rolling Stone*, any number of places in addition to your work with *The New Yorker*, and you just become this giant in environment writing.

Bill: Well, I mean there's more story to it, as there often is. I wasn't writing for those places at the same time, because I quit *The New Yorker* the day Si Newhouse bought *The New Yorker* and essentially fired Mr. Shawn. At the time it seemed a matter of high principle, but in retrospect I think it was, I think I must have realized, in some part of my twenty-seven-year-old psyche, that this was actually a really good excuse to leave what could have been a kind of velvet prison, a wonderful place to write, but ... So I moved. I not only left *The New Yorker*, I moved to the Adirondack Mountains, to the great wilderness of the American East, sort of out of the middle of the city into the middle of the woods. And that's really when my writing started to take a very different turn.

Dean: The first book of yours I ever read was *The Age of Missing Information*. And I was reading this and I just thought (A) it was just a beautiful book, but (B) it was just such a great idea. You take twenty-four hours of cable television—eighty channels?

Bill: A hundred channels.

Dean: A hundred channels, twenty-four hours, and you record it. So you've got 2,400 hours of television to watch. So you watch that, and then you spend twenty-four hours on the top of a mountain. Okay, so what did 2,400 hours of television teach you, and what did twenty-four hours on top of the mountain teach you?

Bill: Well, there's a lot of stories, a lot of things in the book. It was a very interesting project—on one level it was a very horrible project.

Dean: Well, the mountain couldn't have been that bad.

Bill: A year of watching television every day, all day long as your job is just about as much fun as it sounds like. And one of the best results was that we were able then to get rid of the TV without feeling like intellectual snobs. You know, I'd given it its due.

There were a lot of lessons that came through and the book is filled with observations about time and sufficiency and things. But if you boil down everything that came through that coaxial cable for that twenty-four-hour period, a sort of day in the life of the information age, I think the most powerful message that came through all the time—and it's really the message of a consumer society, of which TV was the most profound anchor—is: you're the most important thing on Earth. You're the center of the universe. This Bud's for you! We've come to describe this idea as human nature after fifty or sixty years of conditioning in a highly consumer society. And anytime anybody proposes anything that sounds at all contrary to that ... "Well that would be impossible; that goes against human nature."

Clearly it's a part of your nature, that sort of selfish, self-absorbed part. But for most of human history other things have been at the center of people's ideas: their identity, their relationship with the natural world, with God, with each other, with the community, the tribe, have been how people defined themselves. So it was very interesting to think about our culture as one in which most of the taboos and limitations that come with being part of something larger than you have now been effectively cast aside and we've been taught to think of ourselves in units of one, very powerfully so. And, of course, when you're outside—no great news here—the kind of overwhelming feeling is precisely the opposite. You're small, and everything else is large. But in a nice way. In a beautiful way. Everything seems sufficient. You don't sit by the pond and think, "Boy, that pond would be better if there were more rocks in it." It's just, there it is. So it's probably a good thing to have done.

Dean: I want to talk about *End of Nature* because more than twenty years ago, you started saying things about climate change and global warming, and I don't recall seeing many other people than you talking about that in the popular media. And now, it just seems in the last five or six years like it's become a major thing. Is that fairly gratifying, from your perspective, to say, "Oh, people are finally starting to pay attention to this"?

Bill: Well, it would have been nice had it happened rather more quickly. I mean, I was twenty-seven when I wrote *The End of Nature*. And my view as a twenty-seven-year-old was that I would write a book, people would read about it, and then we would do what we needed to do to deal with the biggest problem we had faced, and that's the way the change would happen. And in fact actually a lot of people read it; it was in twenty-four languages or something, and on all the bestseller lists. But oddly enough it didn't actually change the entire trajectory of the world's economic system.

Dean: Yeah, a Harvard guy would think that way, wouldn't he?

Bill: Pretty much.

Dean: You know, you've been accused of being just this doom-and-gloom guy for more than twenty years. And there's a whole groundswell of folks who say, all this stuff that you cite, it's just a—in fact, I think the quote is, "the biggest hoax"—that global warming, the biggest hoax on the public. And they look back to like 1973, that *Limits to Growth* report, that looked like the end of the world, and that didn't turn out to be true.

Bill: I just went back and reread all the *Limits to Growth* stuff for this new book of mine that's coming out in a week or two. It's amazing to go back and read that set of reports and see in fact how very close to the mark they were. A team of Australian academics just put out a long paper examining all the assumptions that the *Limits to Growth* people had made about what was going to happen, and they were unbelievably prescient. I have a piece in the current issue of *Scientific American*, and it accompanies a piece by a number of scientists, talking not only about carbon in the atmosphere, but about eight other tipping points—nitrogen systems, you know, a long list of things—and for each of them we are either over or very, very near what seemed to be the profound tipping points. With carbon, we've clearly had way too much in the atmosphere already.

Dean: So why do these people come out who say, "It's just a political hoax"?

Bill: Well, let's think about it: most Americans, polling shows, clearly understand that climate change is happening and real, and if most Americans think that way, the overwhelming majority of people in other parts of the world do so too. I was in Copenhagen when Senator Inhofe, the source of your quote about this being "the biggest hoax" we've ever seen, a senator from Oklahoma, came over to Copenhagen to do his shtick, and he had a press conference, and it was actually quite funny because most of the press there was European, and the first four or five questions that he got from European reporters were some variant on, "What are you smoking?"

And he just sort of packed up and left after a while because he wasn't getting the respect that his theories normally get in our press, which loves finding conflict where there isn't any. The fossil fuel industry is the single most profitable industry on the planet. Exxon Mobil made more money last year than any company in the history of money. There are an extraordinarily large number of reasons—forty billion, in that case—why you'd resist the notion that we're going to have to get off fossil fuel. And now it's become a piece of the true cross for a kind of right-wing, tea party strata in this society. Not because there's any kind of science to indicate that climate change isn't real.

Dean: You know, something flipped in you. You went from being a kind of journalist to an activist, and I'd like you to describe the 350 organization. You went from being a guy who wrote about it, to the guy who's trying to get everybody to change the way they live. Did that have anything to do with—didn't you get really sick on one of your trips? Didn't you get dengue fever? And are those two things related, where you did this shift?

Bill: I think, at some level, everybody who writes about things like this is greatly in the hope that it will cause change. And as I've said, I've had more time than most people to figure out that writing alone isn't going to cause the kind of change that we need, perhaps, since I was once young when I started all this work. So, I can tell you that story. I went to Bangladesh, and they're having their first big outbreak of dengue, which is a mosquito-borne disease whose incidence is up about 200 percent in the last decade across Asia and South America because mosquitoes profoundly dig the warm, wet world that we're building for them. And there were lots of people dying all over Dhaka. Bangladesh is a great place—a beautiful, green, fertile, wonderful country—that's going to be completely wrecked. The Bay of Bengal is rising, the salt already pushing up into the glaciers at the head of the Ganges and the Brahmaputra are beginning to dwindle, on and on and on.

But this was acute, not chronic. I was spending a lot of time in the slums, so I eventually got bit by the wrong mosquito; I got sick. I remember going to the hospital. There was a ward bigger than the room we're in now, just people on cots, sitting there shivering from this—I highly recommend not getting dengue. I was shivering, but mostly I was just sitting there thinking, "This is unbelievably unfair." I mean, there's 140 or 150 million people in Bangladesh, so half the U.S. population. But when the UN tries to measure how much carbon each nation emits into the atmosphere, you can't even get a number for Bangladesh. It's a rounding error in the calculations. People take bicycle rickshaws; not that many people are connected to the grid. The 4 percent of the world population who live in the U.S. produce 25 percent of the world's CO_2. If you want to do kind of first-cut moral mathematics, if there's a hundred beds in that hospital in Dhaka, twenty-five of them are on us. So having seen that and things like it, it made it harder to shut up or easier to try to figure out something to do beyond writing and speaking.

And so it was probably four or five years ago when I started trying to learn how to organize. Because it became very clear to me that what we were missing—the reason we weren't getting any action on climate change—was that there wasn't any movement about it. We had Al Gore and we had scientists and policy people and economists, we had the kind of superstructure of a movement, but we'd never managed to bother to build the movement that went with it, that would give it any kind of political heft or power. So completely trial by error we started trying to figure out how to do this. We started in Vermont; we started very cluelessly. I had no idea. I called up a few of my writer friends in Vermont and said, "Here's what we're going to do. We're going to go up to Burlington"—which is our main city, has about 50,000 people, so it's not so main a city, but it's as good as we've got—"and we're going to sit in on the steps of the federal building, and we'll be arrested, and there will be a little story in the paper, and we will have done something." And, you know, writers are as clueless as we were: "Oh, yeah, that's a good idea, let's do that. What a good plan."

Dean: That'll get the carbon out of the air.

Bill: Somebody called up the police and said, "What will happen if we do this?" And the police said, "Huh, nothing will happen. Stay there as long as you want."

So we organized—I started sending out emails that said, "We're going to go for a walk." And a couple weeks later, we left. We left from Robert Frost's old summer writing cabin up in the Green Mountains, because he's kind of our patron saint, and because we thought that most clichéd of all high school English class poems, about the road not taken, was sort of apropos. And off we walked for five days. We'd sleep in farm fields at night. I'm a Methodist Sunday School teacher, so I called up all the kind of Methodist mafia and we had potluck suppers. You know, Methodists are very good at potlucks; that's kind of our main sacrament. We got to Burlington, and there were a thousand people walking. Now, we're in a big, sophisticated cosmopolitan place. In Vermont, a thousand people is a lot—I mean, except for University of Vermont hockey games, that's as many people as there ever are in one place at one time.

We got all our congressmen and people running for Senate and stuff, and they all come down and meet with us, and they all sign this raggedy piece of cardboard we'd been carrying that says, "If I'm elected, I'll work to cut carbon emissions 80 percent by 2050," which was at the time a very radical idea endorsed only by scientists, not by politicians. But they all signed, including the Republicans. The woman who was running for Congress on the GOP ticket, who almost won, she'd said two months before what too many politicians say: "I'm not sure global warming is real; more research needs to be done." Well, come to find out the more research that needed to be done was on the question, "How many people will walk across Vermont and ask me to change my mind?"

Empirically, a thousand was sufficient. So that was good. I mean, it was a good thing. The bad thing was to open the paper and read this story the next day that said this thousand people was probably the largest demonstration about climate change that had yet taken place in the U.S. This was 2006. That was sort of the moment when we said, "We don't have a movement; we have to get one; can we do it?" We decided to try, we meaning me and six undergraduates at Middlebury College, which is a place about the same size as Point Loma Nazarene. We didn't have any money, but we started sending out emails to people saying, April 2007, April fourteenth, will you organize something like this where you are? And we hoped maybe we'd organize a hundred of these things, which would have been a hundred more than there'd been.

Instead, it turned out there were people all over the U.S. who had already changed their light bulbs, already figured out that changing their light bulbs was not actually going to solve climate change, were kind of in that difficult place of wanting to take action, but also feeling that this was simply too big for any action that they took to have any effect. And so the prospect of doing something together with a lot of other people was very nice. And on that day in 2007 we managed to have 1,400 simultaneous rallies in all fifty states, and three days later both Clinton and Obama, then running for president, endorsed this 80 percent by 2050 target, which made us feel... I think, smug would be the technical term for what we felt.

The only problem was that six weeks later, in the summer of 2007, the Arctic began to melt very rapidly. And by the time it was done melting, it was clear that our targets were out of date, that we needed action much sooner than 2050, and it was clear we were going to have to try to organize around the world, which is when we started this 350.org thing, which is a whole 'nother long story.

Dean: I do want to—just tell them what 350 means, and then I want to move on.

Bill: In January of 2008, Jim Hanson and his team at NASA, the sort of foremost climatologists in the world, put out a paper saying we now know enough, between the paleoclimatic data that we have, and real-time observation of phenomena like the Arctic ice melt, to tell where the red line is. And the red line is at 350 parts per million CO_2. Any value for carbon in the atmosphere greater than that, they said, was not—how did they put it? And this was in a peer-reviewed paper—they said it was "not compatible" with the planet on which civilization developed and to which life on Earth is adapted. Pretty strong language, stronger still when you realize that we're well past it already: 390 parts per million CO_2, rising by about 2 parts per million a year. That's why the Arctic is melting. That's why Australia is on fire. You know, down the list.

And that's why we have to actually change much faster and much more dramatically than will be convenient or pleasant or politically easy or anything else. And that's why we then launched this global campaign, using that fairly obscure scientific data point as the rallying cry. I'll show some pictures tomorrow of the first set of results, which came last October, when we held—the same group of students, now graduated from Middlebury, sort of set out in eighteen months to organize the planet. There were seven of them, which is good, because there are seven continents. The one who got the Antarctic also got the Internet, because that's kind of its own continent. And we did our job. We found people all over the world who cared deeply, and on last October twenty-fourth, we managed to have, simultaneously, 5,200 demonstrations in 181 countries. CNN said it was the most widespread day of political action in the planet's history. It owned Google News for 36 hours; it was on the front page of every newspaper on the planet almost, the next day. And it meant that when we got to Copenhagen, there were 117 nations that endorsed this quite radical target, which was unbelievable, given that it was an entirely citizens' kind of grassroots movement that in eighteen months had done this.

The only problem was that it was the wrong 117. It was the poor and vulnerable nations of the planet, and we have not yet convinced the powerful and deeply addicted nations of the planet to do what needs doing. So, on we go.

Dean: In conclusion, I'm going to ask you to do something. I'm going to ask you to read—

Bill: Uh-oh.

Dean: I'm going to ask you to read, starting at the line I've got marked there. Okay, this is the last several lines from *The Age of Missing Information*, written twenty years ago, almost. Just start there.

Bill: I have—this must be, let me just look and see what this is.

Dean: You might want to check the front of it and make sure it's yours.

Bill: No, it's mine. It's been a long time since I've seen this book, but this was just—at the end of this, there was just kind of some stream of consciousness, I was just sort of reporting what was on all these channels at one point in the morning, so I guess this is what this is.

Dean: Read it all the way to the end.

Bill: "The financial markets, according to ABC, 'are waiting for the new unemployment figures. It all has to do with how those new unemployment numbers show up. Too many new jobs could tip the Fed into raising interest rates.' Car sales rose a cheerful 4.1 percent in the first ten days of April, but business travel to St. Louis will be delayed one hour and five minutes due to fog. The traffic copter notes that 'someone on the shoulder of Muddy Branch Road is changing his tire.' On Country Music Television a singer laments that 'pretty girls are a dime a dozen, and I only got a nickel to my name.' Some oldsters are sitting on a sofa being interviewed for a plumbing ad—'When I was a girl, water didn't come to us, we went to water. We had a well, and we pumped her. Colors? I don't remember any. Styles? We had styles of dresses, not faucets.' On *Now You're Cooking*, a lady is making pigs-in-a-blanket with a Super Snacker. 'We have a pact in our house—the first one up plugs in the Super Snacker.'

"And on the pond, the duck is just swimming back and forth, his chest pushing out a wedge of ripples that catch the early rays of the sun."

Dean: Bill McKibben, thank you so much for being with us.

Bill: Thank you.

18

Nurturing a Prophetic Imagination: Missiology as Ecclesiology
Jamie Gates, Larry Bollinger, Robert Gailey

Introduction

To conclude our reflections on Nurturing the Prophetic Imagination, we give critical attention to one of the central debates in evangelicalism as it relates to the mission of the church: Holistic versus Managerial missions. We make the case that developing a more faithful and robust ecclesiology will help Christians move toward the more radical prophetic traditions of our faith. In the prophetic imagination, missiology is ecclesiology. Said another way, the mission of the church is to be the hands and feet of Christ in and for the world.

Holistic versus Managerial Mission(s): Adventures in Missing the Point

The debate over holistic versus managerial missions has occupied scholars and practitioners in evangelical circles for decades. A number of resources exist that offer definitions for these concepts and describe the current debates/dialogue in the theoretical and practical world of missiology.[1] For clarity, we give here a summary of our perspective on these two approaches as they relate to missiological principles and practices for Evangelical churches.

The terms holistic missiology and managerial missiology were coined within the same ideological camp, that is, by those who prefer the practices and concepts represented under the rubric of holistic missiology. Because the terms have essentially "stuck," anyone who embraces the philosophical principles of managerial missiology starts out from a defensive posture. Before embarking on a position, managerial missiologists often find it necessary to justify their stance in light of the number of challenges already leveled at their ideas. This is dangerous in that it can render their arguments and ideas impotent without proper consideration.[2]

Managerial missiologists have made some important contributions to the Church that are worthy of consideration. Their deep concern for stewardship and the faithful use of God's resources to ensure the good news being spread to the ends of the earth has often brought greater financial accountability among churches and Christian agencies.[3] They have shown a concern for efficiency and

---

1. Levi T. DeCarvalho, "What's Wrong with the Label 'Managerial Missiology,'" *International Journal of Frontier Missions*. Vol. 18:3 (Fall 2001); C. Rene Padilla, "Holistic Mission," *Lausanne Committee for World Evangelism,* Occasional Paper No. 33, (September 25 to October 5, 2004); and David Hesselgrave, "Redefining Holism," *EMQ.* (July 1999).

2. DeCarvalho.

3. See, for example, the founding of the Evangelical Council for Financial Accountability in 1979.

effectiveness as it relates to mission(s) practice that has helped mobilize resources in unprecedented ways. There has been a concern for accurate measurements and strategic planning that has helped garner the Church's attention to ensure disciples are sought "from every tribe and language and people and nation" (Rev 5:9).[4] In some instances, such as AD2000,[5] Joshua Project[6] and Operation World,[7] greater collaboration among numerous agencies provided the opportunity for a more powerful witness and wider influence than any one agency could have done on its own.

Biblical evidence suggests that wise stewardship brings about positive and hopeful results. While DeCarvalho suggests that in the Bible, "management and stewardship (Greek *oikonomia*) are synonymous,"[8] Nehemiah reminds us that leaders who are adept at counting the costs, organizing efficient labor, and wielding masterful rhetoric to inspire loyalty, must also be faithful to call God's people to treat others fairly in order to be reconciled to God and to one another (Nehemiah 5). The book of Acts describes the fruitfulness of good ecclesiology, which included bold preaching, sound teaching and authentic Christian witness, and led to significant church growth. This growth was often described in numeric terms, like 3,000 believers added in one day (Acts 2:41). While increasing numbers was not the primary "goal" of the fledgling Church, nevertheless, as the disciples "were together and had all things in common," they praised God, for "the Lord added to their number those who were being saved" (Acts 2:44–48).

The Bible also reveals how Paul was quick to use his Roman citizenship and the privileges that citizenship provided him for purposes advantageous to the Church (Acts 16:37, 22:25, 25:11, 27:24). The mission('s) strategy of the early Church often was determined by geographic and political considerations (Acts 8:4, 11:19–21, 19:21). The first example of a planned compassionate ministry program in the early Church was when the disciples divided up their labor and placed the responsibility for feeding widows to a committee of seven leaders in the Church. The disciples did this so they could devote themselves to "prayer and to serving the word" (Acts 6:1–7).

These positive contributions from those who espouse a more managerial approach to missiology do not negate the important criticisms that also have been leveled at this perspective. Too often management principles and practices have upended sound ecclesial practices. A shift in focus to purely numeric growth and acquiring converts (rather than nurturing true disciples to live

---

4. All biblical references are from the New Revised Standard Version.
5. http://www.ad2000.org/
6. http://www.joshuaproject.net/
7. http://www.operationworld.org/
8. DeCarvalho.

as a peculiar people of love and thanksgiving) empties the gospel of its true power and provides a surface-level Christianity that often uncritically mirrors prevailing cultural norms to the detriment of the Kingdom. In many instances, compassionate services have been pursued as a cover for purely evangelistic purposes. In these instances, the so-called "rice" Christians who emerge may look good recorded in annual statistical reports, but the Church fails to develop changed communities or nurture lifelong, mature believers. The results are at worst a veneer of Christianity that is easily ripped off, such as witnessed in the horrific Rwandan genocide. This type of Christianity is often slowly lost to the creeping influence of other ideologies/faiths or through pure neglect, as explained in the parable of the sower (Matthew 13:1–23). A shallow Christian faith easily conforms its understanding of Christianity to fit the dominant culture rather than allow the word of God to transform culture through believers faithfully following God's will (Romans 12:2). It is to these criticisms and others that holistic missiology principles were offered as a counter-approach to "managerial missions."

The advocates of holistic missiology have also made significant contributions to the work of the Church around the world. From the 1974 Lausanne Covenant to today, many leading evangelical minds—like Samuel Escobar, René Padilla, James Engel and William Dyrness—have argued that the mission of the Church includes ministering to the whole person, not just a person's spiritual condition.[9] Leaders in the holistic missiology movement seek to promote the idea that the purpose of life in the church is more than merely to nurture a "vertical" orientation regarding a person's relationship to God but that it includes a person's "horizontal" orientations as well. These horizontal relationships include a person's brokenness with others, with one's self and with one's environment.[10]

One of the most positive aspects of this ideology is its beautiful witness to the world that Jesus Christ loves and that Christ cares for the whole person, for communities and for the entire world in its complex brokenness and sin. Proponents of holistic missiology have rightly helped the Church see that Christ's great commission to go proclaim the gospel and make disciples of all nations was to be fulfilled through Christians living out and proclaiming Christ's greatest commands to love the Lord with all one's heart, mind, soul and strength and to love one's neighbor as oneself (Matthew 22:22–23, Mark 12:30ff).

Yet, just as with managerial missiologists, holistic missiologists fail to respond to some deeper issues that are important for the Church to consider.

---

9. For the equivalent of the Joshua Project in this perspective, see the Micah Project.
10. Bryant Myers, *Walking with the Poor: Principles and Practices of Transformational Development* (Maryknoll, New York: Orbis Books, 1999).

Practitioners of holistic missiology often misplace their focus on "doing" service toward others, rather than on "being" present in more substantial ways. Because holism involves serving the needs of the whole person, a "messiah complex" can push people to do more for others out of obligation rather than a loving response to grace. It is easy to forget that it is God who supplies all our needs. Another critique leveled against holistic missiologists is that they describe any action or service that is expected to serve humanity as equally representative of the gospel. Sometimes in a desire to treat people "holistically" the verbal proclamation of the gospel is either watered down to generic spiritualism or left out entirely from the equation. And, just as managerial missiologists can be distracted by obsessing about numbers of converts, holistic missiologists can be equally distracted by obsessing about the layers of human need they seek to address.

Both sides of this debate have contributed significantly to our understanding and practice of mission(s). Yet, it is also clear that while the debate rages, both sides are spending a tremendous amount of energy and money toward "proving" one side against the other side. We argue below that while the managerial versus holistic debate is interesting and somewhat helpful, it may well distract us from a deeper and more fundamental discernment that demands greater attention and energy from our Church and a deeper dialogue among us all.

Missiology as Ecclesiology

We want to re-center the discussion of mission(s) in the broader context of ecclesiology. We feel that any discernment about mission(s) needs to start with the question "what does it mean to be the Body of Christ?" This question is theologically prior to and wrapped up in questions about the character of our mission(s). We cannot address the concerns about holistic missions versus managerial missions without first understanding what it means to be this people gathered by God as faithful and embodied witnesses to the peaceable reign of God proclaimed by and incarnated in Jesus.

Any reflection on the mission of the Church should start with theological discernment, use our deepest theological language and tell our most central theological story. Too many discussions about mission or missiology put the cart before the horse, planning out how we do church without substantial time and energy discerning what it means to *be the Church*. Our missiology often starts with the latest insights from the social sciences (e.g., anthropology, sociology, psychology, management, etc.) rather than deep theological reflection. We often quote a few scriptures like Matthew 28:18-20 or Luke 4:14-21 and assume these are self-evident guides for understanding the call of all Christians without spending much time thinking about what it means to be the Body of Christ, "a chosen people, a royal priesthood, a holy nation, God's own people, in order that we may proclaim the mighty acts of the One who called us out of darkness and into God's marvelous light" (I Peter 2:9). We call this "gathered people" the Church.[11]

As God's gift of grace to a broken and sinful world, the Church is an expression of the love found in the character of God, the incarnation of Jesus and the gift of the Holy Spirit. As creator and sustainer, God is always and everywhere in all ways calling all to reconciliation with God and with one another, and the particular vehicle chosen to proclaim and live out this call is the Church. This proclamation and embodiment is most fully witnessed to by the life, death and resurrection of Jesus, the incarnation of God's love. We then also have been given the gift of the Holy Spirit, the consolation and power to initiate and sustain the Church.

As a response to this gift, we are to be a holy nation, a peculiar people of love and thanksgiving. In John 15:12 Jesus tells the disciples, "This is my commandment, that you love one another as I have loved you." As a holy nation, we are not simply a voluntary gathering of like-minded people who come together to develop their personal religious or moral well-being:

> Not a natural or traditional grouping, this is a people formed by God's undeserved mercy. And more, this people has an important task to fulfill: to proclaim God's mighty acts ... Transformed by the receiving of God's mercy, this people has been empowered to witness to God's creative and redemptive activity.[12]

On the night that he was to be betrayed, Jesus broke bread with the disciples and inaugurated what has become a sacrament of God's presence in our midst. *Eucharist* means "thanksgiving" and marks a central part of our identity and calling. We are to be a people that remembers and retells stories of God's faithfulness and love as an act of thanksgiving. But more than retelling the stories of God, the Church that truly lives the *Eucharist* is a Church that embodies the reconciling work of God in Christ. Through the Church as the incarnated presence of God in history, we are not just remembering God, but God is re-membering (reconciling) a people lost and alienated from God and one another.

The Church does not have a mission; it is God's mission in the world. It is to be a sign, a foretaste, an instrument of God's reign in the world. We are to be both the messenger and the message of the gospel (*euangelion*, lit., "good news"). One danger of interpreting the gospel as "good news" is the temptation to read

---

11. The Greek word translated church is *ecclesia*, which literally means "the gathered."
12. Dietterich, Inagrace and Laceye Warner, *Missional Evangelism*, (Eugene, Oregon: Wipf and Stock Publishers, 2002), 3.

"news" as mere words and images abstractly communicated as in a newspaper or television report and not in actual lives. But, as Bryan Stone points out, "We need not denigrate proclamation ... to insist that at the heart of evangelism is the Spirit's formation of a people into a distinctive set of habits, practices, disciplines, and loyalties that together constitute a visible and recognizable pattern before a watching world."[13]

The new creation to which evangelism witnesses is God's peaceable reign—a work of prophetic imagination that both demands and makes possible a distinctive reordering of loyalties, priorities and relationships and of the way power and resources are shared and distributed. The first Christians called this new social option *ecclesia*. To speak of *ecclesia* is to speak of a calling to be the people of God in public, a new and transnational nation gathered and assembled as a visible politics in and for the world.[14]

We must not reduce the Great Commission down to a few verses at the end of Matthew 28 or the story of God down to the moment where Jesus declares the purpose of his ministry as recorded in Luke 4. We need the entirety of scripture to remember the word and works of God, to see more clearly the ongoing revelation of God's presence in the world, to discern more fully the signs of the times in light of God's story, and to discern how God calls us to participate in this hopeful movement of the Spirit.

In order to discern together the movement of God in the world, we will need to develop disciplines of prayer, scripture reading and faithful, embodied witness to the love found in Jesus. We cannot be satisfied with strategies that create mere converts. We are called to "make disciples." This requires much longer and deeper engagement with people and places than is typically a part of mission(s) strategies. As Emmanuel Katongole reminds us about the Church: "The most urgent task facing Christian agencies in Africa is not humanitarian intervention, but community building. Moreover, the task is not simply one of church planting, but of building up local ecclesial communities characterized by disciplines of memory and lament."[15]

As we have tried to make clear throughout this book, we cannot underestimate the importance of lament, confession and forgiveness as important habits of this peaceable Body we are to be. As we have seen, Katongole encourages us not to shy away from the painful memories of the Church's past. We must mourn the Church's complicity in the violence to which it has contributed throughout history, from the Crusades to the Inquisition, from the

---

13. Bryan P. Stone, *Evangelism After Christendom: The Theology and Practice of Christian Witness* (Brazos Press: Grand Rapids, 2007), 319.

14. Ibid., 177.

15. Emmanuel Katongole, *Violence and Christian Social Reconstruction in Africa: On the Resurrection of the Body (Politic)*, 2.

conquistadors to colonialism, from slavery to apartheid, from the Holocaust to the genocide in Rwanda.

Cultivating a discipline of lament is thus a way to re-establish a link between the hope for the future and the memory of a painful past, a past which Christians must learn to name as "our" past and whose pain we can claim as "our" pain not simply because we are its victims, but its perpetrators. Lament thus cultivates the anger necessary to see that there is something fundamentally wrong with the way the Christian story has been easily conscripted in the performance of violence. It is thus through lament that one may begin to appreciate the extent to which violence has become a seductive temptation and a powerful spell for Christians.[16]

Again, Katongole reminds us of the dangers of ignoring our complicity in the pain of the past in our attempts to "grow the Church" in Africa: "One must also resist the consolation of those well designed programs, heavy on numbers, Western dollars, and mobilization, that seek to move on too quickly towards reconstruction without attending to the past."[17]

As the Gospel of John reminds us, "By this everyone will know that you are my disciples, if you have love for one another" (John 13:35). As witness, people will have to be able to look at the Church and say, "This is what God's love looks like":

> As they rejoice in the blessings of the gospel, it will be the quality of relationships, the dynamics of mutual love, the concern for the stranger and outcast, that serve as the evangelizing community's trademark and credentials.[18]

If we are to bear with one another in love (Ephesians 4:2), mutuality is key: "Without a substantial experience of mutuality, communal discernment is simply impossible ... [we are called] to set aside the time and the space to slow down and develop the skills of listening to and learning from one another."[19]

In 2002, co-editor Jamie Gates co-facilitated a different kind of mission(s) trip to Tecate, Mexico. Point Loma Nazarene University's (PLNU) director of Student Ministries, Josh Sweeden, had planned a weekend leadership training retreat where the group would not be playing soccer with neighborhood kids, leading a Vacation Bible School, building anything, doing street evangelism, showing a Jesus film, serving in a soup kitchen, or preaching. Profesora Cynthia Ovando-Knudson co-facilitated the trip. A professor of Spanish language and

---

16. Ibid.
17. Ibid.
18. Dietterich and Warner, 12.
19. Ibid., 15.

literature, Cynthia is more Mexican than she is American. She has the linguistic and cultural affinities that gave her the skills and the heart to listen well. Both leaders grew up as children of missionaries and have deep histories and sensitivities to being part of a global Church. The entire weekend was dedicated to one thing: listening.

Josh made arrangements for the group to meet some of the pastors with whom he had developed deep friendships. Everyone the group met with was asked a question that was difficult to answer and difficult to be received. The pastors were requested to be open and straightforward about the difficult aspects of receiving so many "*gringo*"[20] mission(s) teams from "*El Otro Lado.*"[21]

One of the pastors smiled when the term *gringo* was used. He recognized that the group was being confessional. He said that not all of the teams that come from *El Otro Lado* were in fact *gringo*, only the ones who wouldn't listen.

Using the name *gringos* was a confession by the group of their complicity in the gross disparities created by the border between the U.S. and Mexico. *El Otro Lado* is more than just a phrase meaning "the other side" in Spanish. Living in San Diego, Jamie's Spanish-speaking brothers and sisters often use this phrase in reference to the United States. Rarely is *Estados Unidos* used; *El Otro Lado* has become a standard reference for the side of the border from which the group had come. It couldn't have been a better lesson for that weekend—the group was from "the other side." And members thought they had just arrived on the other side. They were the "other."

It was as if the group's confession gave each person they met permission to speak about difficult relations and dynamics. Perhaps the most truthful and prophetic comments came from the caretaker of the campgrounds where the group slept. In telling about leaky pipes and cracked walls, about the old bunk beds still with the PLNU stamp on them and the newer buildings that mission(s) teams had built over the years, the caretaker reminded the group not just of the materiality of their faith and their fellowship, but of their participation in a church that is also a global economic body.

In his conversation about his difficulty in getting parts from *El Otro Lado* for the new showers in the old cinderblock dormitories, the caretaker made the uneven reality of the border come alive. Parts and people flow south across the border almost at will. Yet, crossing the border north for even the most mundane of needs is a monumental task. The social/economic/political/psychological/

---

20. Like the terms *Mzungu* (central Africa) and *Murungu* (southern Africa), *gringo* is a slang term used as short-hand for those from the privileged north, citizens of the United States or Europe, most often assumed to associate with some variation of whiteness. The term can be simply shorthand for those from *El Otro Lado*, or it may also carry a pejorative connotation. Context determines its specific meaning. We indicated that we in fact meant the less than flattering meaning of the word.

21. Literally "the other side" in Spanish.

theological fence between north and south determines fellowship far too significantly. Those from *El Otro Lado* could zip down for a weekend leadership training retreat by flashing a driver's license to the border patrol; the caretaker and the pastors in Mexico had to apply three months in advance just for the chance to get a temporary permit to buy supplies or visit the PLNU campus just 20 minutes north of the border.

Cynthia asked the caretaker to reflect a bit more critically on the mission(s) teams that came down so often from *El Otro Lado*, particularly the difficult ones. The caretaker showed her a slab of concrete with a half-crumbled wall in the middle of a courtyard. He explained that there are a lot of very talented people with a lot of construction experience and expensive tools that come to help out. But the same dynamics that make it difficult for him to get supplies to fix the showerheads also make him cautious to use the latest and greatest technologies in his construction projects. He often chooses to use a simpler technique and technology because it is something he can fix once all the talent and tools leave.

When the caretaker has one of those teams that just won't listen or do things the way they need to be done in Tecate, he has them build a wall or two on that slab of concrete. When it's time for the team to go back to *El Otro Lado*, the team celebrates the work they've done together, prays, and parts in peace. The caretaker then tears down the wall and gets it ready for the next group that has too much to give and not enough time or patience to listen and learn. The group later dubbed this the "gringo wall" as they realized how profound a sign this wall was in representing their inability to listen to one another, to be reconciled to one another, to be agents of reconciliation as the Body of Christ in the world, to be witnesses to the reconciliation that God has already made possible in Christ.

The borders erected by the dominant ideologies and institutions of our time make it increasingly difficult for us to be a sign and instrument of God's reign. Philosophical individualism, the modern nation-state, and hyper-consumer capitalism are labels we use for three main interrelated counter-formations to the kind of people we are called to be. A faithful church will help us develop the vision and habits to recognize how modern philosophy (even in its "postmodern" form) prevents us from recognizing that there is "no holiness but social holiness."[22] The God of "individual autonomy and freedom" fragments the Body of Christ into competing, supposedly autonomous individuals settling for a "personal relationship with Jesus."[23] If the Church is to live "the creativity of an

---

22. This is a famous phrase from John Wesley found in Preface (§5) to *Hymns and Sacred Poems* published in 1739. "The Bible knows nothing of solitary religion. There is no holiness but social holiness."

23. We are not saying that a deep relationship with God through Jesus is not of central importance to being Christian. Nor would we want to deny the reality of a God who reaches out

imaginative remembering and communal reenactment of the story it has been gifted," it cannot reenact "an autonomous production by solitary, tradition-less individuals."[24] Our faith calls for a way to re-imagine how God relates to persons as members of one Body.

A faithful Church will help us develop the vision and habits to recognize how modern politics (especially in its "nation-state" form) can hinder us from being "one body, one spirit" (Ephesians 4). As we learn from the "Pledge of Allegiance" in the United States, nation-states vie for our loyalty at the expense of our catholicity. National borders tempt us to be citizens of particular geographies rather than recognize our home only in God. National priorities tempt us to sacrifice our children in the name of national ideologies like "life, liberty and the pursuit of happiness." "How does a provincial farm boy become persuaded that he must travel as a soldier to another part of the world and kill people he knows nothing about? He must be convinced of the reality of borders, and imagine himself deeply and mystically united to a wider national community that abruptly stops at the border."[25]

God's reign is fundamentally a peaceable reign. Love for our brothers and sisters cannot respect such borders and faithfully witness to the God who "in Christ was reconciling the world to himself, not counting their trespasses against them, and entrusting the message of reconciliation to us" (2 Cor 5:19). In God's reign, "There is no longer Jew or Greek, there is no longer slave or free, there is no longer male and female; for all of you are one in Christ Jesus" (Gal 3:28). The politics of evangelism stands in contrast to (and offers a salvation from) a politics of domination, exclusion, national idolatry and individualistic rights."[26] Our faith calls for a *koinonia* that is non-conforming to the violent fragmentation of identity and community enforced by modern nation-states.[27]

A faithful Church will help us develop the vision and habits to recognize how modern economics (especially in the form of hyper-consumer market capitalism) prevent us from being "one faith and one baptism" (Eph 4). Globalization's elevation of efficiency, expediency and productivity to the ultimate of human virtues makes it increasingly difficult for us to slow down and listen to the Spirit of God and to one another. Particularly for the church

---

to touch the heart of every person and who calls for a response from every person. Our point here is that God calls and shapes first and foremost a people, a social body with a deep history, diverse membership, and common discipleship. We do not deny the existence or importance of the self, merely its secondary character.

24. Stone, 318.

25. William Cavanaugh, *Theopolitical Imagination: Discovering the Liturgy as a Political Act in an Age of Global Consumerism*, (T&T Clark: New York, 2002), 1.

26. Stone, 318.

27. The imagination of a modern nation-state is enforced as much with an imagination that makes real the false division between Democrat and Republican, Liberal and Conservative as much as it is enforced with the barrel of a gun, a standing army, or nuclear weapons.

in the North, and increasingly for the Church everywhere, the principles and habits of the global economy can so easily deform our desires and keep us busy supporting our "goods and services" that we don't set aside the time and the space to slow down and develop the skills of listening to and learning from one another.[28]

If we are truly one faith with one baptism, the marks on our body will look like the fruit of the spirit: love, joy, peace, patience, kindness, goodness, gentleness, faithfulness and self-control. Growing fruit takes careful cultivation. These are hardly the marks of modern hyper-consumer capitalism that so readily exploit market-style exchanges (commodifying love), manufactured desire (reducing joy to happiness you can buy), niche marketing (fragmenting us and undermining possibilities for peace), over-productivity and Mc-instant consumption (making patience obsolete), self-sufficiency (making mutuality seem unnecessary), self-help (making goodness irrelevant), planned obsolescence (making faithfulness unfashionable), **aggressive accumulation** (making gentleness seem like a weakness) and preying on addictions (making self-control next to impossible).[29] Our faith calls for a community that can practice an economy that "stands in contrast to (and offers a salvation from) an economics of scarcity, consumption, greed, utility, and competition."[30]

There is much to confess in our complicity with powers and principalities that are constantly at work seeking to divide the Body of Christ and prevent reconciliation with God and each other. But, in Christ, God has already established God's reign. This reconciliation has already been made possible in Christ. Signs of the Kingdom are all around us. God is growing among us a prophetic imagination. God is giving us eyes to see and ears to hear. We believe we are at a moment when God is calling the Church to nurture the prophetic imagination.[31]

Nurturing the Prophetic Imagination

Imagine a Church that reflects regularly and together as a catholic body over the central question: *What does it mean to be the Body of Christ in the world?*

---

28. See Dan Bell's excellent article "What is Wrong with Capitalism? The Problem with the Problem with Capitalism." http://theotherjournal.com/2005/04/04/what-is-wrong-with-capitalism-the-problem-with-the-problem-with-capitalism/ See also William Cavanaugh's article "World in a Wafer: The Geography of the Eucharist as Resistance to Globalization," http://www.jesusradicals.com/wp-content/uploads/wafer.pdf

29. See Phillip Kenneson's poignant social analysis of the challenges of modernity to our ability to cultivate the Fruit of the Spirit in Christian community—*Life on the Vine: Cultivating the Fruit of the Spirit in Christian Community* (Downer's Grove, IL: Intervarsity Press, 1994).

30. Stone, 178.

31. See Walter Brueggemann's *The Prophetic Imagination* (Augsburg Fortress Publishing, 1978),

Imagine a Church that sees its mission to develop a catechism (ideas, practices and relationships, also known as discipleship) that will not only help us learn how we are to be in the world but also provide credible alternatives to reigning secular ideologies and institutions.[32] In particular, imagine a discipleship that prevents us from being "one body and one Spirit, just as you were called to the one hope of your calling, one Lord, one faith, one baptism, one God and Father of all, who is above all and through all and in all" (Eph 4:4–6). Imagine if all our churches renewed something akin to the monastic life[33] or served as local seminaries training the Body to study scripture and Christian history deeply alongside a careful reading of contemporary times. Imagine if our universities became resources to help facilitate such profound nurturing of the prophetic imagination.

Imagine a Church that marked time by the Christian calendar rather than the rhythms of any particular nation-state, industry or ethnic preference. Our various "independence days" and national holidays would no longer make as much sense, our 9–5 work day would become secondary to the rhythms of prayer and *koinonia*, and our celebrations of ethnic uniqueness would become subject to our celebration of unity in Christ at the Eucharistic table. Celebrating Advent as opposed to the "Christmas shopping season" might help us to reform our hyper-consumer addictions. Disciplining ourselves deeply together for the 40 days of Lent may help us slow down and listen more carefully to the cries of those who regularly go without. Restructuring time may call us to restructure the rest of our lives to be more consistent with being the Body of Christ.

Imagine a Church that structures its universities to nurture the prophetic imagination; that nurtures in students, faculty and staff a serious engagement of the radical call of both Matthew 28 and Luke 4, sending graduates into all the world to make disciples of all peoples, the kind of disciples who nurture the deep love of Christ, a love that brings good news to the poor, release to the captive, recovery of sight to the blind, freedom to the oppressed and a social life lived faithfully in the year of Jubilee! Imagine a Church whose universities structured education in such a way that wealthy students and poor students could work together in solidarity with those that suffer around the world, where neither would amass the kind of debt that forces them into well-paying upwardly mobile jobs but frees them to creatively follow Christ among the Dalit

---

32. E.g. nation-state; consumer-based markets; globalization; modernization; neo-colonialism; capitalism/socialism; modern neo-liberalism.

33. "[T]he restoration of the church will surely come only from a new type of monasticism which has nothing in common with the old but a complete lack of compromise in a life lived in accordance with the Sermon on the Mount in the discipleship of Christ. I think it is time to gather people together to do this ... " Extract of a letter written by Dietrich Bonhoeffer to his brother Karl-Friedrick on the 14th of January, 1935. (Source: John Skinner, Northumbria Community).

("Untouchables") in Calcutta, and to preach from there to the impoverished souls on Wall Street.

Imagine a Church whose university professors, staff and students were all engaged in ongoing discipleship and theological training together for the sake of the Church. Imagine a Church whose universities dared to develop a curriculum that took the Fruit of the Spirit as its outcomes measure rather than the accreditation of a professional association. Imagine a Church whose universities habitually marshal the combined resources of all its theologians,[34] including those with strengths in medicine, economics, languages, literature, science, social analysis, etc., to engage in hopeful alternatives to the deepest of social injustices. Imagine a Church that developed liberal arts educational institutions outside the United States that were as well-resourced as those inside the United States. Imagine if the resources of all of these universities were marshaled to reflect deeply on how to live together in an economy of abundance rather than scarcity, where all work together to develop regional productive capacity for those without enough and those with too much learn to live with less in solidarity with those who go without.

Imagine a Church that spends the time and energy it takes to develop disciplined practices of love and mutuality, practices of listening to one another, hearing one another, acknowledging the profound gifts God has granted each of us. Imagine a host of what we now call "Work and Witness Teams" spending all that money to go, provide the materials and wages for local contractors to do the building (i.e., providing some jobs along the way), and spending the travel teams' time in persons' homes sharing stories of life and faith. Imagine teams coming from the two-thirds of the world without easy access to travel, sponsored by churches with plenty of resources, as agents of reconciliation. Imagine the wisdom such trips could generate around discerning God's economy and just how much consumption is enough.[35] Imagine a Church that develops sister-church relations with brothers and sisters in another part of the world, where those church members start to care for one another in all facets of life, including listening to each others' interpretations of scripture together, praying together, learning about one another's cultural worlds and redistributing resources as each has need.

Imagine a Church whose love for God and one another woos us to deeper practices of contrition, confession and forgiveness like what is starting to

---

34. All Christians are theologians and biblical scholars, just with various degrees of historical study and depth of wisdom. We need special care and attention for those we call out particularly for the task of studying the history of Christian thought and practice, the interpretation of scriptures and the training of clergy.

35. See Ross and Gloria Kinsler's *The Biblical Jubilee and the Struggle for Life: An Invitation to Personal, Ecclesial and Social Transformation* (Orbis Books, 1999), and *God's Economy: Biblical Studies from Latin America* (Orbis Books, 2005).

happen in South Africa. We are all in need of repentance for our complicity in the oppressive structures and habits of apartheid, a system that divided even the Church into racially segregated life, particularly oppressive for South Africans who were not white. Gauteng district (in and around Johannesburg) is now a district that refuses to be divided by race into "white," "black" and "coloured" districts. But this structural change is only a beginning; the structural move only makes way for the much harder work of actually living together, eating in each others' homes, joining each others' churches, supporting each others' compassionate ministries—the hard work of truly listening to one another.

Imagine a Church whose membership no longer reflects the borders (divisive social constructions) of our fallen world. Imagine restructuring the zoning of church districts/political geographies to cross international borders, especially in border cities like San Diego/Tijuana. Imagine the prophetic engagement of a church that reconceptualizes a notion of "parish" where the church had to think and act with San Diego/Tijuana as one parish. Imagine a Church willing to face the challenge of inviting everyone to the same banquet table without marginalizing those who have been left out for a very long time (I Cor 11). Imagine a Church in the United States that faces head-on the challenge of not letting the Spanish-speaking voice be drowned out by numerically and fiscally stronger voices so used to speaking as and for the Church.

Imagine with us a Church marked by generosity and reciprocity where the people of God work together and direct resources until all who are able to can find meaningful and productive work that pays them a livable wage and offers them long-term job security so they are able to support themselves and their families, a place where disciples are "of one heart and soul" and where everything is "held in common" so that there is "not a needy person among them" (Acts 4:32, 34). Imagine a world where churches, Christian organizations and businesses led by believers in every country are characterized by how their wages are more evenly distributed across the organization, significantly narrowing the gap between the highest paid and lowest paid workers, and where capital is brought to bear on maximizing job creation and job sustenance over and above maximizing profits and individual or shareholder wealth creation.[36]

Imagine with us a Church marked by its concern to identify with, embrace, suffer alongside and mobilize its resources and voice to walk alongside those who suffer and are outcast by society. Imagine a Church that needs no social outreach structure or arm because the entire Body of Christ is engaged in and working towards providing the hungry something to eat, the thirsty something

---

36. See Steve de Gruchy's "Of Agency, Assets and Appreciation: Seeking some Commonalities between Theology and Development," *Journal of Theology for Southern Africa* (Nov. 2003): 20–39, for an excellent essay on giving voice to poor people and advocating for their equal participation in work and in theological reflection.

to drink, the stranger a place to stay, the naked clothes to wear, the sick comfort and care and those in prison visitors. Imagine a Church whose life exudes peace, justice, love and grace particularly focused on the "least of these" at the local, regional and international levels. Imagine a Church that took its commitment to go into all the world and make disciples (and not just converts) so seriously that it would limit its expansion to those areas where it could develop significant resources/capacity/infrastructure for both proclamation and embodiment.

The Body of Christ is both messenger and message, a peculiar people of love and thanksgiving, ambassadors of reconciliation in a broken and fallen world, bearing witness to the peaceable reign of God in word and deed. We are indeed called to be a Holy people with discipleship practices that woo us into the life of holiness. This is a world that God is already mending, healing the rift, *tikkun olam*.[37] As we, the gathered (ecclesia), remember and reenact the story of God in the Eucharist, God is re-membering us (uniting, drawing us together) as the Body of Christ, the Church. Our mission is to become this radical, prophetic Christian community for the sake of the salvation of the world.

Kyrie Eleison. Lord have mercy.

---

37. *Tikkun olam* is a Hebrew phrase which translates to "repairing the world." It is important in Judaism and is often used to explain the Jewish concept of social justice.

Contributors List

Stephan J. Bauman is president and chief executive officer for World Relief.

Larry Bollinger is the chief executive officer of Nazarene Compassionate Ministries, Inc.

Karen D. Crozier is Assistant Professor of Practical Theology and Christian Education and Director of Diversity at Fresno Pacific University, and Special Assistant to the Provost, Peace and Justice Initiatives.

Michael Eric Dyson is a popular author, radio host and University Professor at Georgetown University.

Robert C. Gailey is Associate Professor of Business and Director of the Center for International Development at Point Loma Nazarene University.

Jamie Gates is Professor of Sociology and Director of the Center for Justice and Reconciliation at Point Loma Nazarene University.

Emmanuel Katongole is Associate Professor of Theology and Peace Studies in the Kroc Institute for International Peace Studies at the University of Notre Dame.

Brad E. Kelle is Professor of Old Testament and Director of the Master of Arts Program in Religion at Point Loma Nazarene University.

Nathan R. Kerr is Associate Professor of Religion at Trevecca Nazarene University.

Jin S. Kim is founding pastor at Church of All Nations (PC USA) in Columbia Heights, Minnesota.

Rebecca Laird is Associate Professor of Christian Ministry at Point Loma Nazarene University.

Michael E. Lodahl is Professor of Theology and World Religions at Point Loma Nazarene University.

Mark H. Mann is Associate Professor of Theology and Director of the Wesleyan Center at Point Loma Nazarene University.

Karl E. Martin is Professor of Literature at Point Loma Nazarene University.

Bill McKibben is a best-selling author, environmental activist, and founder of 350.org. He is also Schumann Distinguished Scholar at Middlebury College and a fellow in the American Academy of Arts and Sciences.

Dean Nelson is founder and director of the journalism program at Point Loma Nazarene University and host for the annual Writer's Symposium-by-the-Sea.

Kathleen Norris is a best-selling poet and essayist. She currently resides in Hawaii.

Maria Pascuzzi is Dean of the School of Theology at St. Thomas University (Miami) and was founding director of the Center for Catholic Thought and Culture at the University of San Diego.

Brent D. Peterson is Professor of Theology at Northwest Nazarene University.

Orlando R. Serrano, Jr. is a doctoral candidate in the department of American Studies & Ethnicity (ASE) and Dornsife College of Letters, Arts, and Sciences Fellow at University of Southern California.

Lee Van Ham is a retired Presbyterian (USA) minister and is director of Jubilee Economics Ministries.

Wendy Wellman Sinnema is Savings-Led Technical Advisor in the Economic Development Unit for World Relief.

Jacquelyn E. Winston is Associate Professor of Church History at Azusa Pacific University.

www.ingramcontent.com/pod-product-compliance
Lightning Source LLC
Chambersburg PA
CBHW051104230426
43667CB00013B/2440